LIFE BALANCE
How to Convert
Professional Success
into
Personal Happiness

LIFE BALANCE
How to Convert Professional Success into Personal Happiness

*Powerful Techniques
for the Successful Practitioner*

ALAN WEISS, Ph.D.
Author, *The Ultimate Consultant*

JOSSEY-BASS/PFEIFFER
A Wiley Imprint
www.pfeiffer.com

The ULTIMATE
CONSULTANT
Series

Published by Jossey-Bass/Pfeiffer
A Wiley Imprint
989 Market Street, San Francisco, CA 94103-1741   www.pfeiffer.com

ISBN: 0-7879-5509-4

Library of Congress Cataloging-in-Publication Data
Weiss, Alan, (date)
  Life balance : how to convert professional success into personal happiness / by Alan Weiss.
      p. cm.
Includes index.
  ISBN 0-7879-5509-4 (alk. paper)
  1. Psychology, Industrial. 2. Self-actualization (Psychology) 3. Life skills. 4. Success in business.
I. Title: How to convert professional success into personal happiness. II. Title.
  HF5548.8 .W4337 2003
  158—dc21

                                                                                2002154426

Jossey-Bass/Pfeiffer books and products are available through most bookstores. To contact Jossey-Bass/Pfeiffer directly call our Customer Care Department within the U.S. at 800-274-4434 or outside the U.S. at 317-572-3985, or fax to 317-572-4002.

Jossey-Bass/Pfeiffer also publishes its books in a variety of electronic formats. Some content that appears in print may not be available in electronic books.

Printed in the United States of America

Acquiring Editor: Matt Davies
Director of Development: Kathleen Dolan Davies
Developmental Editor: Leslie Stephen
Editor: Rebecca Taff
Senior Production Editor: Dawn Kilgore
Manufacturing Supervisor: Becky Carreño
Interior Design: Gene Crofts
Illustrations: Lotus Art

Printing 10   9   8   7   6   5   4   3   2   1

In fond memory to
Mrs. Grouthuesen, Mrs. Stephenour, Mrs. Fleming,
Miss Mandelkern, Mrs. O'Brien, Mrs. Bowman, Miss Barratini,
Mrs. Lipert, Mrs. Johnson, and Mr. Heitman—
my grammar school teachers.

I still remember every name and every personality.
I can't say that about my high school, college, or graduate instructors.
That's because I learned more from those I named than I ever suspected,
and to this day I continue to put it to good use.

Also by ALAN WEISS

Books

The Ultimate Consultant Series:

    Great Consulting Challenges and How to Surmount Them (2003)

    Process Consulting (2002)

    How to Acquire Clients (2002)

    Value-Based Fees: How to Charge—and Get—What You're Worth (2002)

    How to Establish a Unique Brand in the Consulting Profession (2001)

    The Ultimate Consultant (2001)

Organizational Consulting (2003)

How to Sell New Business and Expand Existing Business (2002)

Getting Started in Consulting (2000)

The Unofficial Guide to Power Management (2000)

How to Market, Establish a Brand, and Sell Professional Services (2000)

Good Enough Isn't Enough (1999)

How to Write a Proposal That's Accepted Every Time (1999)

Money Talks (1998)

Million Dollar Consulting (1992; rev. ed. 1998, 2002)

Our Emperors Have No Clothes (1995)

Best Laid Plans (1991)

Managing for Peak Performance (1990)

The Innovation Formula (with Mike Robert, 1988)

Booklets

How to Maximize Fees

Raising the Bar

Leadership Every Day

Doing Well by Doing Right

Rejoicing in Diversity

Audiocassettes

Peak Performance

The Consultant's Treasury

The Odd Couple®

Winning the Race to the Market

Videos

Stories I Could Never Tell: Alan Weiss Live and Uncensored

Alan Weiss on Marketing

Alan Weiss on Product Development

Newsletters

Balancing Act: Blending Life, Work, and Relationships (electronic)

The Consultant's Craft

What's Working in Consulting (editor)

About the Author

Alan Weiss began his own consulting firm, Summit Consulting Group, Inc., out of his home in 1985 after being fired by a boss with whom he shared a mutual antipathy. Today, he still works out of his home, having traveled to fifty-one countries and forty-nine states, published twenty-one books and over five hundred articles, and consulted with some of the great organizations in the world, developing a seven-figure practice in the process.

His clients have included Merck, Hewlett-Packard, Federal Reserve Bank, State Street Corp., Fleet Bank, Coldwell Banker, Merrill Lynch, American Press Institute, Chase, Mercedes-Benz, GE, American Institute of Architects, British Standards Institute, and over three hundred similar organizations. He delivers fifty keynote speeches a year and is one of the stars of the lecture circuit. He appears frequently in the media to discuss issues pertaining to productivity and performance and has been featured in teleconferences, video conferences, and Internet conferences.

His Ph.D. is in organizational psychology, and he has served as a visiting faculty member at Case Western Reserve, St. John's, Tufts, and half a dozen other major universities. He currently holds an appointment as adjunct professor at the Graduate School of Business at the University of Rhode Island, where he teaches a highly popular course on advanced consulting skills. His books have been translated into German, Italian, Spanish, and Chinese.

The New York Post has called him "one of the most highly respected independent consultants in the country," and Success Magazine, in an editorial devoted to his work, cited him as "a worldwide expert in executive education."

Dr. Weiss resides with his wife of thirty-four years, Maria, in East Greenwich, RI.

Contents

Introduction

In "The Ultimate Consultant" series I thought it was appropriate to conclude with this seventh book on Life Balance largely because I've never wanted to work harder, despite all of my success. I've always wanted to work less, because I've seen my work as the economic fuel for the engine of my life.

The old apothegm is that no one on his death bed ever regretted not spending more time at the office. Yet during our lives and careers we often seem to confuse our priorities and shift our focus, so that we end up with clients who know us extremely well and families to whom we are strangers.

In the mid-1990s I began to write about lifestyle and life balance, and the response was so great that I launched occasional workshops on the subject and began an electronic newsletter called *Balancing Act: Blending Life, Work, and Relationships*™, which quickly grew from forty subscribers to about 5,000 at this writing—with virtually no promotion. (It's free, and you're welcome to subscribe with an email addressed to join-balancingact@summitconsulting.com. Past issues are archived at my website: www.summitconsulting.com.) I've included over three dozen examples from the readers of that newsletter in the chapters ahead. They range from the objectively useful good examples to the frighteningly familiar and poignant bad examples.

Clearly, this is a subject that is important to entrepreneurs, innovators, and solo professionals, as well as to people toiling away in organizational life. The aging "Baby Boomer" population has created a heightened sensitivity to issues of work/life balance, but the lessons and techniques are applicable for all. Frankly, I've seen too many successful people—consultants being chief perpetrators among them—establish miniature "corporate welfare states" in which employees and assorted hangers-on benefit at the expense (in health and wealth) of the owner and originator.

If you've achieved success in this profession—or expect to (or you wouldn't be reading my books)—then you deserve to enjoy that success in support of your life priorities. In the pages ahead I intend nothing less than to show you how to do that. I've included an appendix with 150 specific techniques. But most critically, just as I've explained in previous books exactly how I've obtained clients, overcome challenges, and garnered high fees, here I've provided specific approaches and ideas about how to relish and enjoy success.

That's not a bad way to end this series, or to begin the rest of your life.

Alan Weiss, Ph.D.
East Greenwich, RI
March 2003

Acknowledgments

My thanks to Terry Giblin and Bob Cohen for slowing me down. They are too valuable to be charging by the hour, but I guess that's just my good fortune.

LIFE BALANCE
How to Convert
Professional Success
into
Personal Happiness

PART ONE

Balance at Work

CHAPTER 1

Identify with Contribution Not Task

It's Not Where You Start, but Where You Finish

There are studies in the psychological literature which suggest that people who identify themselves with their titles and job descriptions are devastated when that formalized identify is removed. Hence, a layoff removes more than that person's paycheck. It removes his or her persona.

However, when one identifies one's self with an ultimate contribution, that continuity of identity transcends jobs, environments, and cultures.[1] *This is a totally mental state.* That is, we determine with whom and with what we identify ourselves. Every salesperson probably has a job description with "salesperson" prominently printed and expected procedures for sales calls explained at length. But the best of them know that their job is to bring in new business, not to make sales calls.

---

1. This is the point behind the ancient parable of the three stonemasons, one of whom was shaping stones, another of whom was constructing a wall, but the third of whom was building a cathedral.

Advice from the Readers of *Balancing Act*[2]

Dr. Dean Ornish says that the greatest cause of disease is stress and conflict in the workplace. Given that preventing, resolving, and teaching others how to resolve conflict is my life work, I have an unending amount of work that could keep me busy forever. Personal mission has always been very important to me. It is what drives and governs the strategic choices I make about projects and assignments I get involved with. One of the things I have learned is that no matter how much energy and commitment I have, my ability to be a contributor, to making people, organizations, and culture healthier and more effective, will be greatly diminished if I neglect personal balance.

One of my early teachers brought this truth into clear relief when he provided a dozen long-forgotten examples of modern and historical figures with a huge potential for contribution who had burned out at an early age because of their inability to sustain a level of personal balance. People in the entertainment field immediately come to mind who failed to realize their potential in terms of the joy they brought to others—Janis Joplin, John Belushi, Freddie Prinz.

Twice in my life I have run into the brick wall of burnout. When you don't "Stop" when you are out of balance, your body forces you down. My suggestion: When you find yourself drifting over the edge, intervene as a matter of choice before forces more powerful than you force you down.

Stewart Levine, author, *Getting to Resolution* and *The Book of Agreement*,
www.ResolutionWorks.org

There are people in Mensa, the high IQ organization, who continually whine that they're not appreciated and are even discriminated against in the workplace because of their "gifts." The truth, of course, is that they are basically unsuccessful and unfulfilled people who have adopted Mensa and its high-intellect connotation (although not validation) as their identity. Take the Mensa membership away and you have a person seeking an identity.

---

2. These pieces of advice were submitted by readers of *Balancing Act: Blending Life, Work, and Relationships,* my free electronic newsletter. To subscribe, send an email to: join-balancingact@ summitconsulting.com or visit my website and click on the Balancing Act icon (www. summitconsulting.com).

The manager of a major advertising office for *The Los Angeles Times* once complained to me that his major problem was with a long-term employee who rarely stirred from his desk to make field calls. He set a bad example, apparently, and his tenure made him virtually untouchable.

"What is his revenue production?" I asked.

"About $75,000 per month," said the manager.

"And what's average?"

"Less than $50,000."

"So what's your point!" I shouted. "He's outperforming everyone by at least 50 percent!"

"Yes, but it's important to get people out of the office. You can't be successful selling from the office."

Instead of finding out what the guy with his feet on his desk was doing right (constant phone calls and personalized "tweaking" of ad content and location), the manager had installed his own set of "rules."

Don't laugh—I've seen consulting firms measure the number of proposals submitted to prospects rather than the actual business that resulted!

In the workplace, our balance and equilibrium are largely a function of identifying ourselves with contributions (finishing points) and not tasks (starting points). No one ever gave a medal to a runner because of excellent form at the starting line.

THE INPUT/OUTPUT RULE

The input/output rule holds that outputs trump inputs. That is, the result is far more important than the activity.

People tell me all the time that their work is like a fungus, slowly growing all around them, climbing the walls and insinuating itself through their lives.

They can't seem to get a grasp on retarding the steadily encroaching obligations (somewhat reminiscent of Steve McQueen and friends in the classic 1950s horror movie, *The Blob*).

Is the only answer to hold out until we're completely engulfed and absorbed by the morass?

When Lincoln was asked by women from temperance organizations to fire Ulysses S. Grant because he drank, Lincoln said, "I can't fire him. The man fights. I ought to send a barrel of his favorite whiskey to all my other generals!" It's the output that counts.

The problem is that we take our eye off the finish line and, instead of getting there as quickly as possible within the rules of the game, we start to pay attention to how we're wearing our uniforms, what the crowd is yelling, whether the field is thoroughly groomed, and how the other competitors look. Track and field coaches uniformly admonish runners to never look back, because it slows you down, distracts you, causes stress, and tells the competition you're worried.

"Even if you're on the right track, you'll get run over if you just sit there."
                                                                —Will Rogers

---

On which side of the "fence" below do you spend most of your time?

Professional Actions

- Write reports
- Conduct "events" (such as focus groups)
- Research and analyze
- Commute and travel
- Upgrade software/ improve office

- Deliver advice
- Implement new procedures
- Coach, counsel, and monitor behavior
- Influence and persuade clients
- Acquire new business

Personal Actions
- Repair things around the house
- Read or watch things out of routine
- Debate how to do something
- Feel obligated to do things
- Work at home and/or after hours

- Recreate
- Experiment with new interests
- Discuss what to do
- Feel freedom to do things
- Play during the week

We fill our lives with accreted material which, like stalactites, forms a mass which hangs in our way and eventually impedes all progress. We must stop the dripping mess.

If the greater percentage of your time is on the left, you are being overwhelmed by tasks and "jobs," many of which can be eliminated. Some aspects of the left column must be done, of course, to achieve what's in the right column. But the left is the means to the ends on the right, so *at least two-thirds of your time ought to be spent on the right side of the "fence."*

If you want to get rid of unnecessary tasks and inputs in your work and life, try using this template ruthlessly and candidly. If the situation fits any of the criteria (and certainly if it fits more than two or three times), eliminate it.

Criteria to Eliminate Tasks and Re-Deploy Your Time

1. If you stop doing this for two weeks, will anyone care? *Example:* Don't respond to certain email requests. Do they continue or disappear? Were you enabling that behavior by responding to it?
2. Can you get the same result from other tasks that *you already perform*? *Example:* If you keep addresses and contacts in a contact management system, in your email address book, and in your personal digital assistant, can they be combined or can you rely on just one of them?
3. Is the reason you began doing this still valid and as important today? *Example:* Are you sending out marketing materials that are out-of-date, no longer reflect your current thrust, and/or have not produced results for quite some time?

4. Are there people not doing this who get the same or better results than you? *Example:* Do you network with other professionals who never follow up on leads after the first call and who actually have a higher rate of new business acquisition than you do?
5. Did someone else ask you to do this for his or her purposes, not yours? *Example:* Are you sharing things, copying things, or otherwise conveying information for which there is no quid pro quo and you are merely extending a courtesy far beyond the original intent?
6. Does this take up a disproportionate amount of time compared to the result? *Example:* If you're using 25 percent of your computer capability to effectively handle 98 percent of your needs, does it really make sense to take weeks to master another 25 percent for the final 2 percent of your needs?
7. Is there someone else who would love to do this? *Example:* If you have staff, can you delegate? If you don't have staff, can you find hourly help, a college intern, or your children? Do you really have to address envelopes yourself?
8. Can you get better at it and reduce the time required? *Example:* By learning to "touch type" you can save at least an hour a day, five hours a week, twenty hours a month, nearly two weeks every quarter. Is that worth a couple of days of lessons?
9. Can you reduce this to an "on demand" instead of a "mandatory" status? *Example:* Never mention a written report to a client. Never offer one. If the client requests one, say that you usually do it interactively with a few discussion points. Only if the client absolutely requires a written, formal report should you consider doing one (I'll still resist).
10. Can you live with the consequences of not doing it? *Example:* By not following up on low-level leads, you might miss one piece of business every two years, but save yourself forty hours in the process. For me, that's a no-brainer.

Everyone has equal time, about twenty-four hours a day. When you say "I don't have the time," you really mean that you choose not to spend it in that fashion. That's rather damning when you say it about a kid's soccer game or a spouse's social event.

WE BUILD OUR HOUSES; THEY SHOULDN'T BUILD US

Winston Churchill once observed that we build our houses, and then they build us. He was referring to Parliament, but the point seems to apply universally.

We construct "nests" and comfortable homes at work to which we flock and within which we seek succor. We chant that life is about change, yet we seek to fend off the advance of change at every opportunity.

Advice from the Readers of *Balancing Act*

On January 1, 2001, my wife, Barb, who was four months pregnant, my one-year-old daughter, Sarah, and I drove home from a friend's house. Barb and I barely spoke to each other, and when we did, it was in short, angry bursts. Tension filled the air, and big tears rolled down Barb's face.

On January 1, 2002, Barb, our two children, and I drove home from her parents' house. The two kids were sound asleep. Barb and I laughed and spoke to one another in a calm and loving manner. We enjoyed each other's company and shared stories about the past year in a very enjoyable manner.

What made the difference?

In 2000, I worked all day every day. When I was in St. Louis, I worked until 5 p.m., had dinner with Barb and Sarah, and then went back to my office to work some more. The rest of the time I traveled with business. In case you're wondering, all work and no play makes for a very dull boy and a very bad marriage.

In 2001, I almost never worked in the evening. Many times I went to the playground with Sarah. The four of us (Ben joined us on May 30th, 2001) had picnics in the backyard during the week, went on three vacations, and generally enjoyed our evenings together. As you might recall, 2001 was filled with anxiety, a poor economy, and terrorist attacks. Yet it was the best year ever for my family and me. The increased balance also enhanced my self-esteem, dignity, and the quality of my life and work.

> Dan Coughlin, President, The Coughlin Company, Inc.,
> a firm specializing in enhancing the effectiveness
> of top performing executives, groups, and organizations

Take a look at your work and you just may find that your existence as an entrepreneur is no less bureaucratic and habit-bound than is that of your corporate friends and clients. We allow our work structure to become calcified and rigid because we tend to seek discipline and methodical consistency—not bad traits by any means—but we confuse rote-like repetition with consistent results.

In other words, we once again mistake ends and means.

Here are some examples of—and suggested remedies for—those inflexible practices which add to the arthritis of our business lives, eventually creating a near–rigor mortis in our professional conduct. Too many consultants who began as free-thinking, experimental, and risk-taking entrepreneurs have evolved into people with blocked business arteries and systems scleroses.

The Business Plan

The worst thing about a plan is that you hit it. I've had clients who bragged about instilling a corporate-wide belief in a 5 percent growth in the northeast and then rejoiced when that figure was hit. The problem, of course, is that the growth should have been 13 percent and could have been, except that everyone was fixated on hitting 5 percent and then called it quits in order to celebrate.

The only reason for a business plan is to have a cogent, well-supported document for lenders should you wish to borrow money. There are two problems with this, however:

1. Early in your career, no one will lend you money no matter what your business plan says, unless you have collateral in the form of assets, equity, receivables, and so on.
2. Later in your career (as you are now, presumably, reading this series), when you don't need loans, they come at you like hail on a stormy day, pelting you with offers, checks, and credit lines.

Business plans are, by definition, self-limiting and unnecessary to successfully run a solo practice or even a small to medium-sized firm.[3] Business plans are convenient tasks that enable people to think they're actually accomplishing something when they're better off spending that time trying to market and

3. Note that I'm not saying you don't need a strategy, just that you don't need a business plan.

bring in new business. Don't do them. They waste time and, worse, establish illusionary structures within which to operate, except they really won't protect you from the elements or constitute any tangible asset at all.

What every entrepreneur does need is a marketing strategy; that strategy can be based on something as elemental as three components: What market need are you trying to fill? What competency do you have to fulfill that need? and Are you passionate about doing so? Any more sophisticated techniques—such as branding or alliances—can only arise *after* those three determinations.

An Office and/or Staff

Since most of us are refugees from the corporate world, I have no idea why anyone would voluntarily want to go to an office every day, nor do I comprehend why anyone would want to manage a staff.

I've found that most people who crave offices do so because of a belief that the office validates their identity as a legitimate professional. (I know that I believed that until my wife talked me out of the idea when I launched my practice.) It's a self-esteem issue. There is a minority, I suppose, with space too cramped or interrupted at home to effectively set up an office there, but that's rare. And the problem with any external office is that it creates a regimen, a responsibility, and a reason for performing certain habits (such as opening and closing it, paying the utilities, communing with business neighbors, and—heaven forfend—commuting).

A staff of even one creates problems with personal concerns, tax responsibilities, benefits, potential legal liabilities, theft, loss of confidentiality, poor client service, and a host of drawbacks that far outweigh the status. My rules have always been: First, do it yourself; if you can't do it yourself, contract it out by the hour; if you can't contract it out by the hour, outsource it; if you can't outsource it, do it yourself.

A friend and alliance partner of mine with a very successful practice attributed a large part of it to her full-time assistant, who arrived at my friend's home office every day and labored from nine to five. The fact that she was cheerfully incompetent and actually *caused more work than she ever completed* was lost on my friend until I encouraged her to test the waters without her trusted assistant. The test was so successful that my friend has just completed her first "anniversary" without her assistant. She is happier and wealthier than ever and has informed me that she's glad she thought of it! (This, of course, being the sign of a successful consulting engagement—the client thinking it was all really her idea!)

My wife talked me out of an office in 1985, when I had been fired and had no income, and when being an independent consultant was a dream far from any reality. "If it turns out you really need an office," she reasonably pointed out, "you can always get one later."

After fifteen years of working at home and building a seven-figure practice, I totaled up the expenses for my once-desirable office over that span, including presumed rent, insurance, utilities, equipment, furnishings, repair, secretarial presence, taxes, and so on. The sum, to my astonishment, came to $450,000. (That's only $2,500 per month.)

Ironically, that is almost exactly the amount that it cost me to send two children to very expensive private schools from kindergarten through undergraduate degrees. That was an eye-opener, and clearly still another shining moment for my wife.

And now, with my kids in the workforce for several years, all that tuition money is ours . . .

Offices and staffs, aside from the severe financial burden they create, also critically hinder our choices and our freedoms. Don't allow them to build your house.

Advisory Boards

I'm a big fan of advisory boards when a consultant is getting started. They provide valuable independent advice, contacts, feedback, and an instant respectability and credential. However, there comes a time when they outlive their usefulness.

Advisory groups (clients, attorneys, accountants, publicity people, other entrepreneurs, and so on) have their own agendas and, as well-meaning and objective as they may be, *can never be intimately familiar with your own passions, goals, and unique dynamics of family, friends, interests, and so on.* There comes a time when becoming an Ultimate Consultant means you've outgrown such advice.

> We evolve. We can't carry all the baggage we've sometimes justifiably needed at given moments with us throughout our lives or we'll be forever bogged down. Good ideas aren't always eternal—and are seldom even long-lived if not constantly honed and altered to fit our changing conditions. Even hermit crabs continue to seek new shells to use as they grow.

This doesn't mean you've learned everything you need to learn. I'm constantly surprised at how stupid I was just two weeks ago! But it does mean that *your sources of input, feedback, and calibration must change.* I've seen too many otherwise successful consultants actually retarded in their growth and wasting their time because a once-effective board of advisors is providing input for the consultant of three years ago instead of the one actually sitting across the table.

The best boards of directors have rules with term limits. You should have at least the same. And if you insist on an advisory board, change it regularly so that the new people enter at a point contemporary with your current achievements. Better still, abandon these boards (which truly successful entrepreneurs quickly outgrow and leave behind) and obtain your feedback from people who are slightly more successful than you, from clients, from trade associations, from extended reading and travel, and from situational research.

In other words, get out of the house and onto the road.

PRISONERS OF "DELIVERABLES"

What you and I do is very important; *how* we do it is far less important. Yet talk to any consultant (or read the consultant's marketing material or visit his or her website) and you'll find an exegesis about *how.*

We are enraptured of our deliverables, and that awe ruins life balance. A six-step sales process, a model focus group, or a psychometrically dazzling survey is worthless if the client results aren't met. Worse, the accent on deliverables consumes vast amounts of time that could otherwise be spent at the beach or with the dogs.

Advice from the Readers of *Balancing Act*

Two thirty in the morning, and I was still in my office. I couldn't believe it. I had been working since 7:30 a.m. the day before. I looked up at the clock and my throat locked.

I felt like a vise was wrapping tighter around my neck. *This damn business,* I heard myself saying; but it wasn't the business, it was me. I had vested every ounce of energy and every spare minute of my life into making my direct mail business prosper.

Fifteen years had passed, and yes, it was the roller coaster ride of my life. I loved every minute of every day, but my family was growing and my husband was beginning to stop asking if I'd be home for a late dinner.

My life was completely out of balance. Why hadn't I seen that before? I began visualizing the noose around my neck getting looser. Visualizing my throat beginning to open. Was I having a heart attack? What was happening? This business wasn't fun anymore, and it was literally sapping my life's breath away.

Adapt or sell. Take control of my life or give it up to whatever issue hit that morning when I walked in the door. After a few minutes I knew the answer—it was time. I would find a buyer and do something different that gave me the thrill I loved and also the life I deserved.

Sometimes balance is just knowing when you're teetering over the edge. Sometimes finding it requires drastic change. My head hadn't listened, but when my throat locked, I knew that my body had.

Beverly Post, Certified Business Coach,
Next Level COACHES-*Get There Faster*

Clients' behavior has exacerbated this mischief. The lower level the buyer, the more the buyer seeks deliverables as evidence of "success." I want to throttle low-level people who are unhealthily interested in the following:

- Number of days you'll be on site.
- Timing, number, and length of reports to be submitted.
- Numbers of meetings held.

- Manuals, booklets, guides, and other paraphernalia to be produced.
- Numbers and outlines of workshops, seminars, focus groups, and so forth.
- Documentation, technical studies, guides, and analyses.
- Job descriptions, performance aids, and templates.
- Forms: succession planning, hiring, exit interview, career tracking.

When a buyer starts to yammer about deliverables, explain that your "deliverables" are results, that is, the achievement of the buyer's business objectives for that project. You'll want to minimize the amount of "stuff" that gets in the way of the expeditious achievement of that goal.

In many cases I've seen consultants all too readily reduce their role to that of apprentices who have been told exactly what's wrong, how to fix it, what tools to use, how much time to invest, and so on. They are a pair of hired hands being directed by a client who allowed the problem to emerge in the first place, who couldn't then correct it without external help, but who feels perfectly qualified to direct that hired expertise in how to resolve the problem!

This is hubris raised to art form. But it's hubris with assistance, since consultants often feed the process through their own lack of self-esteem.

We must educate the buyer early if we don't want to stay onsite late, and that means dispensing with the ridiculous notion that deliverables are important. There should be no such category in your proposals. There should be no such vocabulary in your presentations. And there should be no such concessions to your buyers.

The entire concept of "deliverables" is a chasm on the road to life balance.

It's not where you start; it's where you finish. A deliverable is never a "finish," but merely a way station on the road to finality. I know that you may be thinking, "But it's impossible to achieve results without undertaking a variety of tasks and producing an assortment of deliverables along the way. They are rungs in the ladder." Perhaps, but why use a ladder if there's an escalator, or an elevator, or a helicopter?

Here's the key difference: Let's say that you've decided that focus groups are going to be a primary methodology to determine employee sentiment on an issue and to gain some of their ownership in a needed change. So far, so good. But here are two important differences between what I'm espousing and what most consultants actually do:

I was presenting my views on leadership development to three low-level but legitimate buyers at Con Ed, the huge New York utility. Things had been going well, I thought, until a woman asked me what my binders would look like.

"What binders?" I asked, confused.

"The binders for all your program materials," she told me, "because we're very proud of the look of our materials."

"I don't even know if there will be binders," I replied, now annoyed, "because leadership doesn't come out of binders; it comes from changed behavior on the job. You'll know it because your labor relations improve and your public image is enhanced and safety violations decline, not because everyone has a binder on his desk."

"Well, if you can't produce a decent binder, I don't see why we should hire you!"

The other two broke up the growing battle, and I didn't get the job. I don't regret that. I do regret not clobbering her with a binder, though. I would have done Con Ed a great service.

1. The number of focus groups is up to you, not the client, and the number is immaterial in terms of value (and, therefore, your fee). You may estimate that twelve groups are needed, but find that after seven you're getting repeating patterns and that your work is done, or that after twelve you're still getting such diversity that you'll need another six. It doesn't matter—you're determining need in real time based on your consulting expertise, and there is no investment difference for the client. And certainly *the client should not be determining the number of focus groups.*

2. There are no immediate deliverables attached to the focus groups. That is, there are no weekly reports, interim reports, periodic briefings, Power-Point™ slides, or summary documents produced. The information from the groups is integrated into your project analyses and recommendations.

> One of the main reasons that clients demand time-consuming deliverables is that consultants advertise, promote, and offer them. Stop doing that.

The "deliverable" here is the project outcome: An accurate sampling of employee sentiment and the involvement of employees in designing the nature of the changes needed. If you accomplish that without one deliverable, the client will love you nonetheless. If you don't accomplish that, despite producing one hundred deliverables, the client will never ask you to return.

No buyer, in my experience, says, "Get me that guy with the great deliverables" (or, more prosaically, "Get me the woman who runs such a good focus group"). What the buyer says is, "Get that consultant who got our employees behind the change with a minimum of resistance."

CASE STUDY

In late 2000 a long-time buyer at Hewlett-Packard asked me to undertake a project to help determine the proper client interaction for a true "solution sale." It was a small focus, and she had a very limited budget, but really wanted my help. I'm located 3,000 miles from her.

We agreed on the results of our modest study and also that it was silly to use up the budget on travel costs in an electronic age (and with technological giant HP!). Since HP managers often reported to and collaborated with colleagues who were on other continents, why should a consulting relationship be any different?

We successfully concluded the project in ninety days and produced a model to be evaluated for a solution sales mentality and reality. During that entire period I never set foot on an HP site, and the "deliverables" were phone calls, email, hard-copy reviews, and designs. The client actually created almost all the actual documentation in HP-friendly formats.

Oh, and as a result I was engaged for a nine-month follow-up project to assist with the pilot solution sales implementation.

Deliverables usually require that you "deliver" something other than results, outcomes, and objectives. Some are essential in helping to move the project along, but I would maintain that only a small fraction of deliverables fall into that pragmatic category.

Eleven Guaranteed Techniques to Dramatically Reduce Deliverables

Hence, I suggest you carefully weigh the following before entangling your time and limiting your life choices in convoluted and lengthy deliverables:

1. Is what you're doing really critical to project progress, or is it "make work" to show that you're present and doing something? *Example:* You don't have to be onsite to review documents, to make calls to your client's customers, or to design alternative approaches.
2. Is there an easier way? *Example:* Many interviews can be done by phone instead of in person, and many surveys can be done better by electronic response rather than by hard-copy returns.
3. Is it redundant? *Example:* A sample is just that—you don't need to involve the total population of larger operations to get accurate feedback. If you've provided a briefing, do you really need to back it up in writing? Must people receive a copy of everything you do in slide format?

Consultants tend to agonize over "Am I doing enough?" Try asking the converse when about to propose a project: "Am I offering too much?" If you want to increase your *fees,* fair enough, then increase your *value.* But that has nothing to do with increasing your deliverables.

4. Is it too long? *Example:* I've never found I needed more than thirty minutes for a one-on-one interview if I have tactical, highly directed questions and if I'm willing to move quickly. Yet many consultants take three times as long, mainly because they ask vague questions and are afraid to cut off digressions.

5. Is it an arbitrary client request and not a methodological need? *Example:* Clients will often request you do things "as long as you'll be here anyway" or because "we've done this in the past." Resist such superficial requests. There is no reason to spend time in the finance department if that area is unrelated to the project and has no one with useful information or perspective.

6. Is it merely a favored alternative of yours? *Example:* Consultants mindlessly conduct lengthy, boring, and time-destroying needs analyses because they include them in their approaches in robot-like fashion. Most of them are completely unnecessary and silly. Just because you *can* do something doesn't mean you *should*.

7. Does Occam's Razor apply? *Example:* More on this in a following chapter, but in most instances, the easiest explanation is also the most probable. Are you going around the block to get next door? Don't bring in heavy equipment when you merely have to ask a few people to change a procedure.

8. Are you mistaking activity for value? *Example:* You're better off seeing the buyer once a month and offering real value than you are appearing twice a week to perform tasks with subordinates.

9. Are you allowing yourself to be delegated to the delivery obsessed? *Example:* Many buyers will mistakenly conclude after the proposal is signed that they are done until a final report is produced, and the consultant is delegated to the implementers. It's incumbent on us to resist this demotion. The subordinates *will* be delivery-oriented, so we can't be exiled to that strange land.

10. Are you falling in love with your methodology? *Example:* I've watched consultants who let projects go to hell while they were installing their magic software, or implementing their seven-step sales process, or constructing an esoteric and complex quality assurance bureaucracy. Don't become a slave (or be awestruck) to your own devices. Every technique is simply a means to an end, and not an end in itself.

11. Is the buyer involved? *Example:* Buyers hate "busy work," details, implementation, and small picture stuff. That's great, because if you establish a close partnering with the buyer, you too will have to focus on getting things accomplished quickly with a minimum of superstructure and infrastructure. It should be a lean and mean ship.

THE STRATEGIC VS. THE TACTICAL

We must take a "big picture" view of our jobs, careers, and projects. Too many consultants not only don't see the forest, but they don't see the trees and they don't see the leaves. They're busy examining the veins in the leaves. This is not a strategy for life balance.

A fundamental advantage I've found is to view things first and foremost *from a strategic standpoint* and not a tactical one. It's not that tactics aren't important, but that we tend to be *strictly* tactical. That's why consultants seldom have cogent marketing, pricing, growth, retirement, and—yes—life balance strategies.

> View your work and your life through a telescope, not a microscope. You'll gain a true perspective of the world and your place in it, and your decisions will be far easier, more relevant, and much more successful.

Tactical blinders are an occupational hazard. We become adept at project management (the ultimate, and perhaps most boring, of the tactical pursuits). We organize and plan,[4] follow up, budget, correct problems—we tend to be the quintessential tactical marvels.

But at what cost?

The timeless graph in Figure 1.1 shows the relationship between strategy and tactics. I would suggest that, while the ideal condition—for a client or for ourselves—is in Quadrant #1, we actually spend most of our careers if we're not careful in Quadrant #2. Even Ultimate Consultants, highly successful, profitable, and retaining long-term repeat business, are basically reactionary and operational, not proactive and strategic.

---

4. Planning and strategy are, of course, two entirely different disciplines, the latter involved with goal setting and the former with implementing. The phrase "strategic planning" is a huge oxymoron. For more about these distinctions, read *Top Management Strategy: What It Is and How to Make It Work* by Ben Tregoe and John Zimmerman (Simon & Schuster, 1980) or my own *Best Laid Plans: Turning Strategy into Action Throughout Your Organization* (Las Brisas Research Press, 1994; originally *Making It Work,* HarperBusiness, 1990).

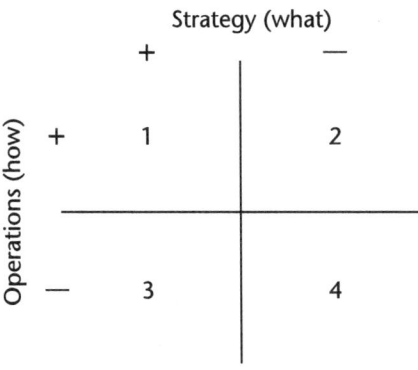

Strategy (what)

Operations (how)

	+	—
+	1	2
—	3	4

Figure 1.1. The Relationship Between Strategy and Tactics

If you don't believe me, here's a quick test. You don't have to send it in for grading, and you don't have to share it. But you do have to be honest:

Strategy Assessment

1. Do you tend to wait until the last minute or even neglect to put away retirement funds, which are deductible amounts from taxes, or do you commit these funds early in the fiscal year from initial profits?
2. Do you take vacations as time permits and add them on to business trips, or do you plan them well ahead and work your business around them?
3. Do you tend to think about new products and services when you see the competition's success with them, or do you lead the pack in innovative and original products and service offerings?
4. Are you a late adapter to technology, struggling to adjust and make it work for you, or do you integrate the newest developments into your practice and your life to ease your load?

If you're not becoming more strategic as you mature, achieving greater success, and continuing to learn, then there is something basically wrong with your philosophy. Moreover, you are not improving your life balance, but rather eroding it.

5. Are you still selling and marketing in the same fashion that you did years ago, or have you now developed more passive income, alliance partners, and non-labor-intensive alternatives to sustain your business and lifestyle?

6. Are your margins stable or even eroding from increased overhead and stagnant pricing, or have your margins increased dramatically as you've improved your value proposition and decreased costs of doing business?

7. Are you still a "well-kept secret" outside of your immediate clients and community, or have you created brands that attract new business at virtually no cost to you?

8. Are you continuing to travel at about the same rate as years ago, or are you controlling where you go and when?

9. Do you continue to accept unattractive clients and questionable projects to put bread on the table, or can you now afford to be selective, sometimes rejecting a prospect and/or firing a client?

10. Do you still struggle to find time for your family, interests, passions, and non-career pursuits, or are you able to immerse yourself in personal pleasures and private interests whenever you like?

I don't think this test requires a scoring sheet. You know where you stand. If you are reading this series—and the seventh and final book in this series, no less—then the second half of each question ought to be your honest selection. If it's not, you owe it to yourself and your loved ones to make some changes immediately.

And if you're not at the Ultimate Consultant stage, but are reading this book to prepare yourself to arrive there, then use these questions as your template to make important professional decisions along the way.

When you are faced with key decisions (and this applies to personal issues as well as professional, although I'm primarily talking about your business here), then ensure that

- You analyze what the longer-term implications are.
- You're never penny wise and pound foolish, meaning that you're willing to invest today for a return in the future.
- You maintain the perspective of what the decision means in light of your client's existence and your own existence. (Few things we ever do have endless import, and none will affect the future of Western civilization.)

All Things Being Equal?

A great fallacy about life balance is the idea of equal measurements. No one sleeps a fourth of the day, works a fourth, plays a fourth, or eats a fourth. Compartmentalizing life offers little reprieve. Charting the day and scheduling every minute—even rest time—often creates an even greater sense of imbalance.

Disregard equal. There's no such thing as an equally balanced life. If I could spend 80 percent of my waking time with my family, 10 percent working, and 10 percent in personal development, I would consider that balanced. Would anyone else? Doubtful, but who cares?

Do I get to balance my time like that right now? No, but I'm heading toward it! And when that time comes I may appear to be the most out-of-balance person on the planet to those who wear imbalance and workaholism as a badge.

You alone get to determine what balance means for your life. Once you discover it, pursue it with ease.

Paul Evans

- You determine what the impact will be on your goals for the next several years, and not just for today or tomorrow.
- You factor in the implications for your personal life. (I've had the good fortune to be able to turn down business over the past decade that would have compromised my ethics, my comfort, my family time, and/or my passions. That's a position few people attain, regardless of wealth, since it has more to do with philosophy and beliefs than with bank statements and income.)

Any profession is a means to an end. It is the economic fuel for your life. If you believe that your life is the fuel for your career, not only will you run out of gas, but you'll probably crash and burn. You retire from a job. You never retire from your life.

It's not where you start; it's where you finish. The runners on the outside lane of the track with the staggered start have no advantage over those on the inside starting farther back. They all have the same distance to cover.

The point, I think, is to keep your eye on the goal and not to waver. It turns out, most of the time, that your life will outlast your career.

ALAN'S ULTIMATE LESSONS

Maintain your sense of humor at all times. It creates tremendous perspective and enables you to laugh at yourself, first and foremost. Those who have the worst life balance are those who take themselves too seriously. Nothing we do affects the fate of humankind, but everything we do affects us tomorrow. I defray hostility with humor, create relationships (as an introvert) with humor, and keep my sanity with humor.

One morning before 10:30, my copier ran out of toner, my laser printer ran out of toner, my postage meter ran out of postage, my fax ran out of paper, my email crashed, and my car developed a leak in its left rear tire. I started out angry and quickly fell apart laughing at this modern version of Job's lot. I decided to take care of everything before lunch, then attend to my normal commitments, but then arrange a reward.

I resolved to take the next day off and never get out of my pajamas. I spent the next day in heedless hedonism, watching old movies and ordering food to be delivered.

My wife asked if I were ill. I told her no, I was just recovering from a bad day. She told me she wished she were I. I take that as a great compliment.

Now I'm hoping that things go so comprehensively haywire again, because I'm going to spend the day after that at a spa . . .

CHAPTER 2

Leverage— Archimedes Was Right

There's a Reason Why the "Big Eight" Have Slimmed Down

When the major audit firms entered the consulting business, a lot of consulting firms became quite alarmed, and a great many solo practitioners began to think about other lines of work. I began to salivate. It was apparent then, and is even more apparent now, that the "audit mentality" was not going to create consulting excellence, and a legion of technicians didn't exactly create an office of fine consultants.

Now, instead of a "big eight" we have barely a "moderate four." The Mercedes of the bunch, Andersen, showed at Enron what happens when your external, independent, objective advisors, well, ain't.

Solo practitioners have tremendous advantages for their clients and for themselves. The operating principle here, however, is *leverage*. There are a multitude of accountabilities, tasks, jobs, and objectives, but the key is not to personally be responsible for all of them. Moreover, whereas larger firms revel in complexity, since it raises billable hours and seems to create an impression that those hosts of hired hands actually are needed, solo practitioners and small firms should focus on simplicity and clarity. (There is a great word in Spanish—"claro"—which means "exactly" or "obviously." I want to say to clients fourteen times a day, "Claro!" I guess I need more work in Barcelona.)

If you want to balance the working side of your life, then simplify, simplify, simplify what you do. Claro.

REDUCING WORK TO OCCAM'S RAZOR

I alluded to the law of Occam's Razor in the prior chapter. This is the eponymous product of William of Occam (1285–1349), an English philosopher. In the course of his work on nominalism, he proposed that things shouldn't be needlessly multiplied in complexity and that the most obvious and easiest-to-access answers are usually accurate.

In modern times we've tended to say, "If all else fails, follow directions."

There are fail-safe mechanisms you can use to reduce the time you spend investigating, analyzing, recommending, and implementing. I've reduced them here, following my own advice, to their simplest and most facile possible form.

CASE STUDY

One of the people in my mentor program told me his interviews were taking over an hour to complete on a subject as simple and direct as "Who are our customers and why are they buying?" The reason was clear to me once we role played. He was asking strategic, philosophical, and subjective questions, rather than objective, specific, and tactical questions.

The question "How do you feel about our buying environment?" will create an avalanche of reflection and supposition, most of it probably inaccurate. However, the question, "What evidence did you use to tell you this was the actual buyer?" focuses the respondent on a particular piece of factual information ("He told me it was his budget and that he had hired our predecessors").

As opposed to relationship building, don't start at 50,000 feet when you're implementing. Start at ground level.

My suggestion is that you have a travel hobby. For years, I carried around a violin on all business trips. I could spend hours in hotel rooms practicing things that I never seemed to have time for at home. One day, a security screener tried to pry off the back of a very expensive violin with a screwdriver, so I started leaving it at home. I switched to magic. I now stow magic notes, photocopies of tricks from magic books, and DVDs in my traveling case. All I need is a few coins and a deck of cards and I can be amused for hours. I've never been on a flight that felt more than about fifteen minutes long.

Engaging in something that is totally absorbing is meditative and mind-clearing. As a result of these practice sessions, I've been able to learn all sorts of difficult sleight of hand that other magicians never seem to have time to practice. I've been acknowledged by other magicians as a world-class finger flicker and have become one of the main authorities on sleight of hand in the New York area.

What these two things have in common is an additional principle: Have some things that you would like to get to but can't seem to get to that are appropriate to traveling or can be pursued during the inordinate amount of time that we are forced to wait for things. Don't make them compulsively driven activities that prove that you can make every moment count. Make them delicious moments that you can anticipate, so that long flights or other long waits become eagerly awaited interludes, rather than long stretches of boredom or "required" activities.

George Silverman, President and Founder, Market Navigation, Inc.

Remember "for want of a nail . . . a kingdom was lost"? A recent zillion-dollar Mars probe was lost because one group of scientists used metric measures and another group, at a different site, used inches. Most answers are right in front of our noses, and most of the time involve merely common sense.

Reducing the Complex to the Basics

1. Ask "Why?"

By asking "Why?" as often as you can, you'll arrive quickly at a "root cause" or a basic need. Stopping too soon will leave you at symptoms, not cause, and "feelings," not facts. The process might look like Figure 2.1 if the client presented a problem such as "Our sales are below forecast."

Sales are below forecast only in Region #1, and that's because three key people left for a better package at the competition and the client's own new compensation package is six months overdue. So do you as a consultant want to start with improving sales forecasting or compensation design and delivery?

You may think this is a "no-brainer," but these sequences occur *in the majority of client work as initially presented.* A good therapist finds the cause of the presentation made by the patient. A good consultant should do the same with the client.

After all, we are corporate therapists.

2. Ask for Objective Information

When two employees walk into a manager's office and complain about a supervisor, the immediate deviation of behavior is not the absent third person, but the two doing the complaining. It's dangerous, time-consuming folly to work on a project that has a basic premise such as "Morale is lousy over there," "That department is politically aligned against us," or "They just aren't team players."

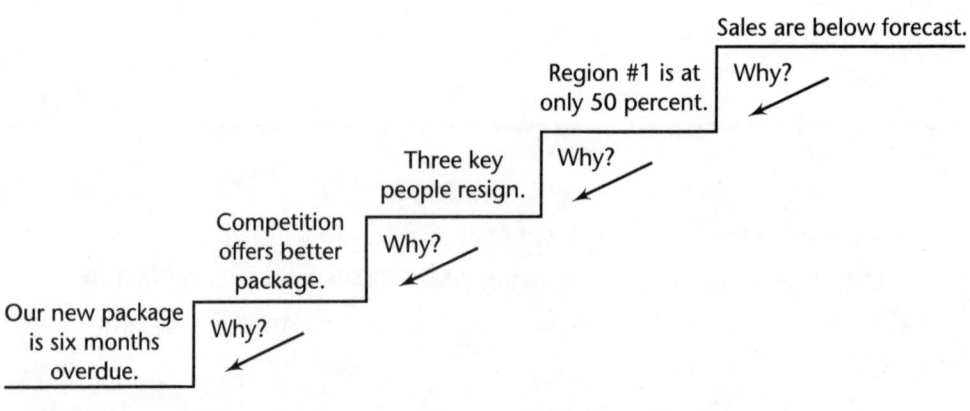

Figure 2.1. Asking "Why?" to Find a Starting Point

I once asked a manager what exact, observable behavior led her to believe that "morale is low" and she responded, "Because employees are not supporting the United Way campaign this year." That it was a recessionary period, wages were frozen, and 15 percent of the workforce had been terminated entirely escaped her radar!

Similarly, I've found that most training solutions are in search of problems that aren't there. Managers love to throw dollars at training because then they don't have to deal with the harder parts, such as feedback, reward, evaluations, modeling correct behavior, and so on.

Any time you're asked to design training of any type, ask: "What behavior leads you to believe that people need skills development? How, specifically, are they underperforming?" About 75 percent of the time the answer will be attitudinal or environmental and have nothing to do with skills or competence. Training won't do a thing but make people even unhappier.

3. Ask for Evidence

This is related to behavior, but includes non-performance issues as well. When the buyer says, "Our retention rate is far below the industry average," ask, "What's your evidence for that belief?" The buyer will often cite the claims of an employee who "knows the competition," or some number being floated around the Internet, or simply company mythology.

Get in the habit of asking your client about evidence and of separating fact from fiction. Most cultures have a valid body of knowledge, but *also* have a corporate mythology that unfairly demands equal consideration.

These three devices—asking "why," using observable behavior, and seeking factual evidence—will use Occam's Razor to slice through complexity and confusion. They are the early aspects of the "lever" which, with a little force, can move mountains.

Archimedes claimed, "Give me a lever and only a place to stand, and I can move the world." I think you and I, therefore, can easily move a client to more solid ground.

If you think the search for life balance is challenging while working for a company, try starting one. Beginning a business, non-profit or otherwise, demands that you make actionable decisions that ultimately reflect your priorities, daily if not hourly. You learn very early on that relationships built on integrity and trust are at the very core of your business and your family, and that without proper attention, both will wither.

One year and two months ago my husband supported me in my dream to start a consulting business—we picked up our pooch and left comfortable jobs, our wonderful home, and loving friends and family to move west across the Pacific to start anew. Knowing no one in the islands was one of hundreds of obstacles to upset our balance.

Achieving it has taken on new meaning as a new marriage, a new state, and a new business have called for us to live more simply than we have ever been accustomed to, to exhibit more patience than we thought possible, and to be unfailing with our show of love for each other, whether through humor, affection, or conversation. But one year later, we are enjoying a balance we see others struggle to grasp.

Absent are the close friends, family, and the pride and comfort of home ownership; however, the fulfillment resulting from a loving and fun marriage, a healthy and happy pooch, and a growing business provide a newfound happiness we are unsure how we did without.

Tanya Goodwin-Maslach, President, Linking Visions Consulting

WORKING SMART AND NOT HARD

Most people work too hard, not because they have to but rather because they confuse hard work with effective work.

If you watch great athletes, they perform with a precision and efficiency in their actions that preserves their strength, whether hurdling, cross-country skiing, or swimming. All effort is directed to the most productive use of their bodies. If you don't believe that, try swimming across a pool with your fingers spread like fans, rather than cupped, or try hitting a tennis ball with a backpack strapped on.

A client told me that it was imperative to better educate independent distributors about the quality of their products, since those distributors influenced the end-customers. When I asked what evidence they had for that belief, they told me, honestly, "It makes sense."

When we went to distributors and asked them what influenced them to order from which manufacturer, they told us uniformly: "Our customers are builders. They tell us by brand what they want, and we deliver. We only suggest alternatives when their preference is out of stock or otherwise unavailable."

The builders told us that they ordered those brands that were of equal quality but also readily available, so that they never had to stop a project to await materials. So the key to the entire sequence was ensuring that the products were either kept in distributor inventory or available for shipment within three business days.

The dealers were simply classic "middle men" who had no preferences about brands!

Yet, curiously, most people go through life with a figurative pack filled with bricks strapped on their backs. I call this wasted effort "going around the block to get next door."

There is a wonderful story of a man seeing a friend searching in the street at night. "What happened?" he asked.

"I lost my keys," was the reply.

"Did you lose them right here?" said the man, starting to help in the search.

"No, I dropped them down the block when I left the restaurant."

"Then why are you searching here?" asked the man incredulously.

"Because the light is better here."

There are several reasons for working hard and not smart, but the most critical is the search for perfection. We are tentative and hesitant to proceed unless we feel we've done everything possible to ensure success. However, most success is actually accomplished *en route to the goal,* meaning that the adjustments and modifications made along the way are the keys, since they are in reaction to real-time events and not hypothesized events.

Graphically, the waste of seeking perfection looks like Figure 2.2.

When you're 80 percent ready to move, move! The report, presentation, evaluation, meeting, workshop, or whatever will not be improved demonstrably by demonically seeking to improve that final 20 percent. Moreover, *that final 20 percent of improvement is seldom perceived by the other party.* In other words, the workshop participants, meeting attendees, reader of the report, person being evaluated, and other recipients can't appreciate the distinction of that final fifth.

What they can readily appreciate are any adjustments you make that improve their lives. Consequently, rather than a workshop that has every minute structured, question-and-answer sessions that are spontaneous (and may be highlighted by some "I don't know" responses) are welcomed. Rather than an evaluation that seeks to document every aspect of a subordinate's performance, an interchange during which the subordinate performs a self-evaluation (or one for you) may be far more valuable.

Life and work are about success, not perfection. This fact demands that you be willing to live with moderate degrees of ambiguity. Once you are comfortable doing that, you will be working far smarter and with less effort.

BEYOND PERFECTION

I've interviewed both actors and athletes who tell me that you can over-prepare a part and over-practice an event. An actor commented that "You want to be at your peak during the actual performance, which means that you don't want everything down 'pat.' You want some adrenaline rushing."

Other reasons we work too hard include the following:

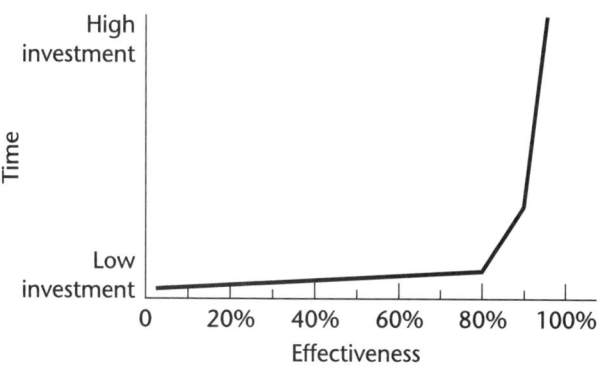

Figure 2.2. The Hard Work That Results from Seeking Perfection

- We confuse input with output. Sales calls don't matter, business acquisition does; calls accepted per hour don't matter, happy customers do; and number of trips per day don't matter, but on-time performance does.
- We are uncomfortable with ambiguity and seek to eliminate it rather than work within it. There is no way to eliminate ambiguity in any endeavor. We can reduce it, but that final 20 percent can't be eradicated, and trying to do so creates onerous work.
- We are incorrectly measured on activity instead of result. We often accede to being evaluated on the basis of how much we do, rather than on what we produce; how often we show up, rather than meeting our goals. In grammar school, attendance was a big deal, and there was trouble if you were absent too often. Yet some kids with flawless attendance performed poorly, and some with spotty attendance performed superbly. Are we still measuring the wrong things as adults?
- We subscribe to a murderous work ethic. Our philosophical and/or spiritual bent is that we should work hard because it is somehow more noble and fulfilling to do so. That may have been true when farmers had to clear acres by hand if their families were to survive, but we now live in a day when the government pays farmers *not* to grow anything.
- We over-commit. We've lost sight of the fact that we can't really help others unless we help ourselves, and we assume that we can help others without surcease or relief. Thus, we are often working on rundown batteries and reserve power because we're carrying the load for so many others. I know

people who serve on six boards of directors. They are doing a poor job on all six, *because no one can do an outstanding job as a director with that kind of load.* We're better working effectively and intelligently on a few things, rather than inefficiently and in a bedraggled way on a host of things.

- We don't focus. I'm always impressed by the top hotel concierges. They may have several people at the desk, messages to return, and two people holding on the phone. But they give unimpeded attention to the person they are helping at the moment. Consequently, when each person is served, he or she is served well and feels that he's received special treatment. This is far better than doing a slapdash job on everyone's requests. We have to focus on the immediate issue at hand and resolve it in a high-quality manner.

- We underestimate the value of "down time." We need time to play, relax, recreate, enjoy our family, or just sit and recharge our power supplies. The more we enjoy life, *the less we believe that we are being "cheated" by the work demands made on us.* My observations are that people who lead fulfilling and rich lives—and allot themselves time for personal fulfillment even in the midst of tough work challenges—are those who perform their work the best. Despite the "workaholic" imagery, I've never met one whom I felt was doing his or her best possible work. The support your work provides for your life balance will be repaid by the quality of the effort you feel comfortable and justified investing in your work.

The very most out-of-balance people I've met are those who try to shortcut both work and their personal lives and relationships. They cheat at both ends, and it shows. Neither aspect of their lives is fulfilling, so neither is capable of fueling and supporting the other. This is a death spiral for balance.

It's important to realize that you can proceed when you're about 80 percent prepared to do so, but not much before. Below that number, you're just trying to get things out the door, put in appearances, and provide lip service. We

Advice from the Readers of *Balancing Act*

My life feels more balanced when I focus on my big goals and tolerate some of the "mess" that comes with pursuing them. Big goals include having a solid marriage, good relationships with my children, and meaningful friendships; providing value to my clients; being a reliable and challenging colleague; providing service to people who are less advantaged than myself; and maintaining an attitude of lifelong learning.

I am able to have this sense of life balance in large part because of my marriage. We have been able to trade roles, and that has freed us to do things that we might not have done otherwise. Currently, my husband is in school. He does most of the work of running our household, including answering calls from our now adult children and caring for two cats and two golden retrievers. In 1988, our roles were completely the reverse after I quit my job as a stockbroker and went to school.

We have learned (along with the kids) that you can skip class to go see a post–World Series parade for the Atlanta Braves, even if the school says it is an unexcused absence. It is possible to get a haircut on a weekday, conduct a business meeting on Saturday, and live on Chinese takeout for multiple days in a row. Getting lost while on vacation can lead to fascinating discoveries if you don't worry about what you were "supposed" to be doing at that moment. Lessons worth knowing, in my book.

Constance R. Dierickx, Marietta, Georgia

have to be confident and comfortable to find that proper place between being unprepared and sufficiently prepared, although not perfectly prepared.

Assess your work life:

- Are you taking work home regularly?
- Is your desk awash in projects and demands?
- Are you behind on your reading?
- Are you missing deadlines?
- Do you fail to return phone calls and emails promptly?
- Are people regularly "pestering" you for things they're owed?
- Are you unable to complete what you had planned on a given day?

If you answer "yes" to *any* of these conditions, then you're working too hard and not very smart. The good news is that you can change these conditions tomorrow by focusing on how you use your time.

HOW TO HAVE MORE TIME THAN YOU NEED

Next to "How do I raise my fees?" I'm probably asked this question more than any other: "How can I make better use of my time?"

Since there is no point in making more money if you don't have the time to enjoy it, I can make a point that the second question might be more important—or at least premonitory—to the first. Time is the great equalizer. We all, kings and working stiffs alike, have twenty-four hours in a day. It's a non-renewable resource. Yesterday doesn't recur. And it's completely discretionary. "I don't have the time to give you feedback" actually means "I have more important things to do at the moment than to give you feedback."

So here are three ineffable conditions:

- The resource constant for all of us is availability.
- It is finite and non-replenishable.
- It is discretionary.

If you want to manage your time so that you have optimal use and effectiveness of it, then these are the three parameters within which you must work. Fortunately, they provide plenty of latitude. Unfortunately, they are usually perceived as inflexible and unalterable.

So these next few pages may be the most critical aspect of the book for many of you. Here's how to have more time than you need.

1. Plan Your Day, but with Flexibility

Well-run medical practices *do not* schedule wall-to-wall patient appointments. They allow time for the inevitable late patient, unexpected extra care needed, or otherwise unanticipated crisis.

Plan your day so that you can handle the expected, but leave time for the unexpected. Do not, ever, schedule wall-to-wall meetings (more on this below).

Allow time between appointments or activities to take some breaths, check on messages, or correct a problem.

If you're working on the basis of an eight-hour day, consider the half-hour before and after lunch and the hour from four to five as "non-schedulable," for example. Never schedule tight connections, whether in an airport or between meetings in the same city.

2. Make a List

Even if you have an electronic organizer, computer calendar, or sophisticated Filofax™, make a brief list each evening of what you *must* accomplish the next day. The list should be relatively brief—having to accomplish thirty things is a recipe for collapse and frustration.

Keep a pad near the television or near your bed. As you recall a *must*, note it. Use that list to keep you focused on your next day's success. For example, reading *Business Week* usually isn't a *must*, but buying your wife's anniversary card or reviewing the Henderson report before it goes to your boss just might be.

If you must sacrifice activities, make sure they are not *musts*.

People moan about time loss and ask, "Where has the day gone?!" The day has gone the way of the dodo bird, because you've forced time to become extinct. People weren't paying attention and didn't care as the last birds were hunted, and they don't care today as the last minutes of their lives disappear.

---

3. Avoid Meetings at All Costs

I'm not talking about marketing meetings, which are our life's blood, but rather every other kind: Meeting during implementation, meeting with non-economic buyers, meeting where a phone call or email would otherwise serve perfectly, meeting for the sake of "getting together," and so forth.

Meetings that aren't for direct sales purposes are a colossal waste of time, because you can't control the flow completely and they are forever starting and ending late. Don't automatically agree to a meeting *unless it's with the economic buyer or a prospective economic buyer,* before or during the engagement.

I have completed entire projects without one meeting. If you must have them, keep them one-on-one. *Meeting wastefulness is in direct proportion to the number of people present.*

4. Ruthlessly Eliminate the Non-Essential

We allow "necessary evils" to creep into our lives. They take the form of discussions with people we do not find interesting, routine follow-ups, reviews of reports others have already reviewed, upgrading computer software, dealing with repairs, and so on.

Don't provide interim or final client reports if the client hasn't requested them (and don't, for heaven's sake, offer them as a "deliverable" in your proposals). Don't give out your cell phone number and don't keep it on. Your job is to respond quickly, not instantly, and nothing you or I do has implications for world peace. Keep your office phone forwarded when you need time to concentrate.

Don't create work for yourself. If you focus on the results and objectives of any project, then support only those activities which will quickly and effectively lead you there. *Most consultants visit the client site more than they need to because they feel that's how to justify their value.*[1]

5. Scrutinize Your Reading

Do you see that big pile of magazines, flyers, reports, newspapers, and assorted other periodicals on your desk, on the floor, and sliding off the sofa? Throw them all out if they've been there over a week.

You must read *The Wall Street Journal* and your local newspaper every day, and you should read a few monthly magazines on your profession and your major clients' businesses. But that's it. All the rest is extra. If you can get to it

---

1. I'm not going to get into the wastefulness of hourly based and per diem fees here, since you shouldn't have come this far in the series if that's what you're doing. But if you've picked up this book first for some reason, I refer you to the third book in The Ultimate Consultant Series, *Value-Based Fees: How to Charge—and Get—What You're Worth* (Jossey-Bass/Pfeiffer, 2002).

without disturbing the rest of your time flow, great. If you can't, then dispose of it. (After all, if you're not getting to it effectively and you're reading the seventh book in The Ultimate Consultant Series, then how much do you really need it?!)

As a rule of thumb, if you can't read a newspaper on the same day of publication or a magazine during the same week you've received it, jettison it. Periodicals are meant to update you, not to serve as archival reminders. Seriously consider reducing your subscription lists every six months and, when you consider a new subscription, find *two* existing subscriptions you can cancel. These things accrete like lime deposits from the roof of a cave. Pretty soon you've got magazine stalactites.

It may be okay to develop piles of recreational reading material—novels and magazines about hobbies, for example—although even that drives me crazy. But with business literature, peruse it or lose it. Better still, cut off the supply of anything that's not useful enough to demand your rapid attention.

6. Delegate

Most of you reading this are solo practitioners, but that doesn't mean you can't delegate. In fact, delegation is one of the greatest time-reclamation devices that exists.

Delegate everything and anything that doesn't need your personal touch (computer repair, background research, statistics, errands, and so on) to the following people as befits the situation:

- Your kids, spouse, or partner, who can occasionally help out (collate a mailing or call places for information).
- Client personnel, often in a better position than you anyway (develop historical data about the situation or contact their own clients).
- A college intern, receiving credit for working with you (research some likely prospects or work with the computer repair people).

- An hourly subcontractor (do your monthly books or create a new design for your brochure).
- Neighbors and friends (pay them to staff a phone "hot line" or to call in for you when you're on vacation overseas).

There is no reason why your "personal touch" is needed for the repetitive, the mundane, or the non-essential.

7. Combine Downtime with Uptime

We must suffer through certain "time indignities," including waiting for late-arriving clients or prospects, commuting time, missed connections, waiting for repairs, spending time on "hold," and so on. But within these time traps resides opportunity.

Always have something to read in your briefcase, including a book for pleasure. Use a headset in the office so that you can work while you're listening to that extraordinarily melodic music on "hold."[2] Use your cell phone to make calls while you're waiting for your car or in a long line at the airport. Use CDs or tapes in your car for business education or personal enjoyment.

I'm not a "type A" personality, yet I've never understood people sitting on an airplane for two hours staring vacantly into space or pacing up and down while waiting for a late meeting to finally begin. That time is either valuable or wasted, depending entirely on your discretionary use of it.

8. Get Tough

Finally, just say "no." Hang up on the telephone solicitors (best line: "Sorry, but I don't respond to phone solicitations as a matter of policy"). Don't talk to strangers on airplanes or trains (best line: "I'm a fundraiser, would you like to take part in my work?"). Put filters on your email, using both subject (for example, Buy Stocks) and sources (for example, Stocks@getrich.com).

Make your home office sacrosanct, if that's how you work. Your family and friends wouldn't stop downtown to bother you, and they shouldn't do so

---

2. But not so you can work while carrying on a conversation. "Multi-tasking" is for computers, but not polite or effective with a client, colleague, or acquaintance.

in your home office either. Don't allow "reverse time use" to ruin you, wherein *you're* running errands for others, minding the dogs, and amusing the kids.

You wouldn't throw money out the window. Don't treat time any differently.

Leverage is about getting the most accomplished with the least input. It's maximum acceleration *and* mileage on a small amount of fuel. This is possible because, instead of dealing with the limitations of the internal combustion engine and the laws of thermodynamics, we're dealing with the human mind, talent, and innovation.

Advice from the Readers of *Balancing Act*

You deserve quiet time. You deserve time every day, alone, by yourself, for meditation, contemplation, reflection, prayer, daydreaming, or just plain sitting still. I'm not talking about television watching or book reading time. I'm not talking about quality time with your kids. I'm not talking about time for doing hobbies or artwork. It's not about cleaning your desk or making your agenda for the day or lists of things to do. I'm talking about time when you can be by yourself, with yourself, doing absolutely nothing.

We think we have to be infinitely available to our jobs and families. 24/7/365 is our latest business model. We have telephones, faxes, pagers, cell phones, and wireless email. Where does that leave time for us? Turn everything off for your quiet time. Let your family know you're taking a break. Believe it or not, the world can function without us for a few minutes.

If you don't know what to do with your quiet time, just breathe. Watch your breath flowing in and your breath flowing out. The Vietnamese Zen Buddhist monk Thich Nhat Hanh wrote a wonderful poem to go with your breathing: "Breathing in, I calm my body/Breathing out, I smile./Dwelling in the present moment/I know this is a wonderful moment."

Enjoy your quiet moment. It's spiritual replenishment. It's like going to the cosmic gas station to get a fill-up. Decide to take some quiet time in your life. You deserve it!

Marcia Sacks

FOUR CHOICES FOR ACTION

If you want to achieve maximum leverage for your time and energy, there's a secret about the actions we can take that very few people truly understand: There are only four choices.

I know that sounds radical, overly simplistic, and just ridiculous in a complex world of work, business, influence, bargaining, and so forth. But if you observe those people who are truly outstanding at minimizing their investment (energy, time, resources, and so forth) and maximizing their results (profit, growth, repute, etc.)—as I have for a quarter of a century—you'll find that they tend to make things easy. Remember Occam's Razor.

In Figure 2.3 you'll see that we are always dealing with the past or the future. (We may be making decisions in the present, but they are in reaction to something that has already transpired or in anticipation of something we want to transpire or prevent.) And we are dealing with either cause or effect.

Consequently, "fixing" a problem may mean that we are merely dealing with the effect (symptom) to ameliorate its impact or truly removing the cause to eliminate the underlying root cause.

Example: If your boss is habitually twenty minutes late for the start of an important staff meeting each Friday because his assistant meets with him first to go over early messages, you can take *adaptive* action by not scheduling any important matters or key decisions in the first twenty minutes. However, you can take *corrective* action by rescheduling the meeting to begin before the

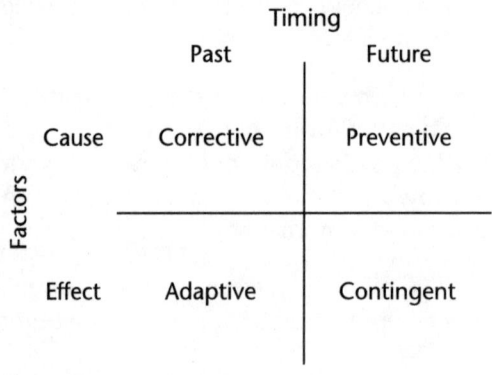

Figure 2.3. Four Types of Actions

boss's assistant arrives (or meet with the boss and explain why punctual arrival is a "must").

Another example: If your email is out of control with hundreds of messages from mostly unimportant sources every morning, you can adapt by having an assistant filter out the truly important items for your later review. Or you can remove the problem by changing your email address and providing it to very few people.

Most of us wind up adapting to things we should actually correct, meaning that we add very costly activity and resource use to our day. Ironically, the better "adapters" we become, the more we tend to do it and forget about problem correction altogether.

If your car leaks oil, you adapt by checking the level regularly and pouring in another quart frequently. But you correct by finding the source of the leak and repairing it. Adaptive actions seem less costly (a quart of oil versus a major repair), but *they actually consume increasing amounts of our time and only put a "bandage" on a condition that will generally grow worse.*

We should focus more on corrective action—removing the cause of our problems and refusing to live with them (the "necessary evil" bromide). That is the route to a leveraged, stress-free environment.

In terms of the future, we can prevent a problem by seeking to eliminate its likely cause and/or deal with its manifestation at some point by being prepared to cope with the effects. *Example:* A fire marshal and approved electrical accessories and "no smoking" signs are all preventive measures for various causes of fire (careless smoking, electrical overload, poorly stored combustibles, etc.). However, insurance, emergency exit drills, and sprinkler systems are designed to ameliorate the effects of fire, should it occur (loss of life, property, money, etc.). We need both kinds of protection.

Usually, the more likely that a given cause will occur, the more we need to maximize our preventive actions. The more unlikely the cause, the more we need effective contingent actions to deal with the effects, since we're not investing in prevention. The former would be represented by maximizing customer service for clients who are constantly sought by our competitors. We would want to prevent as many sources of unhappiness and poor service as possible. The latter would occur when we buy "key person" insurance for an important owner or officer. We can't do much to prevent an unforeseen accident—say, being hit by a beer truck—but we can have something prepared to lessen the impact of the loss on the business.

When your child seeks out colleges, the preventive action may be coaching to maximize performance on the SAT exams (and a college fund established many years before), but the contingent actions may be "back-up" schools (and an equity line on the house).

Any of these actions can be "interim" or "permanent." An interim action is intended for a finite period, while a permanent action is intended as the final solution. You may take the interim adaptive action of frequent oil additions until the permanent corrective action of fixing the leak is possible. You may accept an interim preventive action of keeping the kids out of the pool until the permanent contingent action of a pool alarm or barrier to the deep end is in place.

The problem is that too many "interim" actions become permanent by default, apathy, or sloth. You can see "patches" and "repairs" around a great many houses and offices that were never meant to be permanent: wires that snake around desks and are hung on plants; desks in the hallway; cardboard boxes holding key files which ought to be on the computer or stored in metal files.

To what extent is your work (or personal) life creating and relying on those patches and repairs? How many "necessary evils" have you accepted, and how much time and energy must you invest to support all of these adaptations?

Seek to remove the causes of problems and prevent future causes from occurring. That's leverage. The best adapters will always lose out to people who don't have the problems to begin with. The fire sprinklers and insurance might have worked perfectly, but no one's very proud that the fire occurred in the first place.

Most people whom I encounter with time management problems and poor leverage are those who have built an edifice of adaptations. They remind me of the performers who used to appear on the old "Ed Sullivan Show," spinning plates on the ends of long rods inserted in a table. As the plates spun, their momentum would keep them balanced, but as entropy set in and the plates slowed, they would fall and crash unless the rod was freshly spun.

The performer would frantically run back and forth spinning more and more rods as more and more plates were utilized. It was a hilarious and impressive act. The problem is that at some point the growing amount of plates would be untenable to keep spinning, or the existing amount would finally exhaust the available energy to maintain their speed. Sooner or later, the plates would crash.

And so it is in our lives. There are only four types of actions to contend with: (1) *adaptive* for living with past problems; (2) *corrective* for eliminating their causes; (3) *preventive* for avoiding future events; and (4) *contingent* for coping with them should they occur. Don't mistake coping for prevention or adapting for correction.

Eliminate problems and prevent future ones from occurring. Those are the actions that decrease our investment and maximize our leverage. Archimedes said that, with a big enough lever and a strong spot to stand on, he could move the world.

ALAN'S ULTIMATE LESSONS

Whenever you reach a goal (or even set one to begin with), deal with an issue successfully, or develop a new idea, ask yourself, "What else can I do with this?" Look to leverage your successes and strengths. I find that too many people enjoy a brief success and immediately begin patting themselves on the back before they truly maximize their leverage.

I wrote a few articles on the subject of life balance which were well-received by the publications and their audiences. So I created a workshop that was fully subscribed and then a newsletter that has grown to over 5,000 subscribers. And now you're reading this book. And I haven't stopped with this, although future plans will remain a secret for now.

My lesson is that one success is virtually never isolated, but can be applied to a host of other formats, activities, and audiences. Don't stop with the first success. It's only a harbinger of what lies ahead, if you're willing to take the journey.

CHAPTER 3

Innovation and Risk

We're Here to Make Waves,
Not to Stick Our Toes in the Water

Most people at work tend to lead conservative lives. They are acutely aware of their long-term prospects sitting in other people's hands. They are burdened by peer pressure, hierarchical dictates, and cultural norms. Organizations, in general, are not hotbeds of creativity and change.

The trouble, of course, is that virtually all of us who are entrepreneurs are refugees from those same organizations, yet we carry the conservative baggage with us to our independent new lives. The originators and/or prime movers of such corporations—Sears, Hewlett, Packard, Sloan, Gates, Jobs—didn't create those giants through timidity and reluctance. They took bold risks.

As entrepreneurs, we should be taking, at the very least, prudent risks.

Innovation was defined by Joseph Schumpeter once as "creative destruction." I like to think of it as the constant attempt to set new standards. It is a process of creation, not restoration. Some people confuse it with creativity, but I see innovation as *applied creativity*. And in our lives and work, it's virtually impossible to move forward without risk, and it's impossible to thrive without innovation and new levels of competence.

THE WILLINGNESS, NOT MERELY THE FREEDOM, TO FAIL

We read the clichéd but true experiences of people like Edison all the time—someone whose great discoveries and breakthroughs occurred only after hundreds of times as many misses and defeats. The best salespeople are rejected over 80 percent of the time. The best hitters in baseball are successful only about one time in three. In both soccer and ice hockey, scoring is a rarity.

The greatest risk is often in doing nothing and standing still. Not one vacuum tube manufacturer successfully entered the transistor business, which replaced them. Championship teams that try to preserve the status quo often finish out of the running the next year. As Dizzy Dean observed, "Don't look back. Someone may be gaining on you."

What all this means for life balance in your career is that "playing it safe" is not a viable option and actually creates more stress, rather than alleviating stress. In fact, there are two equally noxious extremes: too much stress and too little stress. Figure 3.1 is a standard psychological bell curve for stress, which was popularized by Judith Bardwalk in her book *Danger in the Comfort Zone.*

On the right side of the chart, excessive stress creates a paralysis of action. For consultants, this may mean that money pressures, sensitive prospect calls, and the current economy may drive one to a near-catatonic state. Instead of boldly suggesting large projects or daring interventions, the tendency may be to ensure that the fees aren't prohibitive and to get the work at any price.

But on the left side, excessively low stress—the result of a couple of large

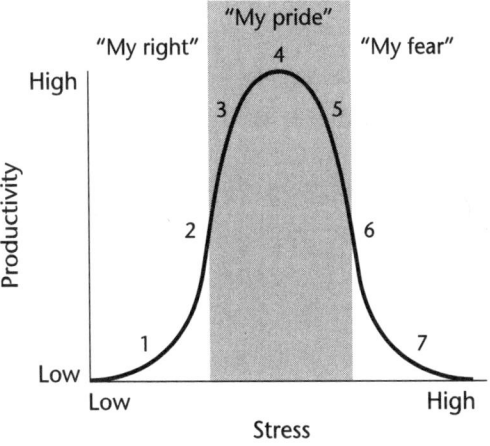

Figure 3.1. Relationship Between Stress and Innovation

When I began my own practice in 1985, I did so because I had been fired and was angry, not because I had created a great business plan or saw a wonderful economic window of opportunity. I viscerally decided that the potential, although elusive, benefits were well worth the substantial and quite real risks.

My friends told me that they had the better side of the equation in organizational life. After all, they had far more security, much less risk, and a guaranteed paycheck. I might be able to earn more than they did eventually—you don't really create wealth unless you own your business—but the overall risk/reward ratio was certainly on their side.

Funny thing: By the early 1990s, not only was I out-earning them by hundreds of thousands of dollars annually, but I had far more job security as the downsizing mania of that decade threw millions of people out on the street, regardless of seniority, competence, and loyalty, and affected millions more through the depressed economic trickle-down.

Risk isn't always what you think it is.

Advice from the Readers of *Balancing Act*

Two years ago I was at a meeting to receive an award for the website I had developed for "my" beer company. All of the sudden I literally started to lose my balance. A very frightening experience: "I am not able to stand anymore—I will fall down." I managed to finish my presentation and go to my car. I started to drive but was afraid to use the highway, and after an hour I was back at the point where I had started. Desperately, I managed to drive twenty miles, than started to realize what was going on. It was not the first time my body had started a protest. Suddenly I realized: "How long can I ignore these signals? It is time to stop." I called my wife and told her that I would not go to my work the next day—an enormous relief.

What happened next: First, I slept fourteen hours per night for a period of six weeks. Over the next four months I was in therapy to find out what had happened. And the answer was terribly simple: I had been doing *their* thing for the last ten years of my life. Trying to live up to *their* expectations ("their" meaning: my parents, my friends, my bosses, and others)—never really thinking about the question: What are *my* expectations (of life, work, relationships)? For the past year I have been an independent consultant and making twice the money in half of the time—doing my thing!

José Evers, The Netherlands

projects underway, an annual retainer that will pay the bills for a year, a windfall from an inheritance, a new book out, and so on—can cause an attitude of sloth. Marketing stops, new approaches aren't of interest, leads aren't followed meticulously, and the consultant simply coasts. Nothing exciting comes of this.

The best place for all entrepreneurs is smack in the middle, where there is sufficient stress to create a sense of urgency, a willingness to take prudent risk and create changes, and a realization that the status quo is insufficient. The happiest, most productive people I know are at position #4 on the chart. They are self-motivated, highly energized, amazingly resilient professionals (inside or outside of organizational life).

The time to take prudent risk is when you are having hard times or moderate success. The time to take stronger risk is when you are doing wonderfully and acting from a position of strength. No risk, no reward. Or as William Penn said, "No cross, no crown."

The areas in which, and degrees to which, we take risks as entrepreneurs might look like this:

Area	Low Risk	Moderate Risk	High Risk
Financing	Use savings	Family borrowing	Home equity
Marketing	Print materials	Major website	Host public workshops
Sales	Work with low-level evaluators	Try to meet economic buyer	Meet economic buyer or refuse to pursue
Fees	Match client's budget needs	Competitive with larger firms	High-end, "Mercedes Benz" of the business
Philosophy	Mainstream, standard intent	New approaches to standard problems	Entirely contrarian and raising the bar
Personal Time	Only when time allows	Planned carefully and coordinated	Fully integrated and often spontaneous
Professional	Adheres to norms and peers	Seen as exemplar of best practices	Trendsetter and often defines new practices
Business Relationship	Vendor	Consultant	Peer; learned counsel
Acceptance of Failure	Personal defeat and setback	Important learning opportunity	Normal part of the job and expected
The Future	Uncertain and threatening	Positive with careful planning	Nimble and willing to build, no matter what

People who tell you they've never failed are in one of three positions: (1) they've never tried anything really worthwhile; (2) they have failed and don't realize it; or (3) they're lying. Failure—and the willingness to take risks which may lead to failure—is the mark of someone whose professional life is remarkably in balance. Trying to avoid failure at all costs is highly stressful (because it's a game that can't be won).

More importantly, you cannot run your professional life on the basis of *not* losing, *not* failing, and *not* incurring setbacks. In this business, we must play to win, not play to avoid losing. Every time you see an athletic team of any nature with a big lead lose the lead and the game in the latter stages of the competition, it's because the coach has opted to play it safe *and try to protect the lead.* That is,

Advice from the Readers of *Balancing Act*

Seven years ago, the consulting firm that I worked for offered a health and lifestyle status assessment to each of its employees. I participated. A few months after completing the status assessment, I received my results and a call from one of the physicians working for the assessment organization. His message was simple: You are at risk for a serious health event if you do not change your lifestyle. I wanted to change, but didn't have a clue how to do it.

After considering a number of options (slowing down, taking up a hobby, changing jobs), I settled on fulfilling a lifelong dream: becoming a martial artist. At age forty-nine and with no previous martial arts experience, I signed up for introductory lessons and started taking classes. My initial objective was to use it to exercise and to learn some basic martial arts techniques. I scheduled classes in my calendar. They were like any other meeting, and the only time I missed class was when I traveled. I would make up the missed classes on the Friday or Saturday of the week I traveled. Within a short time my focus changed and studying the martial arts became an avocation.

In the six years since I started studying the martial arts, I have earned a black belt, improved my stamina, reduced stress, and performed in my job and with my clients at a much higher level. I personally believe that had I not started studying the martial arts, I would have had a serious health event.

Tony Kubica, Warwick, Rhode Island

instead of playing with the intent to win, the team is playing with the intent not to lose. These are two radically different philosophies, and the latter is death to an entrepreneur.

Aristotle said that if we don't seek the truth, it will seek us out and find us. The same applies to risk. It is an inherent aspect of the solo practitioner's life. Trying to minimize it is pointless and futile, but adapting a risk-taking philosophy is aggressive, productive, and, ironically, comforting once you feel the power of innovation.

TESTING THE ENVELOPE

We tend to view experimentation and, in the test pilots' immortal phrase, "testing (or pushing) the envelope," as dangerous and risk-laden. But I've found that in balancing one's career, testing the envelope—stepping out of the "box" you're in—can actually be less stressful and more prone to increase your happiness.

That's because the envelope we're in is not always a comfortable nest, padded and protected to our comfort. We've often locked ourselves into an uncomfortable penitentiary, where we agonize in self-inflicted hard labor to maintain what we believe to be our proper "home."

> The reason to test the envelope is not so much to find more daring pursuits and callings, but actually to find happier, simpler, and easier ways to conduct your business and nurture your career. Old houses aren't necessarily comfortable. Sometimes they're just old and lack the necessary plumbing and conveniences.

How difficult is it for us to "rebalance" our work lives by testing the envelope? A lot easier than you'd ever suspect.

A championship race horse may win ten times the purses over a season as the next-best horse, but it doesn't win each race by ten lengths, train ten times as hard, or receive ten times as much attention. A championship horse wins most races by a nose, but wins ten times the purse of the second horse.

I couldn't imagine how I could earn serious money going out on my own if I charged by the hour. Every reputable, authoritative source advised me in 1985, when I launched my business, to calculate an hourly fee based on the lifestyle and expenses I expected.

But it made no sense, since the most valued senior partners at the top law firms in New York City were then billing at about $500 an hour. That was $20,000 a week, or $1,000,000 on a fifty-week year, assuming a constantly filled week. But I didn't want to work forty hours a week, and I knew that fee level wouldn't play well anywhere outside of New York.

I tested the envelope and arrived at value-based pricing, using my contribution to the project's results as the basis of my fee and asking for all or most of the fee in advance. To everyone in the profession's astonishment, I made this work and have probably earned millions more than another consultant doing my type of work but charging by the hour.[1]

You test the envelope to improve your life, not to endanger it.

You don't have to win by ten lengths, you only have to win by a nose.

The best salespeople easily earn ten times the commissions of average salespeople, but they don't know the product ten times better, don't work ten times the hours, don't have ten times the leads. They work a little smarter, know their territories and prospects a little better, and know just a few more selling techniques; that's all.

I make over ten times what the average attorney or consultant currently earns in the United States, and I work about twenty-five hours a week. And I'm constantly testing the envelope to explore whether I can work still less and make even more.

---

1. See the third book in this series, *Value-Based Fees: How to Charge—and Get—What You're Worth* (Jossey-Bass/Pfeiffer, 2002).

MID-FLIGHT TEST

As the proverbial "lone wolf," it can be tough to systematically test your current status against other possibilities professionally. Here are some guidelines I find useful:

Working Hours
- Do you work more than a forty-hour week?
- Are you denying yourself and your family because of work which must be completed in the evening and/or on weekends?

Travel
- Are you traveling more than 50 percent of the time? (If you're a successful veteran, ask yourself if you're traveling more than 25 percent of the time to places you just don't want to go.)
- Do you travel first class and comfortably, stay in fine hotels, and generally minimize the wear and tear of the road?

Business Acquisition
- Do prospects come to you regularly or must you "beat the bushes" constantly to find them?
- Are your average projects becoming larger in terms of both revenue amounts and profit margins?

If we don't continually test our own status, the default position is complacency or resistance to change. What would you tell a client in that condition and with that mental set?

Methodology
- Do you continue to do things the way you did five years ago, and can you perform most of your interventions "with your eyes closed"?
- Have you learned new techniques, tried new approaches, and become known for a wider variety of skills?

Professional Status

- Do you have one or more brands clearly recognized to be your unique positioning?
- Are you a leader, "voice," or authority in trade associations, and have you published within the profession?

Learning

- Do you know more today than you did a year ago about business, your craft, and the world around you?
- Are you serving as a mentor and exemplar to others?

We are all flying our own test planes. Although the profession is common, it is also highly diverse and each one of us occupies a singular position within it. Someone calculated recently that there were 800,000 different fare possibilities from Los Angeles to New York by air, if you factored in the number of airlines, their varied fares, various discounts (advance purchase, frequent flying, Saturday stay, and so on), and various connections.

How many possibilities are there for us? We have our unique talents, backgrounds, experiences, education, clients, prospects, methodologies, time frames, models—well, you get the idea. There must be at least another 800,000 possibilities for us to configure and represent our practices!

It's very rare for a market, product, service, or even relationship to remain static over long periods of time. External forces change. Why, then, do so many consultants insist on perfecting yesterday's talents? We can't afford to keep getting better and better at what we used to do, but should prepare and anticipate for what's coming tomorrow.

Don't become the vacuum tube business of consulting. Never be merely content. That's not to say don't be happy, but rather to suggest that happiness is a factor of anticipating and enjoying change. Life isn't "balanced" when you're simply standing still.

Ironically, perhaps, your career is best balanced when it is constantly moving, emerging, shifting, altering, and changing. High-wire performers will tell

I facilitate six "Inner Circles" and have five franchisees. Picture twelve entrepreneurs around a conference table for three hours monthly with a focus on vision. Inner Circle defines vision as a snapshot of what we intend to create three to five years out. We state our visions in terms of revenue, head count, locations, and our role; but the real trick is to paint a clear picture of our desired lifestyle. Balanced living is ALWAYS an issue for entrepreneurs, be they founders or third-generation owners.

At sixty, even I struggle with vision. Making hard choices to clarify vision is difficult. Instead of acknowledging our true desires, we're susceptible to what we "should" choose, as if we were seeking our mom's permission.

Two years ago, I purchased a condo in Palm Springs on a golf course, overlooking a lakeside green, with a gorgeous view of the mountains. Cell phones and computers, with my meetings completed by each second Friday, give me the freedom to live 60 percent of my winter months in the desert, free from the Minnesota wind chill.

Year one found me horribly guilt-ridden, feeling like I was lazy (even though I am available 24/7), and fearing that members would think I was retiring. Imagine my surprise when they encouraged me to enjoy what I had earned and said that I was an inspiration to them.

This year has been far better. When I depart for the airport in either city, I don't want to leave. I figure that's as close to balanced living as I am going to get.

Norm Stoehr, Minneapolis, Minnesota

you that it is far easier to balance when moving forward rather than when standing stock-still. You can't stay upright on a bike that has no forward motion (at least I can't). *Movement is the key to professional balance.*

For Ultimate Consultants, the envelope test should be a frequent exercise, because you are the ones who have the best capacity and basis for productive change. The concept of balancing your career by changing it may seen peculiar, but it will serve you well and, if you glance backward, you will probably find that it already has.

If testing the envelope is the tactic to ensure healthy and constructive change, then the overall strategy to embark on when change is called for may just be reinventing yourself altogether on a regular basis.

REINVENTING YOURSELF (REPEATEDLY)

I've written extensively in the prior books in this series about the "success trap." The graphic depicting it is reprinted as Figure 3.2.

Successful consultants can easily find themselves in this perfidious condition, wherein we believe we are moving forward unimpeded but, in reality, are merely coasting on a plateau and no longer climbing. Sooner or later the laws of entropy obtain, and we begin our decline. We are the proverbial frog in the boiling water.

The time to leap to the next S-curve to avoid the plateau is prior to it, while still accelerating upward. The "escape velocity" required to achieve the next level of growth is far more economical at this point than it would be if we had to take off from the plateau to catch the next curve.

> For consultants' careers, the choice is whether to grow or decline, not whether to grow or not to grow. Lack of growth is the equivalent of decline in any entrepreneurial profession.

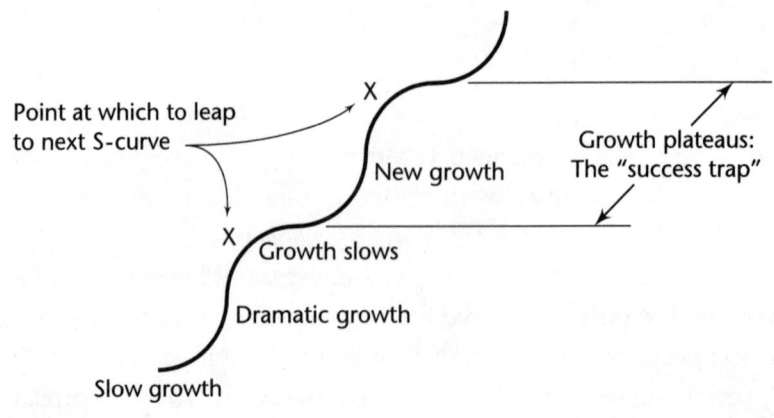

Figure 3.2. The "Success Trap"

For me, the most effective "leaping" mechanism is that of reinvention. Whether you've been in consulting for twenty-five years or entered it as a second career a few years ago, you should be considering "reinventing yourself" every few years. Otherwise, we become ineluctably stale.

Reinvention doesn't necessarily replace who you are and what you do, but it provides for new dimensions and additions. There is nothing wrong with multiple brands, diverse fame, and eclectic notice. All of your dimensions may not be compatible in terms of one website, one set of marketing materials, and one potential client source, but that's fine.

> You reinvent yourself when you establish a new brand, new approach, new recognition, or new methodology that establishes you as an authority and expert in additional fields. The expertise is usually present among consultants who have been successful over a period of years. It's the volition that's missing.

Reinvention is a renewing, vigorous pursuit. The three components of a truly successful career are

1. Market need, which either already exists or you create.
2. Competency to meet that need, which you either possess or can develop.
3. Passion.

If you agree, then you are in a position to constantly reinvent yourself. Needs are constantly changing and enlarging, competencies are continually amassed and enhanced, and passions are infinite.

Try to reinvent yourself at least once every two years. (Don't complain that I don't provide specific goals!) Reinvent yourself with the following in mind:

- You should have a legitimate and sincere interest in the new field. Don't choose something that's hot but not of interest. And don't feel that it has to be allied with what you're now doing. I know a consultant who ventured from her traditional field of R&D commercialization to go into

Arm & Hammer® baking soda was traditionally an ingredient in recipes. But the formulation also had a tremendous capacity to absorb odors. In fact, many people used an open container of the product in their refrigerators to remove unpleasant odors.

The company decided to "reinvent" the brand and advertise it as a deodorizer, without diminishing its importance as a food ingredient. The approach was tremendously successful, and most recently an Arm & Hammer cat litter box product was introduced with that powerful brand connection.

What do you do as a consultant that lends itself to reinvention? For example, there's no reason why an excellent team facilitator can't be a superb executive coach, or a succession planning specialist can't also help people with their career tracks.

It's a matter of the same traits being applied to new environments, whether removing odors or removing conflict.

---

presentation skills. She had made her mark among R&D operations with her superb "pitches" and developed the basics of successful presentations from her own innate competencies.

- You should look at it as a legitimate market and occupation, not as an avocation. We're not talking about a hobby, but rather a new business pursuit. My own criterion is that any reinvention must lead to at least a six-figure annualized business venture.[2]

Take a look at your marketing materials, website, and collateral support. Does it represent you today as you wish to be represented? If not—and the answer for successful people is that it probably doesn't—it's time to reinvent.

---

2. I usually receive open-mouthed stares and incredulous expressions when I tell people that any new business venture that can't generate a minimum of $100,000 annually isn't worth pursuing.

- Choose an area or need or competency divorced from what you now do. The appeal might be to move into an allied area, but that's no fun and not as potentially lucrative. If you're adept at strategy, moving into personal planning might seem like an easy leap, but moving into outplacement might be more radical, more challenging, and more lucrative.
- Don't hook up with fads; find enduring truths. Reengineering, quality, customer driven anything, just-in-time, and "brain theory" are ephemeral and temporary. But leadership, sales acquisition, interpersonal relations, talent retention, and teamwork are eternal needs. Find something that has "legs"—long-term endurance and applicability. I've found that "life balance" is going to have appeal throughout the Baby Boomers' middle and later ages, at a minimum.

You can also reinvent yourself in conjunction with abandoning current focus. When I first went out on my own, I had a strong training background, expertise in the craft, and invaluable contacts among training buyers. I performed in that arena for as long as I needed to put bread on the table, but then began to wean myself away from it. Today, I may do a training program twice a year, and then for a small fortune.

It's tough, for example, to deal in both strategy and managerial skills, because once you're associated with the latter, you lose all credibility with buyers of the former. It's hard to convince someone that you can keynote a convention if you've traditionally been seen as a concurrent session presenter. There's a direct conflict between field and staff, consulting and training, and so on. The escape to the more desirable position is in reinvention.

A word to the technical consultants among us: Technical consultants are among the worst paid in any specialty and, consequently, their life balance is often askew. It is an underpaid, price-sensitive niche. My suggestion to any technical consultant is to reinvent himself or herself into a more general business consultant, albeit with a technical expertise.

Years ago, there were insurance agents. But it's hard to find one anymore, because they have reinvented themselves as "financial planners," replete with scads of impressive initials (dutifully awarded by trade associations) to go after their names. A new brand of dentists has emerged, cosmetic dentists, who specialize in the aesthetics of your smile.

Are you the same consultant you were three years ago? I doubt it.

> You don't build on weak foundations, but on strong foundations. We build on strength, not on weakness. What are you superbly good at, and how can you make that still better?

BUILDING ON SUCCESS, NOT CORRECTING WEAKNESS

One of the primary causes of imbalance in one's profession is the mythological belief that we must constantly be correcting weaknesses. (The analogy is, perhaps, the greater value in raising the bar rather than "fixing" problems.)

If you review most self-help books, tapes, and similar patent-oil products, you'll find they possess an inherent and subtle operating philosophy: The reader/listener/user is somehow "damaged." Very few people seek therapy or counseling because they are feeling great and want to know why. Instead, they go only under duress, when they feel so much pain that they can't stand it any more and when the problem is so far advanced that a huge amount of remedial work may be necessary to restore equilibrium.[3]

We tend to throw ourselves into our work and spend long hours on activities *when we perceive that we are performing poorly (or not up to some arbitrary expert's standards) and must "fix our problem."*

Weaknesses need to be "fixed" when they are flagrant, debilitating, and dysfunctional. If you can't use the language, use silverware in a restaurant like an alien life form, and don't know how to moderate a focus group, you have to learn. But most of our "failures" are caused by the multitude of variables that we can't control in any case.

---

3. This is just one of the many reasons that therapists don't make more money. Their profession is overwhelmingly oriented toward correcting misery, rather than identifying and improving on happiness. Isn't marriage counseling best done when a couple is enjoying their partnership (or even prior to the marriage), and not when they've already contacted divorce lawyers?

The key to navigation through life is knowing where you are. Your current position determines the course you must take. Setting a course without frequent stops to determine your position is the surest way to run aground. With regard to the human condition, it's these navigational fixes that give meaning to the motion.

Here are some tips for navigation that I find useful:

- Make a list of that which is vital to you. Pare it down to that which is absolutely essential in your life. Carry it with you. Post it privately so that it is accessible to you at your workplace. When the frenzy of life overwhelms you, pause to contemplate that which is essential. You will be amazed at how quickly the frenzy dissolves as perspective returns.

- Make a list of the relationships that are most important in your life. Contemplate how you would like loved ones to think of you as they reflect on your relationship. What words would you like them to use in describing you if you suddenly passed away? What would they say today? What steps can you take to make your ideal relationship a reality?

- Schedule a trip to a wonderful national park. Take with you one of those with whom your relationship is vital. Force yourself to forget the future. Immerse yourself in the grandeur of the created order. Delight in the vitality of a chipmunk, a Mexican jay, a white-tailed deer. Bask in the beauty of life in the here and now.

Craig D. Uffman, President, The Uffman Group, LLC, Baton Rouge, Louisiana

---

My son is an actor, which means he's really a bartender (although my wife is quick to point out that he's the "head bartender"). One thing I've found in supporting and following his career is that timing, who you know, and luck are everything. There is questionable talent among a lot of "big names" and superb, unrewarded talent in a lot of regional, unheralded productions. Consulting may not be quite that severe in its social Darwinism, but it's not all that different.

Someone had come to observe me and also to participate in a potential project if my sales presentation succeeded. My acolyte was all primed and I expected the prospect to simply hand me a checkbook in the wake of my powerful verbal skills.

Well, it didn't quite work out that way. Two people in the room were skeptical that the project was even necessary, and the third was adamant that the cheapest price was the major consideration. I couldn't dissuade them, exhausted my supply of rebuttal ammunition, and ran out of patience. We parted friends, but still very much strangers.

Walking down the hall to the exit, my colleague was absolutely deflated. "I'll never make it if you can't convince people like that," he moaned. "Are we going to debrief and find out what we did wrong?" (He meant, of course, what I had done wrong!)

"No," I replied, "we're going to put the top down on the car and drive to a great burger joint I know where they also have Anchor Steam beer."

"You're not depressed?!" he blurted.

"Look," I pointed out, "they were buyers and didn't buy. They failed, not me. They need me, but haven't retained me. There isn't a thing I could have done differently in there to change that, including putting a gun to their heads. The behavioral problem is them, not us; get it?"

Years later, that one-time acolyte, now a highly successful practitioner, told me that the "failed" sales call and its aftermath that day was one of the most important lessons he ever learned from me.

A huge part of what we do depends on the right buyer, with the right need, seeing us at the right time. That's why I advocate branding so forcefully, and marketing "gravity," since these devices tend to attract the right people to you on a regular basis, ameliorating at least two of those variables.[4]

---

4. See my earlier book in this series, *How to Establish a Unique Brand in the Consulting Profession* (Jossey-Bass/Pfeiffer, 2001), and also *How to Market, Establish a Brand, and Sell Professional Services* (Kennedy Information, 2001).

Consequently, our overriding focus, especially as we progress as Ultimate Consultants, should be to focus on strengths. This means that we achieve greater balance at work by improving our efficiencies and effectiveness, increasing the momentum we've already developed in strong areas, instead of overcoming the inertia of a "standing start."

Correcting perceived weaknesses is hard work. Improving on clear strengths is smart work.

Here are some techniques and questions to habitually build on strength and enable yourself to work smarter and not harder.

Strength-Building Exercises

1. Find the distinctions between the business you've closed and the business that hasn't closed and then work to replicate the former conditions. This may be something you did (you insisted on a private meeting with the buyer with no subordinates present), something environmental (you met at a club, not the buyer's office), or something the buyer did (you were told about a clear need before the meeting). Maximize those conditions which led to success.

2. If a given day was particularly successful and/or efficient (you got a lot done), ask yourself what caused that expediency and duplicate it (you kept the phone forwarded, didn't go into town for lunch, or ignored the mail).

3. When anyone, under any circumstances, tells you that you did a great job, don't just say "thanks," but ask, "Why do you feel that way?" The answer is quite often not what you'd assume it to be. ("It must have been my great slides, right?" "No, the room was too dark then. It was the fact that you spent so much time taking our questions individually.")

4. Ask trusted clients or advisors what they believe your value to them has been. The answers are often astonishingly simple and almost always focused on output, not input. It is absolutely stunning how few consultants can articulately and succinctly describe their own value proposition.

5. If you already have successful brands, aggressively explore how else you can promote them, where else they can be publicized, and how much more impact you can achieve from them. (And if you've had great success in other areas, then turn that success into an additional brand.)

6. Orient your practice toward what you're good at and away from what you're not so good at—sort of a success tropism. If you don't like running

workshops but have continued doing them out of habit, since you began in that field, stop advertising them. If you're not very good at facilitating groups, don't include it as a part of your project just because others do. If you hate to socialize (as do I), then decline invitations to client social events that aren't absolutely essential (virtually none is).

7. Review your website, brochures, collateral material, and even casual conversations. Are you advertently or inadvertently promoting inefficient activities and/or interventions you're not good at? For example, why offer a "needs analysis" if they are laborious, seldom all that accurate, and tend to confuse the buyer's priorities? There is no consulting auditor in the sky keeping track of whether you perform needs analyses.

Athletes continually condition themselves—physically and mentally— to repeat those habits and actions that lead to their success until they are second-nature. Then they reinforce them still further. Some people spend a lifetime fruitlessly trying to hit a golf ball out of a sand trap, when they actually should be practicing their already strong fairway shots, *which will keep them out of the sand traps.*

At this stage of your career, don't worry about correcting weaknesses. You got where you are on the strength of your good habits and skills, not by accident. Those "weaknesses" aren't about to magically collude to undermine you tomorrow at long last. You've mitigated them in the past; ignore them in the future.

Your strengths are what "brung you" to this dance. Promote them, support them, exploit them, and let them lead.

ALAN'S ULTIMATE LESSONS

Recently, I spoke at a speakers' school for the New York Tri-State Chapter of the National Speakers' Association. I was the featured, opening keynoter, and the talk went quite well.

Amidst all the accolades and requests for advice, a somewhat unkempt woman came over and told me that she had some suggestions on how I could improve my weaknesses on the platform, such as using notes, smacking my lips, and clearing my throat. I'm accustomed to this, since it happens a few times a year, and I gave her my stock answer: "I'm not interested in your feedback." That, of course, ends the conversation.

Not only are such people overwhelmingly presumptuous, but they are giving the feedback for themselves, not for you. In a larger sense, never allow yourself to be surrounded with people who bring you down, who critique incessantly, and who point out your "weaknesses." Such commentary is invariably made by inferiors who want to bring you down to their level.

Ignore unsolicited feedback and your life/work balance will be enhanced immediately. You'll miss nothing but grief and frustration.

Balance at Rest

CHAPTER 4

There Is Nothing Wrong with Playing to Win

If Winning Doesn't Matter, Why Does Anyone Bother to Keep Score?

A dolph Rupp, the legendary basketball coach at the University of Kentucky, made the rather insightful comment in the subhead above. I bring it up because life is a competitive sport.

I don't believe that personal life balance is synonymous with "mellow," "laid back," "semi-retired," or "vegetative." Many people are at their optimal, highly fulfilled best when they are quite active and very busy. My idea about life balance isn't the presence or lack of activity, *but rather how that activity is distributed.* In other words, working hard and playing hard may be fine, but solely working hard and never playing at all is never fine.

No one goes to the Olympics with the mantra, "Let's go for a bronze!" Despite the Olympic slogan claiming it's really about how you play the game, the competitors don't arrive to ensure a fair deal for everyone and hope the best person wins. They hope that *they* win, and they'll use every legal technique (or worse) to gain a competitive edge. The medals are awarded and tallied, and the flags of the winners are hoisted to the accompaniment of their national anthems.

This "amateur" competition is as serious and relentless as it gets, replete with coaches, legal challenges, lobbying among judges, howling protests, drug checks, and other pleasantries.

My point is that we're often competing against others, against standards, and/or against ourselves. All of that is just dandy, and we might as well become accustomed to it. Because someone is keeping score.

We are.

HOW YOU PLAY THE GAME MAY NOT BE ENOUGH

One of the overlooked or deliberately ignored vital components of our personal lives is that we need to succeed, no less than we do at work or on the playing field. Success provides more than simple fulfillment. It provides

- A momentum and habit of learning.
- Self-esteem.
- External locus for growth.

A Momentum and Habit of Learning

Have you ever been with someone who is intensely uncomfortable in what should be a gratifying event? It may be a party, a social outing, the theater, or a special restaurant, but the individual is uncomfortable and actually eager to simply "get through it." The reason is that he or she is not in the habit of quickly learning about and adapting to new or unfamiliar experiences.

It is not enough to have competed. We must compete with the intent of achieving excellence, not measured by others or by score-cards, but by ourselves.

When we are able to engage in lifelong self-learning, we don't merely gain knowledge, we master a *process* for growth.[1] We are far too reliant in our daily lives on the feedback of others to calibrate for us how we are performing:

- "You didn't answer my question."
- "You've let the maintenance on the car wait far too long."
- "You were really funny at the club the other night."
- "You offended the Johnsons when you made that remark."

The result of the constant, usually unsolicited feedback we receive is that we begin to consciously or unconsciously modify our behavior in such a way as to maximize the favorable, comfortable feedback and to eliminate the feedback that threatens our comfort and self-esteem. (Unsolicited feedback, in particular, is always provided for the sake of the sender, not the recipient.)

When we achieve individual successes—and it doesn't matter in which pursuits—we begin to immunize ourselves against some of the foreign intrusion. We know when we're successful, know when we're unsuccessful, and know whether the lack of success is our fault or not.

The reliance on external feedback to assess our success is a vulnerability that threatens personal life balance because it makes us dependent on others for validation. (My favorite analogy is the speaker who gauges his or her success purely on the ratings of the feedback sheets turned in by the audience, even though the greatest gift the speaker may have provided is to anger the audience and force the individuals to think differently about an issue. Low feedback scores don't mean lack of success in one's objective, on the stage of a conference or on the stage of life.)

However, the ability to create and sustain an inner focus on the measures of success for one's self is quite a different story. We can—through the creation of winning habits and positive momentum—establish our own metrics for success, irrespective of what others tell us.

---

1. I've often reflected that universities, or perhaps even secondary schools, should focus on teaching students *how* to learn and not on *what* to learn, the latter being fungible and inconsistent, but the former being uniform and applicable in almost all environments. They abjectly fail in that regard at the moment.

Think of any event you've been to where someone begins to offer unsolicited critique. It may be of a golf shot, an amateur performance, the wine someone else chose, another person's attire, or whatever.

Nine times out of ten, the person doing the critiquing is actually inferior to the person being critiqued in that pursuit. I've seen golfers with terrible slices offer helpful commentary on partners' drives; women with plastic dress shoes suggest "better" accessories for a friend; and people with no pitch whatsoever comment on how a musical might have been improved.

The problem isn't so much in the *offering* of the advice, but rather in the fact that all too often it's *accepted.*

I am usually critiqued most in my platform work by amateur and clueless speakers; in my organization development practice by consultants who don't understand value-based pricing; and in my driving hobby by people who can't afford to drive the cars I choose to drive.

Always consider the source. If someone critiques your investment strategy, he had better be someone retired at an early age with $30 million in the bank he did not inherit from his daddy.

This internal "gyroscope" of balance is what I call "self-mastery." When one has achieved self-mastery, one has the innate ability to evaluate personal progress against personal standards. That is a powerful instrument to help us navigate through life. Self-mastery is attained through consistent success and the following two factors: self-esteem and external locus for growth.

Self-Esteem

Self-esteem, simply stated, is the acquisition of skills, the application of those skills for success, the appreciation of that success to motivate us for the acquisition of more skills, and so on, in a self-perpetuating cycle, as seen in Figure 4.1.

I used to believe that life balance meant scheduling some free time for golf or hiking, but one letter from an anguished parent taught me otherwise.

The radio business is ferociously competitive. Four times a year we get our report cards in the form of ratings. On one such day we were celebrating; the results proclaimed we were number one. The long, tedious hours of research, preparation, and execution had paid off, and we were deliriously happy.

Phone calls, cards, and letters poured in from our corporate office and friends in the industry, congratulating us for a job well done. Yet the letter I'll never forget came from a woman who was oblivious to the ratings. Her teenage daughter had recently passed away from leukemia. She wrote, "You visited the hospital this spring and went room to room talking with many of the kids who were cancer patients. You spent five minutes with my daughter, took a picture with her, gave her a t-shirt, played around with the equipment that surrounded her, and made her laugh for one of the few times in the past several months. I just wanted you to know that you might not remember her, but she never forgot your visit and kept the Polaroid beside her bed. Thank you so much for your time, however brief, that you spent brightening her life."

It was a profound lesson for me. Life balance is more than measuring work and play. It's finding time to touch others' lives, as well. Sometimes that touch reaches all the way to your heart.

Dom Testa, Morning Show Host, Mix 100 Radio, Denver, Colorado

---

Self-esteem is not about rallies, motivational books, or affirmation statements. It is about the pragmatic acquisition of tangible skills which lead to success, thus prompting the acquisition of still more skills to lead to more success.

Self-mastery demands the ongoing and assertive acquisition of new skill sets that are conjoined and configured with existing skill sets to create success.

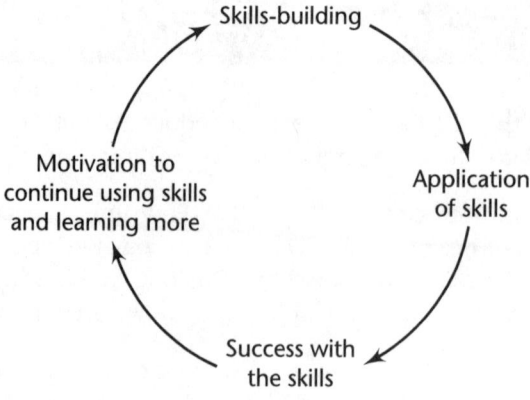

Figure 4.1. Skills Building and Self-Esteem

People are not confident and are not content to acquire skills if the experience is threatening or painful. "Nothing succeeds like success" may be a bromide, but it is based on the logical principle that we're much more apt to be willing to learn if that learning has paid off in the past. (This is why any decent consultant engaged in a major change effort realizes that "small victories" are critical to create the momentum for support that will lead to the major victories.)

External Locus for Growth

The highly regarded psychologist Albert Bandura has studied self-efficacy and has concluded that people who see their learning as externally focused are more resilient, bounce back from setbacks better, and are more likely to succeed than those who see their learning as internally generated.

This may seem counterintuitive at first. After all, shouldn't someone who believes he or she can provide what's needed without external help be more confident and self-assured? But when someone who believes that he can generate the knowledge and competencies required fails, that person has "shot his bolt," so to speak. If I've tried my best with what I have and failed, then I have nothing left and the only conclusion is that I'm deficient. I'm not going to succeed in this endeavor, because I don't have the right tools.

However, when someone who believes that learning is externally acquired fails, she tends to simply seek further outside learning to conquer the challenge. If the prior stock of acquired learning is insufficient, then I'm going to pursue additional sources, since the potential for learning is infinite. The failure, there-fore, is not a personal deficiency but only a temporary lack, which can quickly be overcome. I'll be successful as soon as I obtain the right knowledge (which I'm now in an excellent position to do, having failed the first time and realized what is additionally required).

It's not simply "how you play the game." I don't mean that you must win, or that you must be a ferocious competitor. I do mean that you must play in a way that provides growth irrespective of the final score, win or lose. To achieve that personal growth throughout your life, you must create a habit of success, which results from a consistently high self-esteem, which rests on the acquisi-tion of external skills, learning, and competencies.

Personal life balance is primarily a function of taking control of your suc-cess, and that is best done through the mastery of your personal growth.

CREATING PERSONAL CHALLENGES

I find the greatest challenges to be those that we create for ourselves. I don't mean obsessions, compulsions, arbitrary "shoulds," or other burdensome self-imposed demands, but rather targets for accomplishment, "stretch," and growth.[2]

Personal challenges take place in a multitude of forms, as described below.

The Challenge to Exceed Prior Performance

This is the amateur marathoner or ballroom dancer who needn't win first prize for success, but who wants to better his or her best prior performance. That is a state of continual "winning." Golfers are virtually impossible to talk to when they lower their previously best score.

This is not restricted to athletic endeavor. If you saw half of your child's soccer games last season, perhaps you can see two-thirds this year. If you've been reading three books a month, perhaps you can go to four. If you buy your spouse an unexpected present twice a year, you may try to make it four.

---

2. For a discussion of these "shoulds" and a look at the neurotic condition of trying to build one-self into an idealized mold, see Karen Horney, *Neurosis and Growth: The Struggle Toward Self-Realization* (W.W. Norton, 1950).

Starting an independent consultancy has rewarded me with the ability to integrate work and life—and to enjoy both in the here and now rather than sacrifice one for the other. But I've had a continuing debate with a friend over how to grow my business. "Stop being a consultant," he says, "and start managing consultants. Grow into a big firm. That's the only chance for a big payout that will give you the flexibility to do what you really want to do."

"But I'm already doing what I really want to do," I counter. As well-intentioned as my friend is, I know very well the value of having work balance and enjoying life today. That was made very clear to me on the morning of September 11, 2001.

I was walking into One World Trade Center when terrorist hijackers slammed a passenger jet into its upper floors. Although I made it to safety from that point, I was only two blocks away when another plane hit the second tower fifteen minutes later. As I made it back to my apartment in Greenwich Village in a swirl of confusion over what had happened and what might happen next, I couldn't help but feel enormously lucky. Lucky to be alive, yes, but even more lucky to know that if I had perished that day, it would have happened while I was following my dream, not someone else's. That single thought from that horrible day will always keep me pointed in the right direction.

Liz Lynch, New York City

So long as it's not a compulsion meaning "defeat" if you don't hit the new target, such attempts to better prior performance are healthy and invigorating. (The opposite of a compulsion is spontaneity and freedom of choice.)

The Challenge to Master Something

Many of us groan and mumble, wishing we were better at something we must (or even want to) do on a regular basis, but which always slows our day and undermines our comfort. It may be painting a wall, fixing a leak, arranging some flowers, or training the dog.

There is a tremendous freedom in mastering a task or pursuit that has proven elusive and difficult. Settling down to read about it, study it, gain coaching, or merely keep practicing creates the means to set and conquer a new challenge.

The bromide that "most men lead lives of quiet desperation" may be a bit draconian, but the fact is that most people lead lives with far too many necessary evils and frustrations. The challenge is to eliminate them or to learn to perform them better.

> Personal challenges must be private, constructive, healthy, and at no one else's expense. It's fine to seek to keep the car clean consistently, but not to beat the next car to the corner when the light changes. This should be a private matter, not a public sport.

The Challenge to Try Something New

I can actually grow leeks (big white radishes, great on sandwiches) in the yard, whereas I've never tried to garden at all before. I began smoking fine cigars a couple of times a month when I turned fifty. I've piloted the Goodyear blimp, a B-24 bomber, and a steam locomotive. Some of these things I do repeatedly; some I only had to experience once.

Nonetheless, merely trying something new—whether or not you become adept at it and whether or not it becomes a habit or a one-time event—is a challenge to be met. I've known too many people who refused to try lobster, or visit New York, or drive a stick shift, simply because they were unfamiliar and uncomfortable.

I respect people who tell me they've tried lobster and don't like it, but not those who squeal they can't touch it. If you've been to the Big Apple and don't like it, that's fine, but if you have "no need to go there," I'm baffled.

The Challenge to Try Something Daring

Daring is in the eye of the beholder, of course. For some, it may be relatively tame, such as scuba diving or parasailing. For others, it may be somewhat riskier, such as mountain climbing or parachuting. (For me, ballroom dancing would be high risk for everyone around me, but I'm going to try it under safe conditions.)

A daring feat sends the adrenalin pumping and creates a sense of exhilaration. There's a difference between daring and risking as well. Gambling in a casino is high risk, because the house odds are permanently against you. Scuba diving or even hang gliding has redundant safety measures and strong records of relative safety.

The challenge to try something daring may occur once a year or less. But it's a challenge that seems to grow in appeal as we ourselves grow older and realize that time is running out on some of our dreams. Living one of those dreams every so often helps us to retain our youthful vigor and outlook. We are only as old as we feel.

Personal challenges have the added appeal of being "quiet." We needn't broadcast them or share them. There is no need to create additional pressure through others observing our "performance."

When the only risk is to the ego, there isn't all that much risk.

CASE STUDY

A friend of ours is a fifty-year-old, highly successful businesswoman who owns an upscale boutique. She's a marvelous entrepreneur, leads a very dramatic life, and could simply coast on her success.

Several years ago, however, she began voice lessons with a coach. Her intent was to sing opera and to perform selections in a private recital for friends. For many people the lessons and journey are sufficient, and the actual fruition never occurs.

But our friend held her recital, and we all held our breath hoping that we heard coloratura and not creaks. We heard even better—she was superb—and we all shared in the unequivocal victory.

Why did someone so successful have to take the "risk" of performing difficult arias in public? Some might say she had nothing to lose, but I think she and many of us like her must continually conquer challenges if we are to really taste life.

Only dogs should sit on their haunches.

However, they may be shared, which has the effect of providing others with some of the reward of the challenge well met.

Here are some personal challenges I've been able to observe (or discern) among friends, colleagues, associates, and even strangers:

- Coaching a Little League team to the league playoffs, never having coached before.
- Restoring a classic car without help and without any experience having done so.
- Running for minor civic office, including campaigning and debating the issues (she lost).
- Publishing an op ed piece in the local newspaper.
- Becoming a local competition finalist in Toastmasters™.
- Chairing a fundraising event.
- Changing one's "look," including hairstyle and clothing.
- Taking a spontaneous vacation, with little notice.
- Acquiring a taste for a new genre of music.
- Creating a work of art with no affinity or natural ability.

Personal challenges can be daily or monthly or strictly situational. They should always be fun, and since no one else has to watch, they should always be candid and honest. Pretending that "debriefing" with your child about the school play you missed is the same as having been there supporting her is as bad as kicking the ball out of a sand trap, even though no one is watching or will know.

You will know.

The beauty of the challenge is in the pursuit, not solely in the conquest. My train layout always has imperfections, no matter how faithful I try to make it to the prototype, and it's virtually impossible to continue to lower your running times as you get older. But you can always create new challenges—to run within a certain time of your more youthful marks—that compensate for changing conditions.

Life is about success, not perfection. Success is what you define it to be. I'm suggesting that a major component of success in your life at best is to continually create personal challenges that you pursue with relish and occasionally beat with exaltation. If you stop worrying about someone else's tennis game, or lawn, or time with their grandchildren, or appreciation of good wine, and simply focus

All my life, I've struggled with a personal challenge: I've been interested in too many things. The variety and intensity have been evident to all. One friend remarked that I had a book on every subject.

The advantage of having many interests has enabled me to discuss intelligently most things with most people. However, it has prevented me from really mastering anything, and as a result I haven't made the progress I'd envisioned.

A few years ago, I set out to create the balance that had alluded me. I made a list of all the activities I wanted to experience in life, assigned time lines to them, and created a ten-year plan. The plan listed the activities that I wanted to achieve each day, week, month, and year. I put my plan on the wall where I could see it every day. For several months, it seemed that I hardly made any progress. Then, gradually, as I achieved my weekly and monthly goals, I began to feel for the first time that I would actually experience the rewards of balancing my work with my life.

Several years still remain in that original ten-year plan. I've had to make a few alterations, especially where I had overestimated how much I could accomplish within a particular time period. But, as a direct result of adopting this technique, I have a contract to write a business book, am in the second year of a Ph.D., and I'm participating in a prestigious mentoring program.

Bruce Hoag

on your personal goals for growth and improvement, you'll be healthier and far more content.

There's always someone doing a particular thing better than you are. But only you are doing the range of things you do as well as you do them.

THE RATIONAL CHILD WITHIN US ALL (EVEN THE BIG SHOTS)

Nearly twenty years ago, Dr. Pauline Clance wrote a prophetic book called *The Imposter Phenomenon: Overcoming the Fear That Haunts Your Success* (Peachtree Publishers, 1985). The author interviewed and observed hundreds of executives, athletes, celebrities, politicians, and others who were highly successful in quite visible positions.

What she found was that most of them felt they somehow didn't deserve to be where they were and might well be "found out."

My observation is that this self-doubt has intensified, not abated, over the past decades. We've observed the mighty fall, from Enron-esque corporate debacles to the terrible crimes and cover-ups committed by church authorities. While many of us may believe that people who attain the "high place" are somehow infused with greater maturity, wisdom, and cosmic view, they are actually subject to the same emotions, uncertainties, politics, doubt, and conflict that all the rest of us grapple with. The only difference is that they are playing with larger stakes.

Most of us tend to act like children more often than we'd care to admit. That's because our childhood has usually been our most formative time, and we carry with us the triumphs, defeats, confidence, and vulnerabilities from those years, either consciously or unconsciously.

We scream on the sidelines at our kids' sports events and contests, we feel cheated when we're not praised for a success, we become irate when criticized unjustly (and we believe it's almost always unjustly). As playwright Tom Stoppard observed, "Age is such a high price to pay for maturity."

Our onboard rational child can create uncertainty, but also great pleasure. The best of us retain our childlike wonder and sense of awe. We still sit on the grass bedazzled by fireworks, scream on a roller coaster, and exalt when we win a competitive event (which is more likely now to be Scrabble™ than football).

There is nothing wrong with playing to win so long as winning is not the sole source of your self-esteem and psychic well-being. There is everything wrong with not trying.

Balance at rest is a function of eating life in big gulps. A successful consultant or entrepreneur should be establishing a private and personal existence that includes challenge, learning, philanthropy, self-examination, exploration, and risk taking. I've observed that the best consultants are those who have varied and multi-faceted lives and who take a holistic view of their world and

I was very concerned in the early days of my professional speaking career because what I spoke about was little more than common sense. I didn't have new models, or intricate matrices, or creative theories.

My topics dealt with examining challenges for opportunity instead of threat, finding cause instead of blame, and setting objectives before choosing alternatives. This was not heady stuff. I half-expected clients to demand their money back after I was done. Yet the audiences loved it, and the buyers kept rehiring me. My consulting work is based purely on the same brand of logic and utilitarianism.

Even today, when I've had the opportunity to reflect on the tremendous value of common sense and the need for clients to "hire" it, I still have my moments.

Not long ago I was speaking to about five hundred people when I noticed a man striding up a side aisle toward the stage. I deliberately moved away from his route, beginning to think that he was the one who was finally going to call my bluff and challenge me right there on the stage. He finally mounted the far staircase as I retreated, still speaking, to the extreme opposite end. From there I watched him take out a screwdriver, adjust the thermostat, and retreat back down the aisle.

That one was a false alarm. But you never know. . . .

themselves. This creates a person much more competent to deal with the complexities of client organizations and who can bring a diverse array of talents and perspective to the fore.

Risk aversion, challenge, fortitude, learning, and other vital traits are not segregated between one's personal and business lives. A person has the traits or doesn't, and they will be present or absent in all aspects of his or her life. You don't turn on risk taking at the office, and you don't discipline yourself to learn only at home.

FREEING THE RATIONAL CHILD

Here are some suggestions for freeing that rational child and learning from the child's learning:

- Consciously explore the child's belief system. If you were told repeatedly that you "couldn't even play the radio," you have probably shied away from attempting to master an instrument. Choose an endeavor that you always believed was beyond your affinities and talents, and experience it. You don't have to master it, only to enjoy it.

- Separate the child's feelings from the behavior. Understand that feelings are always valid—after all, they're your true feelings at the moment—but that what you do about them is controllable. A child may throw a tantrum or throw a punch when he perceives a threat, insult, or injustice. But an adult can measure her response and determine how best to subordinate ego and deal with opposition.

- Indulge the child's wonder. I've met adult New Yorkers who have never visited the Statue of Liberty, Kansans who have never seen the ocean, and Floridians who have never skied on snow. We need to get out of our ruts, no matter how comfortable we've made them and how softly we've lined them. I remember going on the parachute jump ride at Coney Island when I was about seven. It scared me out of my mind. I wish it were still operating. I'd go on it again and probably still be scared out of my mind.

- Use the child's energy. We tend to exhaust ourselves on the job, recuperate at home, and then use our recovery to exhaust ourselves at work yet again. Balance at rest demands that we expend some energy to enjoy ourselves. Our personal lives are not merely battery-recharging stations. Whether we go a bit slower on the job, or take an extra day or two a week off, or work a shorter day, we must marshal our energy so that it is allocated over our complete life.

- Discipline the child. We can enjoy life best when there is some discipline, restraint, and order about it. Spontaneity is wonderful. We simply need to apply a degree of control to our activities. Buying an exotic sports car can be the fulfillment of a strong personal goal, but it is profligate if done in lieu of funding retirement plans. Taking a world tour can be tremendously enriching, but it is probably selfish if it means leaving your children for six months. One of the downsides of success in this profession

A good friend of mine has been successful in the brutally competitive executive search industry for decades. He has supported partnerships, offices, and staff on his individual success. He's well into his sixties and going strong.

He has a second home about three hours outside of Manhattan, where he spends almost every weekend. But his weekends are four-day affairs, Friday to Monday. He's in a position, through his success, that allows him to do this; so instead of making still more money or traveling still more or having more business lunches, he and his wife take to the hills.

We all need to change the alignment of our lives as we grow older.

is that it can lead to great disappointment if not planned for and handled intelligently.

The "rational child" is determined to apply those behaviors which have been comfortable and rewarding and to avoid those behaviors which have been uncomfortable and penalized. Our job is to ensure that those perceptions are validated, cleansed, and replaced with accurate perceptions about our present condition.

HOW TO IGNORE THE SCORE AND REWARD THE EFFORT

The "score" helps you measure your effort each time. But it is the effort that counts.

What are the efforts that are important in your life? Are they time with family, involvement in hobbies, contributing to charities, engaging in your spirituality, establishing a legacy? I'm talking about "effort" and not "result" because people who have reached Ultimate Consultant status probably should have more and loftier goals than others. It's impossible to fulfill them all, and they may be moving targets to begin with. It's the effort to make progress toward them that becomes important.

For example, how big a retirement account is enough? How much of your hobby should be completed, or consumed, or realized? (I collect stamps. I know I can never collect all within even my specialty. Does that guaranteed incompleteness make the pursuit irrelevant or a failure? Of course not. It's the joy of the journey that counts.) How much charitable contribution or amount of pro bono work is enough?

CASE STUDY

My wife and I had engaged some new estate-planning professionals to check our previous planning and make sure that we were doing "enough." One of the advisors suggested that the purchase of a certain insurance contract now could save our children at least one million dollars in inheritance and estate taxes when the time came. (There was enough to pay taxes and still provide for them, but this would have been an additional million.)

It sounded like a no-brainer. I asked about the insurance costs.

"It's $30,000 a year, from your current age until death," he nonchalantly informed me. I was shocked at the price, but wondered about being penny wise and pound foolish.

"How old are our children at the point in your diagram where the entire million is saved?" asked my wife.

"They would be in their early fifties," we were told.

My wife didn't miss a beat. "Are you telling us that we should spend $30,000 a year to save our children a million from an already lucrative estate when they would be virtually the age we are now?! I'd rather spend that money every year going on vacations with them while we're all here!"

That was the end of that discussion. All of a sudden, everything was crystal clear.

Life is about success, not perfection. We'll miss a dance recital, forget a birthday, insult a friend, and make an error that loses the game. But if our intent is to do the right thing, and we do it more often than not, we're in the right territory.

"Home is that place," said Robert Frost, "which, when you go there, they have to take you in." Is it better to have a secretary automatically send flowers to a spouse on special occasions without fail and flawlessly, or to choose them yourself and deliver them and forget an occasion every once in a while?

We can't beat ourselves up because we don't achieve perfect results. We should beat ourselves up if we don't even try. Unlike business, where results are far more important than tasks (new business acquisition trumps numbers of sales calls, for example), in our personal lives the effort and intent are every bit as important. It's why the local pharmacy sells belated birthday cards and why *we almost always get a second chance with loved ones (and seldom with buyers).*

We kill ourselves when we keep score of the outcomes of our lives and best intentions, as though it's next month's sales forecast or this year's inventory. There is no "magic number" at which point the results are achieved. We accept the congratulations, kick back, accept our bonus, and take a bow. In life, it's the quality of our continuing efforts that counts.

The more effort required, the more you should savor the accomplishment. If you had to reschedule a trip, take an early breakfast meeting, then hire a car to take you across town to your kid's ballgame or spouse's first art exhibit, then you've accomplished much more than simply showing up at a PTA meeting at seven in the evening. Two-income families and single parents require more effort, and deserve the plaudits.

Don't worry about the final score, because the "score" keeps changing and it's never final in this lifetime. Focus on the effort required to meet your personal, civic, social, family, and interpersonal goals and desires. If your intent is pure and sincere, the results will be fine, even if they aren't consistent.

Advice from the Readers of *Balancing Act*

Life balance to me is all about diversity in life and breaking out of the routine. I have been in information technology (IT) for over twenty years; the past four years I have been an independent consultant. One of the pluses of being an independent consultant is that you never know who you are going to meet next, or what type of engagement you will be assigned.

One of my life-balancing loves is coaching my daughter and two boys' soccer and baseball teams. I, first of all, completely enjoy working with young, eager minds, each at a different intellectual and physical level. It is a tremendous experience to see the fantastic strides each of the kids achieves by the end of the fall or spring season.

The dynamics of practices and games can also be very interesting when dealing with the parents. Fathers are typically trying to relive their childhoods, and mothers believe their children are the next Pele or Babe Ruth. Mothers are also concerned about important issues such as snacks and healthy drinks. Each constituency has to be managed and handled, in most cases with "kid" gloves.

I have actually had parents tell me that I must be a great manager of people in the corporate world from the way I handle the kids. The best compliment I have ever received is when parents told me they loved the way I coach by rotating all the kids in play evenly, unlike "other" coaches. To top it off, parents ask if I can coach their children next season, mostly from the request of their own kids.

Sure the parents purchase a gift certificate or athletic bag at the end of the season for the coach, but my real fulfillment comes from the boys' and girls' smiling faces (sometimes tearful) and their achievements of the current season.

What more could one ask for in the balance of life?

Averill Bromfield, Weston, Massachusetts

Never give up the attempt to improve your life at rest—and the lives of those around you.

ALAN'S ULTIMATE LESSONS

From the time I was about ten years old, I collected stamps. By the time I was forty or so, I had amassed a quite impressive United States specialized collection. I found I was putting more and more time into it, trying to fill the considerable remaining empty spaces.

One Sunday, I sat at my desk and actually said to myself, "I'd love to take a ride today with my wife and explore some new areas, but I'm behind on the work I have to do on my collection." Then I sat up, blinked, and realized that I said "work" and that I was denying myself spontaneous pleasures.

I put away my albums and didn't touch them for ten years. I cancelled all of my philatelic memberships and subscriptions. Cold turkey, I left the hobby.

Ten years later, I hit fifty and decided to embark on a host of new paths, one of which was to renew my stamp-collecting hobby on a more intelligent and pleasant basis. I "reenlisted," bought new albums, transferred everything, and began to once again build my collection, but *when I chose to and without arbitrary time investment and obligation.* "Completion" isn't an option or a desire.

I'm simply having fun collecting when, where, and what I choose.

CHAPTER 5

If You Don't Reward Yourself, You Reward No One

It's Hard to Lead from the Rear

I 'm fond of pointing out on the business side of our lives that "If we don't blow our own horns, there is no music." There's nothing wrong with self-promotion if you sincerely believe you have tremendous value to deliver to others.

Similarly, it's hard to help others if you don't help yourself first. Good intentions don't automatically mean selflessness, sacrifice, or surrender. The airline flight attendant tells us that we should put on our own oxygen masks before we attempt to help our children. You can't contribute as much as you might like to philanthropy and good causes if you don't have all that much to give.

There's nothing wrong with rewarding ourselves, not only financially, but also emotionally, psychically, and physically. It's hard to lead others to safety if we're weak, uninformed, scared, or lodged permanently in the rear of the pack.

Ayn Rand caused tremendous controversy with *Atlas Shrugged* and her philosophy of objectivism, self-pride, and a healthy selfishness. I interpret her writings to mean that each person is entitled to the fruits of his or her talents and labors, so long as people don't infringe on others' rights and do act legally and ethically. Such a philosophy becomes rather interesting in an age of "victimization," where interest groups seek to lower the bar and gain inclusion for everyone regardless of talent, rather than strive to meet the higher standards.

We encounter this among our clients and often live amidst it in our personal lives. And it is anathema to the entrepreneurial spirit and our economic system. This chapter is about honest and deserved reward, not about hedonism or profligacy. But for many of us, it's tough to accept the fact that it's okay to reward ourselves.

TITHE TO YOURSELF

The notion of tithing—providing one tenth of one's income to a religious group or charity—has been popular among a wide diversity of people and causes over the years. Why not consider "tithing to yourself"?

I don't mean, necessarily, a fixed part of your income, although many financial planners strongly advocate such discipline for retirement, debt reduction, college savings, and so forth. But I am suggesting that you consider yourself to be a beneficiary of your own success in some methodical manner.

The notion that denying ourselves makes us better people is somewhat dispelled if we consider the ramifications of that philosophy in terms of what we're actually able to do for others. As humorist George Ade observed, "Don't pity the martyrs; they love the work."

Here are some choices in terms of ensuring that you're participating in the fruits of your own labor.

Discretionary Time

Don't build your personal time around your work schedule or crowd it in interstitially as time permits. Begin by determining the following:

- How many vacations of what duration should we take this coming year (not counting time appended to business trips)?[1]
- What personal events do I want to attend as a high priority (a special athletic contest, a hobby convention, a reunion)?
- What family events are of the highest priority (a birthday, recital, anniversary, and so on)?
- What time do I need for self-development and learning (a graduate course, a retreat, a workshop)?

After you arrive at these personal commitments, build them into your calendar *and plan your work routine and client responsibilities around them.* In the vast majority of cases, consultants have flexibility in scheduling client activities and visits, and if these time commitments are clear in advance, they can become sacrosanct islands, even in tossing seas. But if they aren't clearly committed, then you will tend to do what's best for the client and never consider what's best for you. These are not two mutually exclusive positions. The problem is that we are conscious of the former and keep ourselves in the dark about the latter!

Personal Space and Spirituality

No matter how you define or engage in this—whether with others in ritual actions or by yourself in splendid isolation—we need the time to engage in rejoicing in our existence, examining our motivations, and challenging ourselves for improvement and contribution.

We need "down time." We can't constantly be "on" or in demand, or in charge. I read in a dog psychology book that dogs may be at their most supreme happiness when sitting around doing absolutely nothing. Content existence is enough, and they don't have to be continually "engaged."

I believe that this principle of content existence applies to parts of our lives as well. We need a chance to be introspective, to revel in success and scream about setbacks, and to simply have no demands made on us. There is

---

1. If you have children, this should include with and without the kids. I know of couples with teenage children who have virtually never taken a vacation alone since the first child was born, which is healthy for exactly no one.

I love your books and your newsletter, so ever since you wrote that you suggested we throw out our junk mail for a balanced life, I've wanted to write my "better" suggestion to you.

I tried throwing out junk mail and catalogs and it didn't work for my business, so I tried this and that until I found my best solution, which has been working successfully for years. Now that I manage other businesses, my clients really appreciate it.

This little gesture will cost you a little bit of time and money but makes the world a better place to live. If you are high profile, you've created a demand for yourself. You are going to attract attention. And that needs to be managed. . .

Please do not throw away junk mail or catalogs until you take the time to respond and ask to be removed from their mailing lists. And by the time you've answered the phone only to find out it's an unwanted sales call, please take the time to ask them to "please remove my name from your phone list."

The easiest way to get off junk mail lists or to stop unwanted catalogs is to mail back your mailing label inside a stamped envelope with a note handwritten on the side of the label with these words, "Please remove from mailing list. Save a tree!" This will get you off of more mailing lists faster than any other words I've tried. Mailing is the faster and cheapest method of contact. I prefer the U.S. post office stamped envelopes. This task can be assigned to anyone. For every list you remove yourself from, you are actually removed from 1.5 to three lists. So this process gains momentum over time. It really does help ecologically. It cleans up your life, too. It prevents future emotional annoyances. It aids the economy. It saves charitable organizations valuable marketing dollars. And when you move on, the next "recipient" will thank you.

Madeline Bailey, Beaverton, Oregon

no heroism in being constantly available to partners, families, friends, and other demands that are non-emergencies and non-critical. We all deserve our personal space.

The more successful you are (and the stronger personality you are), the more you will be sought out, at work and at home. You have to provide for some occasional isolated time. I tell executives that a part of their week should be spent with their feet up on the desk thinking about the future, their strategies, innovation, and new paradigms. No one else is doing it, and that's their job.

No one else is thinking about your future and your condition at the moment, and this is your job. People who "tithe the personal space" for themselves tend to be more confident, calm, and considerate, because they don't see normal demands on their time as denying them something.

They're already committed to their own personal reflection needs.

I used to feel guilty about sitting and doing nothing, until I realized that we're never actually doing "nothing" unless we're asleep. (And even then, I've awakened with fresh, new ideas at times.) I'm reminded of those ubiquitous electric golf carts that need recharging periodically. They're just sitting there, but if they weren't they would eventually be useless. We all need to sit and let our batteries recharge to full capacity.

Financial

Consultants are remiss about two financial considerations: retirement planning and debt reduction. The latter, when done systematically, is the same as or better than creating savings, especially if you are wiping out 18 percent credit card debt and savings accounts are only paying 5 percent. And once you miss the cutoff for qualified retirements savings plans, you usually can't make it up later. That investment and deduction are lost.

Your financial tithing should include the payment of your normal monthly living expenses (including recreation), the pay-down of outstanding indebtedness, and the full contribution to the retirement plans for which you qualify. The bromide about "investing back in the business" can be dysfunctional. As solo practitioners, an updated computer or new marketing piece will hardly be exhaustively expensive.

Hint: Make it a practice when you land an especially large account (for example, over $100,000) to "top off" your SEP IRA contributions, or eliminate

Advice from the Readers of *Balancing Act*

The true test of finding balance in your life is changing a negative experience into a positive lesson. My personal example involves the first time I was fired from a job.

I decided I had had enough of government employment and I needed to strike out on my own. Beauty school and my background in sales prepared me for the trade of manicurist. I had told each student where I would be employed after graduation, and that was the result I achieved. That's the good news.

The bad news is that, after a year and a half of my working there, the owner and her family decided that I no longer worked there. This I was told on a Saturday, which everyone knows is the busiest day of the salon week. Clients were told I was sick. They were scheduled with other operators. They were not told I was fired.

I went to the shop to pick up my personal items. It was obvious I was not sick. But my point was to hold my head up and tie up loose ends personally. I did not want someone else responsible for this project. The son of the family was my overseer. It was his job to be sure that I did not abscond with a nail brush or water dish.

The whole episode took less than twenty minutes. I was not going to allow this setback to discourage me. I promised myself to start interviews on Tuesday and left the shop to have lunch and catch an afternoon matinee. On Tuesday, I had an interview, and on Thursday, I started at the new salon. It was much more upscale, much more professional, and I included a raise for myself by negotiating an increase in my commission.

Star Hawkins, Dallas, Texas

an entire credit card's indebtedness, or earmark some tax money. (If you're debt-free, then make extra payments on your mortgage each month, which will go toward principal and considerably decrease your eventual interest payments while immediately building your equity in your home.)

Monthly bills, retirement planning, debt reduction: After that, you can contribute healthily to whatever philanthropies and charities you choose, being in a position of great strength.

Health

As we age, this is more important, perhaps critically important. We need time for exercise, for pre-emptive and preventive medical analyses, and for nutrition.

I've made it a practice either not to attend banquets, or not to eat at them. The food is universally poor, and I usually eat because I'm there (and bored). The same holds true even for first class on planes. Unless the food is very appealing (more common with international carriers), I won't eat it.

Work out regularly. Play competitive sports appropriate for your condition and your age. Our health, nutrition, and conditioning are not things that can be "worked in" when possible. We need to tithe the attention and commitment.

Join a gym, get a trainer, buy equipment for your home, but most importantly, commit and religiously observe this activity. Without it, you can't provide as much energy and support to anyone as you would like.

CASE STUDY

I've known several successful entrepreneurs who died in their forties and fifties. They had "corporate welfare states" in their businesses, supporting dozens of "implementers" and assorted hangers-on. One memorable man told me he would not buy himself the new Mercedes he coveted because his people might think he should have paid them a larger bonus.

Many of these people also had extended families to support: grown children, aging parents, other relatives, former spouses. The burden was tremendous and omnipresent.

Even these burdens can be borne if there is personal time, space, and money. But when you sacrifice in all aspects of your life all the time, you will eventually wear out.

Wearing out in life is usually fatal.

SHORT-TERM AND LONG-TERM PERSONAL REWARDS

What kind of reward system do you have for yourself? It's startling how many people are so frenetically engaged in their activities and work that they never plan for rewards, respites, and celebrations.

Rewards needn't be grand or expensive (although they certainly can be). However, they do need to be frequent. And you can't rely on externally driven awards, which are always nice but unpredictable, political, and rare. Picture your rewards as the water offered periodically to the marathon runner, or the polishing you provide for the car, or the refreshing dip in the pool on a hot day.

Rewards revive and resuscitate, and they are entirely within your control. You don't have to reward yourself with a car, or even a tangible. But life

CASE STUDY

I was coaching a woman who had launched her own business, suffered through the usual perils and uncertainties of start-up, and gradually although arduously created a sustaining profession. As her revenues grew into the low six figures, she told me she for the first time believed she could reach her distant dream reward.

That dream reward was a sporty BMW automobile that cost about $35,000.

"What will tell you it's time?" I asked.

"When I have the money to pay for it in cash, which might be in a few years at this rate of growth."

"But you can easily afford lease payments now and still have sufficient income for all other expenses, retirement, and so on. Why does it have to be in cash? Why not reward yourself now? You can always pay it off more quickly if you choose and have the income."

She looked at me somewhat startled, but said she'd think about it. Three months later she had the car and was ecstatically happy. And her business grew at an even faster pace.

requires periodic booster shots, and rewards are the most painless kind. Here are examples of types of personal rewards you should be considering and building into your lifestyle.

The Reward of Giving

Allot time for the charity you always wanted to help. Show up by surprise at a child's event you wouldn't normally be able to attend. Send a contribution to a good cause. Coach a team or mentor a colleague. Perform some pro bono work. Do you know why so many people are engaged in these activities and why volunteering is so integral a part of our culture? Because it feels good. Helping and supporting others is a revitalizing experience.

> We reward ourselves in subconscious ways all the time. We schedule a commitment to be sure it doesn't interfere with a favorite television show, or get to the movies early to sit in a preferred seat. We simply have to escalate that attitude to a more conscious level of self-fulfillment.

The Reward of Permission

Allow yourself a frivolity, whim, or caprice. Take a day totally for yourself. Eat something you ordinarily think you shouldn't. Go to an amusement park, or a ball game, or the race track, or the museum when the crowds aren't there but you are. Ask yourself what you've been guiltily denying yourself, and then do it.

The Reward of a Gift

Buy something for yourself *that you can use regularly.* It may be a new purse or wallet, or a pair of shoes, or a key chain. Change something old and worn that you've used for years out of habit and have no emotional attachment to (there are a lot more of those things around than we imagine!). Make an impulse purchase.

The Reward of a Change

Stop killing yourself on the subway or train and take a cab or even a limo. Choose a new vacation spot. Break the routine. Exercise in the morning instead of after work, or vice versa. Change the dog's walk to make it more of a pleasure for yourself (I guarantee that the dog won't mind). Try a different "look" with your wardrobe or hair.

The Reward of a Respite

Have another family member take on your responsibilities for a while with an elderly parent or relative. Hire a professional to mow the grass, maintain the pool, or clean the house. Eat out for a week. Fly first class on your own dime. Find a burdensome chore or responsibility and seek help or support with it.

The Reward of Congratulations

We sit back and wallow in our defeats but seldom adequately reward the victories. If you've done something well, *reflect on why and how and rejoice in your choices, judgment, and performance.* Once you recognize why you succeeded, you'll be much more able to replicate the success. Think about your tennis win, your published article, the great family excursion, the way you were able to fix the computer (or car or closet door) yourself. Think about why it happened and give yourself some points in the credit column.

> There are more ways to reward ourselves than we realize if we consider that a reward is simply an action, behavior, or event that makes us feel better about ourselves and provides useful advantages for our future behavior.

What triggers a reward? We can't fill our days with them, and shouldn't there be some criteria to meet to deserve them?

The problem is that we normally make the criteria so tough ("I'll buy the car when I have the cash," "We'll celebrate after the book is published," "Let's wait until everyone is totally happy") that the Olympic high-jump record looks easy by comparison.

The rewards above range from the substantial to the whimsical, from the expensive to the quiet moment of reflection. Therefore, the occasions can vary, but I'd suggest that your "triggers" might include the following:

- *A tough job well done:* The crumbling front steps are finally fixed, or the rift with a family member is eliminated.
- *A clear victory:* You've raised the targeted funds for the scholarship campaign or secured a variance from the planning board.
- *A "loss" in a good effort:* Your underdog soccer team lost in the playoffs, or your proposal wasn't accepted but the other party told you that he or she was impressed and would welcome a renewed relationship in the future.
- *A celebratory ritual occasion:* An anniversary, birth, appointment, milestone, or other event.
- *A periodic occurrence:* Make a point of rewarding yourself in some way on the last day of each month, the first day of each quarter, six months between birthdays, and so forth.
- *A "down" time:* We seem especially intent on denying ourselves when things are going badly in general, yet that's exactly when a reward can break the cycle. Put aside the tough times for a moment and find an appropriate reward.
- *A sharing occasion:* A family, social, professional, or other group event can often be celebrated by everyone. There nothing wrong with a reward for being a part of—no matter how minor—another's good fortune or of the group's success.

INSTANTIATING YOUR DREAMS

Instantiation is the tangible representation of an abstract. For example, if you're talking about the relationship between the shape of an airplane wing, speed, and the lift that results in flight, you'd be best serviced with a model, or at least a drawing, of a wing. If you still don't believe in the power of instantiation, ask someone to describe a spiral staircase. Over 90 percent of those you ask will make a circular or conical motion with their fingers, rather than attempt to describe it ("A continuing ascending structure which circles back upon its own circumference at each successive height").

I came home dejected after a basketball game that we had won by a single point because I thought I had played very poorly.

"How many points did you score?" asked my uncle.

"One point, a lousy foul shot, one out of two," I mumbled.

"So the team won the game by your point," he observed, as if it were as obvious as a ham sandwich.

I cheered up significantly at this revelation and went off to meet my friend for a celebration pizza.

Dreaming is thought to be an exclusively human trait, but I seriously doubt it. If you've ever watched a dog, sound asleep, begin to twitch its paws, whimper, and smack its lips, you can be pretty sure Rover is finally catching that totally elusive squirrel.

Psychologists agree that dreaming is a healthy pursuit—including daydreaming—and one of Freud's most profound works was *The Interpretation of Dreams* (a psychological practice employed on a widespread basis today).

The types of dreams I'm alluding to are "conscious, constructive dreams" or "controlled dreams." They are the deliberate fantasies we return to, foster, nurture, and use for a sense of fulfillment. They may involve playing a violin concerto to a packed symphony hall, writing the great American novel, sailing to Tahiti, climbing a mountain, competing on a game show, or adopting a totally new image.

Positive dreams reflect your aspirations, unused talents, and vicarious needs. Negative dreams are about revenge and vindication. The latter can be positive if they serve to exorcise feelings that will therefore not influence actual behavior. The former are always constructive and can be used to influence behavior.

It wasn't any one big moment but a career of little ones that added up to my dangerously skewed version of the world. My career path led from documentary films to radio broadcasting into television news. Eventually I began viewing life through the lens of a videocamera, and I didn't like what I saw.

I was a television news anchor and reporter for two decades in big markets like Boston, small ones like Santa Maria, California, and medium-sized ones like Austin, Texas. Back in the 1970s in the post-Watergate and Vietnam era, the power of the media attracted me. I thought by hooking people up in McLuhan's global village, the TV would solve most of the world's problems.

For eighteen years I read local news at six and ten. After a while it began to blur. If you think local TV news is boring to watch, imagine what it's like to read every night. On the plus side, I was a local celebrity with media access to the rich and powerful. That was great for the ego but bad for whatever remained of the "real me." I worked from 1:00 to 11:00 and rarely had a chance to read my daughter a bedtime story. In the early 1990s, with all-OJ coverage, my sense of humor tanked and I felt cynical about the alleged "news" I had to read. I got a prescription for Prozac.

I hated my job. Of course, nobody else, including my wife, could understand why. How could they? Being a TV news guy is a "dream" job, but for me it had turned sour. Still, I felt like Howard Beale in *Network*—"mad as hell" and I didn't want to take it anymore. But I didn't have the guts or good sense to quit.

Fortunately, nature seeks a balance and life has a way of balancing your act for you. One morning my thirty-year-old protégé invited me for breakfast to inform me he'd soon be taking my spot in the anchor chair. Far from being angry or hurt, I was genuinely thankful to be liberated from my self-imposed role of "talking head." (People couldn't imagine why I was so happy after being replaced by a young stud twenty years younger.) I was more than ready to break out of the box. I wanted to be free to dream and make new dreams come true. And so I began a mid-life journey to rediscover the parts of the "real me" I'd left behind.

My values changed. Now money, fame, and recognition mean less and less. Integrity, community, and contribution are what turn me on.

Bob Karstens

Ergo, by "instantiating your dreams" I mean consciously striving to turn your positive, aspirational dreams into physical reality. One's reach needn't always be beyond one's grasp.

What dreams have you revisited the most, deliberately and intentionally, over the recent past? What obstacles actually exist to your realistically pursuing them? Why have you allowed them to remain dreams and not acted on them?

Ironically, when we dream of an improved state, altered condition, or new circumstance, we also associate it with the fantasy in which we're engaged. In other words, merely by dint of imagining the desired future we also conclude that that future is imaginary. But nothing could be further from the truth.

Every major-league ballplayer and star athlete probably dreamed of the experience. I think the same holds true for politicians, executives, musicians, doctors, and entrepreneurs, among others. My assertion is that *we tend to become what we dream if we allow ourselves to follow that path.* Picasso told of his mother assuring him that he was destined for greatness, a future view which he shared. "She said if I joined the clergy, I would become the Pope. And if I joined the military, I would become a great general. Instead, I pursued art, and I became Picasso."

It's no accident that an Academy Award® winner will say, "This has been my dream," or a pilot will say, "I dreamed of flying since I was five years old." Martin Luther King, Jr., very deliberately and brilliantly chose the metaphor, "I have a dream. . . ." Dreams have power and magic to them and serve as an abstract destiny. Why shouldn't we concentrate on instantiating them?

WHEN YOU WISH UPON A STAR (MAKING DREAMS COME TRUE)

How does one instantiate a dream? How do you make it a reality? It might seem counterintuitive to suggest that there's method to capturing a fantasy, but I think that there is.

When we moved to the San Francisco area many years ago, the real estate agent, knowing my income and our objectives, showed us fabulous properties in the town of Belvedere in Marin County. As she led us through one house high up on a hill and overlooking the water, I had stopped dead in my tracks.

"Is there something wrong?" she asked.

"No," I said, "it's just a little intimidating when reality catches up with your dreams."

After I had become somewhat accustomed to the experience, I arrogantly asked if the dogs I heard barking would be a constant problem.

"Sir," she sniffed, "*those* are the harbor seals!"

Sometimes we're not totally prepared to live the dream.

First, recognize the validity of the dream or aspiration. Don't dismiss it as "merely a dream" or an impossible fantasy. If you dream of it, whether a yacht, a trip, or a developed talent, it is legitimate.

Second, ask yourself what obstacles are in the route to progress toward fulfillment. Almost all such obstacles are self-imposed, and many are themselves illusory. "I don't have a singing voice" can be remediated through professional coaching. "I don't have the time" is overcome through planning and discipline. "They'd never let me," upon analysis, will virtually always demonstrate that there is no "they."

Third, don't strive for perfection, strive for progress. Playing an instrument needn't be synonymous with a Carnegie Hall debut. Traveling the world doesn't have to include Nepal. Captivating an audience as a speaker doesn't have to include keynoting the Democratic National Convention.

Fourth, break it into achievable, individual elements of progress (see "daily small victories," next page). You can learn the scales before playing Haydn, learn to sail a small boat before owning a yacht, and learn to paint simple objects in the privacy of your den without mounting an exhibit in a gallery. All of those Oscar® winners started with forgettable parts in desultory movies.

Fifth, don't stop dreaming. Keep it alive and extend it if you wish. As you master some aspects, perhaps you might want to enlarge your dream (play an instrument in a band with friends, do stand-up comedy in a local, informal club).

Dreaming is merely a form of visualization, which in turn is a powerful technique to prepare you for the future. If you visualize a meeting and its possible direction, you better prepare yourself to be successful in it. Athletes often visualize their events to prepare themselves for key junctures and challenges. Actors visualize their character's responses and reactions. Visualization creates a familiarity, as if you've been there before, which commensurately improves your confidence and ability to deal with the challenge.

Dreaming is grand visualization. It is a great way to create your own future and balance your life. Because as reality barges in every day to influence you, you'll be simultaneously creating your own future reality.

> There is no reason why we can't fulfill our dreams. That doesn't mean that life is over. It means we should start dreaming bigger.

DAILY, SMALL VICTORIES

I've rarely walked into a prospect's office and walked out with a contract. What I have walked out with most of the time is an agreement for another meeting, a concession that my help may be needed, a request for a proposal, a commitment to provide me with further information, and so on.

I call these "small yeses," which means the sale is being advanced in a positive direction, that is, one that leads toward a mutually beneficial relationship. (See Figure 5.1.)

The "small yeses" have the advantage of being achievable, short-term, readily identifiable, non-threatening to the prospect, and so forth. I believe that almost all sales are consummated through such a progression.

Similarly, our lives move forward based on a series of small, even modest, daily victories. We don't progress based on huge leaps and bounds, from

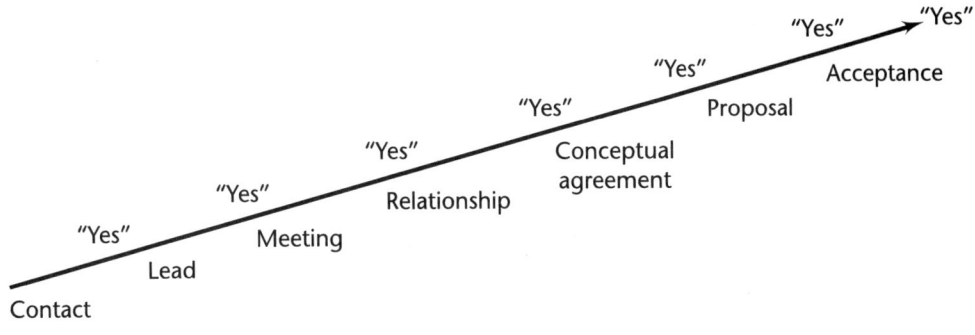

Figure 5.1. The Series of "Small Yeses"

stellar victory to cosmic performance, over and over. In fact, some of the most devastated people I've had to work with are those who pinned all of their hopes—and all of their ego—on "the big one": the promotion, recognition, marriage acceptance, vacation, or relocation. When the promotion doesn't come through, the new house has termites, or someone else is lauded for the new idea, the person hoping for "the big one" can have his or her world collapse.

As you can see in Figure 5.2, betting on that one great event to boost our lives and self-esteem is problematic at best. If none of the "big ones" hit, then our self-esteem rests at rock bottom. But if some do hit, we're on a roller coaster, since we still hit bottom in between the major victories.

> "Authenticity" is a word much bandied about, especially by motivational speakers (who have often seemed to me to be the least authentic people, since they choreograph their laughter and tears and seek to manipulate the audience). I think authenticity is actually about self-comfort, self-esteem, and self-worth, knowing who you are without having to rely on others to tell you who you are.

It's far better to have a constant self-esteem, which means we know that we're never as good or as bad as we hear at the top and the bottom. We are best

Advice from the Readers of *Balancing Act*

As a leader in a large organization, it is challenging to ensure balance in our lives. Deadlines for large projects seem to consume inordinate amounts of time away from our families and other outside interests such as community service. While it is important that we bring balance into our lives, I feel that we often send subtle messages to subordinates about how we feel about life balance.

I remember a large project that required the undivided attention of each of my senior managers. Failure would cost the organization dearly. One of my trusted advisors approached me about a family situation that he felt strongly about attending to. It wasn't an emergency, but I could tell that he really needed to fulfill this obligation. He was a bit embarrassed about asking for the time off. While I knew it would hurt our effort, I determined that he be given the time off. The project moved forward and was a success. In the end, I'm sure that he spent numerous hours making up for his absence, but the critical day was available for his family.

It's one thing for us, as senior managers, to bring balance into our own lives. Probably more important are the messages that we send to our subordinates about life balance. We control, in large measure, the life balance attitude of our organizations.

Thomas R. Warne, Tom Warne and Associates, LLC, S. Jordan, Utah

able to have constant self-esteem when we establish and recognize the small, daily victories in our lives.

Daily, small victories can be found in two dimensions: the routine and the planned.

Routine Small Victories
- Getting through your "to do" list and plan for the day.
- Handling unexpected breakdowns, disruptions, and unhappiness.
- Cheering up others and acting civil and pleasant to strangers.
- Anticipating a future problem and effectively planning for it.
- Performing an unpleasant but vital task.

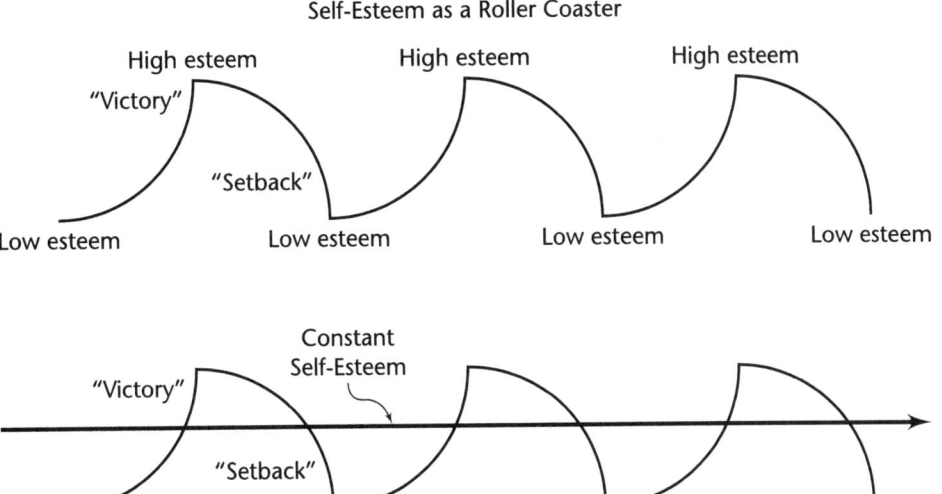

Figure 5.2. Self-Esteem Perceptions Compared

Planned Small Victories
- Moving another person to a "next step" important to you.
- Successfully hosting or supporting a special event.
- Taking a trip with a minimum of aggravation and stress.
- Reconciling a problem or a poor relationship.
- Finding scarce resources to begin or complete a job.

I consider it a small victory if I attend a social event and interact politely and convivially, since I'm an introvert and truly hate small talk and meandering conversation. I like to reward myself for having attained that victory.

Every other day I work out at the gym. I don't like to work out. It's tough work, tiring, and an hour or so of my time that I could use on more enjoyable activities. But at my age, and with my love for food and wine, I have to work out to indulge my true passions. I consider this discipline, *each*

After I addressed the awards banquet of a small business association, people flocked to tell me how much they enjoyed my speech. This is common for any speaker who can make a few valid points and use a bit of humor. But one woman was overly vociferous.

"You're not only the best speaker we've ever had, you're the best any of us has ever seen!" she elaborated.

"You're being too kind," I said, itching to head for the door.

"No, you did things tonight no other speaker has ever been able to do."

"Such as what?" I asked, now truly curious. Was I, indeed, underrating myself?

"No one," she solemnly informed me, "has ever stood on that stage and held a microphone, talked, and walked around all at the same time!"

Stunned, I blurted, "But what about my five key points for small businesses?"

"What five points?" she asked.

Whenever you believe you're walking on water, I guarantee your knees will be wet.

---

and every time I walk out of the gym, still another small victory, and I drive to my favorite coffee shop with the top down on the car to pick up a flavored coffee.

Before 9 a.m., I've had a small victory and treated myself to a small reward. Seem silly? Maybe. But fill your day up with these and you'll be able to overwhelm the negatives, downturns, and "small defeats." Since there are unexpected small defeats and unexpected small victories, *it's the planned victories that will take us over the top and turn the tide of battle.* If you don't plan the victories, then your day may be negative at worst or neutral at best.

In terms of life balance, isn't it best to stack the deck in your favor?

The small victories are different for each of us, usually based on what is more difficult for each of us to achieve. For example:

Difficulty	Small Victory
Organization	Achieving our daily "to do" list
Writing	Promptly responding to correspondence
Socializing	Interacting politely and civilly
Assertiveness	Lodging a well-argued complaint
Confrontation	Engaging a problematic colleague or partner
Ambiguity	Handling two unexpected "crises"
Athletics	Participation in a competitive event
Weight/Appearance	Engaging in an appropriate regimen
Speaking	Addressing a small civic association
Repairs/Physical Labor	Fixing a broken shutter or cabinet drawer
Feeling Rushed	Taking the time to walk the dog

Small victories can be both the exercising of a strength as well as the correction of a weakness. (In fact, the former are more easily accomplished and much more important in personal growth.) For example, I love to write and can do so with some facility, but I still consider it a small victory to have finished this chapter before 10 a.m. as I had hoped to do. (And if I had been interrupted and had to finish it in the afternoon, I'd consider that a small victory also, because I managed to handle an unexpected interruption and nonetheless complete my planned schedule.)

The great thing about small victories is that they are in the eye of the beholder. The bad thing about small victories is that the beholder is too often listening to a little guy on his shoulder whispering in his ear, "You don't deserve this." Flick the little guy off your shoulder and enjoy your victory.

Finally, victories are most often squelched by guilt. Virtually all guilt is self-imposed. There is an anthropomorphic guy sitting on our shoulder, whispering in our ear, telling us what we "should" and "shouldn't" be doing—and enjoying ourselves is always in the latter category.

There is no reason to be guilty about relishing the small daily victories. If we beat ourselves up for doing something wrong or making an error, but fail to reinforce ourselves when we get it right and succeed, then we've created the quintessential paradox in which "tails, you lose; heads, I win."

You have to flick the little guy off your shoulder and then stomp on him just for good measure. He is simply roiling up all the baggage and beliefs from our pasts which no longer have any bearing on our lives today. Listening to others for "approval"—whether the unsolicited feedback of real people or the imagined rantings of a pretend guy on your shoulder—is the most vulnerable position you can be in.

But listening to yourself and knowing when you've failed *and* succeeded, in no matter how minor a manner, is true self-mastery. And if you don't enjoy that ability and provide the necessary rewards to yourself, you'll never be able to reward anyone else properly either. It's hard to provide incentive, models, examples, and accolades from the rear of the pack.

ALAN'S ULTIMATE LESSONS

Positive self-talk is not a pseudo-psychological, mystical pursuit. Some noted psychologists, most prominently Martin Seligman, have documented how people who are positive in their speech turn out to be more optimistic and successful.

When you state that you were "lucky" for receiving an award or accolade, but someone else received one on talent, you undermine your own victories. If you listen to excellent athletes, you'll find that almost all of them relish their victories and credit their training, discipline, and hard work. Star basketball players who stand on the foul line with a key shot in a tough game do not say, "My last three baskets were dumb luck, and I'll be lucky to make this one."

I've found that there is a thin line between arrogance and confidence. Arrogance is the belief that you're good at what you do and have nothing left to learn. Confidence is the belief that you're good at what you do and are continuing to learn.

Be confident, enjoy your victories, and keep on learning.

CHAPTER 6

How Stress Can Help You

No One Moves at All
Without a Sense of Urgency

There is distress and there is eustress. The former is an overload that depresses our energies and dampens our talents. The latter is a turbocharge that creates a sense of urgency and heightened well-being.

Dogs may be content sitting in one place and merely observing the world passing by, but humans generally are not. We need stimulus, challenge, and change. Blood doesn't course through our veins in response to the knowledge that this day will be no different from every other. In fact, people do not hit their peak and realize their untapped potential without exigent circumstances demanding atypical responses.

To put it another way, the mundane doesn't set the heart racing.

Stress has an ugly repute. It should be managed but not manipulated. Organizations that install free health clubs for workers are to be lauded unless they commensurately are piling on the stress every morning with the expectation that the employees will work it out again on the treadmill—pun intended—every evening.

One of the largest costs for organizations these days comprises absenteeism, sickness, and disability claims. And a great deal of the cause of those expenses emanates from stress, according to most literature on the subject. (In fact, even certain forms of cancer and other dire diseases have been associated with stress.) The same holds true for our lives, in that our own "absenteeism" from our daily engagement with the world, family, and responsibilities is caused by stress overload.

One of the biggest "costs" that we incur for our own lives is the accretion of stress and its debilitating effects. Yet one of our greatest strengths flows from the adrenaline rush from knowing that our pride and accomplishments are on the line.

CONSTRUCTIVELY PILING IT ON

Ironically, perhaps, I've found that I become more energized the more I accomplish, and more enervated with the less I accomplish. In other words, there is a momentum of success. The key is to maintain a balance between too little challenge and too much work.

Let's take another look at our stress graphic, shown in Figure 6.1.

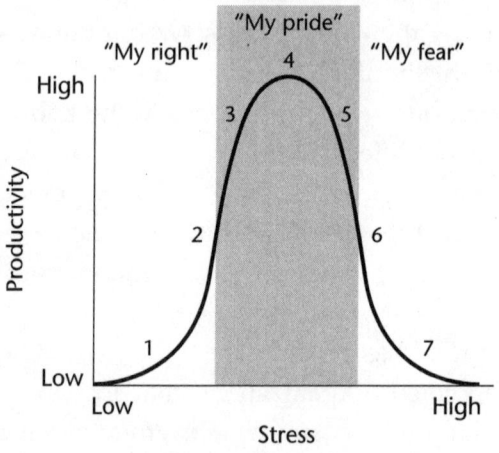

Figure 6.1. Stress Management Bell Curve

Life Balance

There is a difference between stress and anxiety in my opinion. Stress is a generative function that can become dysfunctional if overwhelming. Anxiety is a state of apprehension that is immediately dysfunctional, clouding judgment and delimiting actions.

The ultimate low-stress life is the retiree who has no more work accountabilities and who may have decided to curtail or eliminate most private accountabilities (family, social, civic, recreational, and so on). Those are the "my right" positions #1 through #3, and they represent an "entitlement" philosophy. (It is no accident that "entitlement" is currently such a popular phrase denoting automatic benefits.)

If you sit in your yard each day, or perch in a coffee shop in town, or dangle a fishing line without letup, you've decided to simply exist. But if you forget about the retiree, you'll find that many people lead their daily lives this way, a sort of monotone, predictable, congruent, and repetitive twenty-four hours, *Groundhog Day* reincarnate.[1]

At the right of my chart is the "fear factor," wherein the traditional "workaholic" might exist at point #5 and the completely paralyzed and nonfunctional individual reside at point #7. The stress here is so great that the individual can't move (for example, can't make sound judgments, intelligent decisions, or solve simple problems).

There are many of us subsumed by extended family responsibilities, trapped in bad relationships, grappling with troubled children, confronted by financial problems, and so on. (And there are many more whose trivial problems—such as weight and appearance, competition with neighbors, and buying a new car—take on a distorted but equal kind of gravitas.) In these cases,

---

1. From the popular movie where the protagonist is forced to continually repeat the exact same day every twenty-four hours.

CASE STUDY

As a gift one year, my sister gave me a forty-five-minute session in an isolation tank in downtown New York. The tank resembles a long coffin, is completely dark, and has several inches of warm salt water on the bottom so that you float without a feeling of either wetness or temperature. Oxygen is pumped in. The air is warm and without a discernable current.

You lie down naked in this contraption. The idea is that you are as removed from all stimuli as possible and can think deep thoughts or merely meditate and relax.

I yelled to get out within twenty minutes (I thought two hours had passed and they had forgotten about me). I realized that I *need* stimuli, need some interference, and require some interaction to do my best thinking (and performing). My stress level went over the top in isolation.

Peace and tranquility aren't all they're cracked up to be.

our entire existence suffers, since the results of this stress can rarely be compartmentalized.

> High stress levels are not normally containable. That is, they seep through cracks and crevices to infect all aspects of our existence. And once they begin to overflow all available space, they threaten to blow the structure completely apart.

At the mid-point of entitlement and fear is pride. This level (position #4) is attained when there is sufficient stress to promote urgency, movement, and innovation, but not so much as to tip the scale toward paralysis.

This is why the more we accomplish, the more we can accomplish. The most energetic and enthusiastic people I know are "busy"—they hold social club positions of leadership, have hobbies and pursuits which consume them,

Advice from the Readers of *Balancing Act*

How can one day be one of the best, yet also one of the worst days of your life? On February 26, 1996, we found out, for on that day our son was born but our daughter died. In her short life, our daughter showed us how precious life is . . . it was her greatest gift.

At the time of our daughter's death, my husband and I were embroiled in the corporate lifestyle. Our lives were a whirlwind of international travel, corporate metrics, and continual diary checks. How we managed to enjoy a wonderful marriage (let alone start a family) remains somewhat of a mystery.

By many accounts, we had it all. By our account, we did not. We did not have work/life balance. Our daughter taught us that life was far too precious to continue this way. We set out to achieve work/life balance early in our working lives rather than later. With this goal firmly placed in our heads and hearts, we established ProScribe, a medical communications company, and leveraged the Internet to locate ProScribe in Noosa, a cosmopolitan beachside resort town in Queensland, Australia. We gained incredible flexibility, with time for personal and professional goals.

The success of work/life balance can be measured in many ways, but for us, success is knowing how precious life is and doing all that we can to share that gift. Achieving work/life balance is one of the greatest gifts you can give to those you care about . . . including yourself!

> Dr. Karen Woolley, CEO, and Dr. Mark Woolley,
> COO, ProScribe Medical Communications

serve as coaches and advisors to friends, experiment with new ideas, take vacations, and so forth. We've all seen them. In some cases, we are them.

The more we accept reasonable stress levels, the more we are willing to experiment and innovate, because prudent risk becomes an operating philosophy. We realize that we can't accommodate all that we seek to do merely by doing what we used to do.

It is also the point at which we can maximally stretch, apply, and explore our talents.

Advice from the Readers of *Balancing Act*

After working on my bachelor's degree for *many* years as a part-time student, I had to make a choice. I either needed to go to school full-time and finish my degree, or forget it. I was unable to take day classes and work as a legal administrator for my then-employer, and I couldn't get the classes I needed at night. I left work and focused on school for one year. During that time, I took an internship with Voices for Children. This organization works with volunteers who advocate for children in the foster care system in San Diego County.

After my internship and schooling concluded, I had another choice: go back to work full-time or find something that would allow me time to continue working with "my kids"? I found law office management consulting. Having worked in the legal field for over twenty-five years, I realized my dream of owning my own business and continuing my work as a CASA (court-appointed special advocate) for children in foster care.

Now I have wonderful balance in my life. Some mornings I may conduct a training session on marketing or practice management; that afternoon I may build Legos® with a six-year-old who is in his twenty-second placement. Life is very short, and very special—make it count.

Carole M. Leffler, CML Consulting, Encinitas, California

Herein some suggestions for arriving at and maintaining the "pride position":

- Don't compartmentalize your life. Do what needs to be done when you feel most like doing it, not by arbitrary time standards. (This is a tremendous benefit that we have as entrepreneurs and not nine-to-five workers.)
- Recognize that the more you take on, the more you will have to be innovative in dealing with it successfully (for example, use delegation, technology, your kids, or other means).
- Get a lot done early. Do the toughest things first, and then gradually ease off. Your energy and motivation are highest when they are freshest.

- Isolate setbacks. Your inability to reconcile a family dispute does not make you a bad parent, and the fact that you can't fix the garage door doesn't mean that you're a hopeless bumbler.
- Extend victories. When you accomplish an unprecedented (for you) task or eliminate a huge number of challenges, remind yourself that you can use these talents and approaches repeatedly.
- Consciously manage your stress levels. I know that if I deny myself daily rewards to get "work" done, I'm less effective than if I allocate time for rewards and get to the "work" later. Only you best understand your own psychic needs and emotional balance.
- Don't accept outside interference. This is your life and your stress. Don't allow them to be affected by others' opinions, unreasonable demands, or unsolicited feedback.

WORKING IT OFF

What happens when we find ourselves on that slippery slope heading for position #7? It happens to all of us. We usually describe someone who was at the peak and has since hit the right-side nadir as a victim of "burnout."

"Burnout" sounds so inevitable and unrecoverable. We associate it with "workaholic" or "type-A personality" or some other pseudo-disease for which there is no cure or anodyne.

A curious phenomenon takes place when people at position #1 are suddenly scared witless by a threat and race pell mell to position #7, abject fear, without ever proceeding through positions #2 through #6. The employer, partner, colleague, or other interested party tends to conclude, "Total incompetent—doesn't perform under any conditions." But the point is not to scare people into a profound catatonic state, but merely to instill enough stress to create high performance.

Here are some signs that stress is beginning to take you "over the edge" to the down slope:

- You are taking on more and more responsibilities, interests, and involvements, *but not giving any up or cutting back anywhere.*

- You find yourself unable to get to everything you used to, and jobs and intentions now carry over to the next day or even the next week.
- The books you intend to read are a growing pile on your desk or night-stand, and some you put on the shelf unread.
- You don't read the newspaper every day.
- You have heartburn, headaches, upset stomach, and/or other ailments that you haven't had before so frequently.
- You find that physical tasks have become more burdensome and you're out of breath or fatigued more easily than before.
- You find that more and more people are making unreasonable demands and prompting arguments, including family, friends, and random acquaintances.
- You feel unlucky and think that you can't get a "break."
- You fall asleep earlier than normal, but don't sleep restfully.
- You forget things more often.
- You laugh less and enjoy yourself less.
- You're doing a lot of "failure work," that is, tasks already performed have to be redone because of errors or omissions, from your taxes and check-book to your hobbies and golf game.
- You haven't been to the movies or a theater in months and aren't even sure what the newest releases or productions are.
- You're intensely worried about finances.

All of these conditions needn't apply at once for you to be suffering from too much stress, and conversely, all of them might apply short-term or inter-mittently and you may have no stress at all. But if quite a few are present for quite a while, you can bank on the fact that your stress level is getting too high.

"Managing stress" means calibrating our stress levels so as to remain at position #4 indefinitely. If we do this well, it becomes second-nature. If we don't, it's tough to climb back up from position #7.

How do you work it off? Fortunately, it's not difficult, and most of us need to do it periodically. Here's my formula.

ALAN'S FORMULA FOR WORKING OFF STRESS

1. *Identify the Condition.* Use the indicators above as a template to alert you that you're not going through a temporary tough spot, but rather sliding down the overstressed slope. Be aware that "work off" actions are required. Don't assume that "this, too, shall pass." It won't.

2. *Ensure That You're Physically Healthy.* Go for a check-up (even if you have one annually and it's not the appointed time). Make sure that there are no somatic causes and that your blood pressure, heart, and digestive systems are up to snuff.[2]

3. *Create an Exercise Regimen.* If you're highly disciplined (I'm not), you can do this at home with some basic equipment and/or jogging. Otherwise, join a local gym. In either case, get some professional advice to establish the right cardiac and weight training uniquely for you. In terms of stress reduction, the key here is to do this with absolute regularity. Most authorities suggest every other day, or every day but alternating the activities. If you travel, virtually every hotel has some kind of exercise facilities. (If you already have an exercise regimen and are feeling stressed, change it. In fact, you should change the nature of your workouts every six to nine months in any case for the best results.)

4. *Regulate Your Diet.* I've never seen a "cold turkey" approach to diet that worked long-term. That is, you can't forever deny yourself favorite foods. Ask your doctor or a nutritionist to help create a realistic approach to weight control and diet. For example, I love cheeseburgers, but only have them once a week or so. I stay away from fried foods most of the time. I don't eat rich desserts, but I do eat big steaks. We have to intelligently moderate our diets.[3]

---

2. Just as an example, if constant heartburn is caused by acid reflux disease, there are excellent medications to control and eliminate the problem. This is one of the more common "aging" diseases we all encounter sooner or later.

3. I will provide my favorite diet for weight loss and nutrition, which my wife calls "the stupid diet" because I lose weight on it and she doesn't. Avoid all fried food, bread, pasta, and desserts. Do not eat red meat. Use sugar substitutes in coffee and drink diet sodas or water. Eat all the fish, chicken, non-sugar cereals, fruits, and vegetable you choose. Once a week, you can depart from the restrictions. I find that you lose weight consistently while on this diet, especially if you accompany it with regular exercise.

5. *Eliminate "Carriers."* There are people in all of our lives who bring out the worst in us. They may use passive/aggressive behaviors, exhibit bad habits, or simply be permanently irritating. There is no etched stone with commandments that demands that you do your penance by dealing with them. Keep them out of your life. These are people who carry stress just as insects or rodents carry disease.

6. *Reorganize Your Life.* Get rid of magazine subscriptions for periodicals you don't read or don't enjoy. Rearrange your closet, desk, or garage so that you can find things the first time, every time. Reduce the commitments on your social calendar. Resign from some unpleasant and non-productive committees. Cook less and eat out more. "Reengineer" your existence so that your routines are substantially altered.

There is one good thing about self-induced stress: It can be self-eliminated. We are usually not victims of the cosmos. We are victims of our own actions, albeit with the best intentions. We can choose to stop being victims at any time. Stress is more a result of lack of volition than of poor conditions.

---

7. *Monitor Your Changes.* Test against the criteria above in two weeks or so after you've made the changes. They may not have disappeared completely, but they should be reduced. If they are, solidify your new regimens and routines. If they aren't, then you haven't hit the real causes (that is, the people or conditions piling onto your stress levels). Go back to the drawing board and try again.

"ANCHOR" POSITIONS (YOUR STAKE IN THE GROUND)

The ancient Aztecs were highly militant, and rather merciless. During their years of domination in what is now Mexico, they built a sophisticated and successful society based on high standards and great heroism.

One of the most dramatic gestures of the bravest Aztec warriors was to tether themselves to stakes in the ground, using vines tied to their ankles and

I was dragging through an airport in Charlotte when it became apparent that I would have to take periodic rests in order to lug my heavy overnight bag and briefcase to a distant gate. As I leaned on a railing wheezing, I said to myself that this was ridiculous.

I walked into a gift shop a few yards away and bought a wheeled luggage cart for $20 and got to my gate in better shape. When I got home, I enrolled in a gym, purchased an overnight bag with built-in wheels and a place to attach my briefcase, and began to rearrange some other parts of my life (for example, I was toting around far too much junk for a night or two, so I dumped about ten pounds of flotsam).

I've resigned never to put up with "necessary evils." If I find myself regularly inconvenienced or unhappy, I change something. There is a great restaurant nearby which believes its own press clippings and keeps guests waiting for hours (unless you know the owner), all of this overseen by a rude hostess. We don't go there any more. The food's not good enough to overcome the annoyance.

---

fastened to the stake. (This is the origin of the phrase "to put a stake in the ground," meaning to establish a position.) The warriors would hold their ground and defeat the enemy or be killed (the enemies were equally ruthless), but would not retreat, not even move evasively to any great degree. This practice not only established an unmovable front line, but it tended to intimidate the enemy and bolster the spirits of the rest of the Aztecs.

We all need a similar "stake in the ground" emotionally. The "fight or flight" dichotomy that we face daily too frequently results in flight.

If we're to deal with stress in a healthy manner, we have to manage the stressful events and circumstances and resist their managing us. Jefferson said, "In matters of taste, swim with the current; in matters of principle, stand like a rock." We generally swim no matter how soft the resistance or weak the tide. We flee from stress, which exacerbates its deleterious effect on our lives.

Standing up to stress—confronting it, rebuffing it, challenging it—is vital to subordinating it. We need an anchor position from which we will not be moved.

> If you don't know where your stake in the ground is fixed, then you
> don't know whether you're holding ground, gaining ground, or los-
> ing ground. That means you have no way to judge your perform-
> ance, and your ability to manage stress is undermined by your
> inability to measure your reactions to it.

Here are examples that tend to generate "fight or fight" choices. The deceptive aspect about them is that at first blush confronting them seems highly stressful, but the most stress results from fleeing them and never reconciling or ameliorating them.

- Your partner or spouse is engaged in the "silent treatment," unwilling to share the reasons for his or her unhappiness (and you're afraid that pursuing the causes forcefully will dredge up all-too-painful past conflict).
- A very vocal and intimidating person has advertently or inadvertently asked you to take a position which you detest (for example, becoming fundraising chair for the United Way or being responsible for a repetitive and maddeningly boring job at work).
- The fear of the known (admitting to breaking a cherished possession) is overwhelmed by the fear of the unknown (the degree of potential outrage and rift in the relationship).
- A threat associated with others' experience overcomes your decision to engage in normal precautionary activity (a friend's heart ailment was discovered during a routine physical and now you continually postpone scheduled medical work).
- Your ego may take a bruising and it isn't strong enough to withstand the perceived beating (someone at a cocktail party takes a position you're almost certain is wrong, but you fear the backlash if you speak up and you are proved wrong).
- Your history provides strongly prohibitive reasons for acting (your parents laughed at your attempts to engage in athletics, you never played very well as a result, and you're loath to join the club's softball tournament).

Alan, per your suggestion, I jumped on the chance to move the office back home when a required move (fourth child meant extra bedrooms needed) meant we could look for homes with an existing office.

The move home has added many benefits:

- I've lost some weight due to healthier meals and snacks that are always available and save at least a couple of hours each week in mealtime savings alone.
- The elimination of commute time allows for additional marketing work; I don't feel guilty working on the book and articles early in the morning, as opposed to marketing that had more immediate but perhaps less powerful results.
- I'm spending far more time with the family, not just eating dinner on time. Taking breaks throughout the day with my young children or wife is far more invigorating than anything I could have done at an office.
- I'm saving many thousands of dollars every year.
- Even though the commute could be as little as twenty minutes one way, the daily total loss to commuting was closer to two hours.
- I'm happier, healthier, and less stressed, as is my family because of the move.
- The air is cleaner.
- I've gained more business due to more time invested in marketing.
- I enjoy working more.
- I "play" more often (skeet shooting for lunch instead of rushing out for a bite of bread).

Mark Faust, Principal and Founder,
Echelon Management Institute

- You are guilty about the cause and feel an obligation to permanently atone (you traveled a great deal while your kids were growing up, they and your spouse have never let you forget it, and now you're reluctant to confront them about poor choices in friends, behavior, schoolwork, or other issues).

When I was about ten years old, my friends and I taunted two huge and tough members of the school's junior police force. The two took it very badly and promised to "get us." My friends eventually took their licks, but I constantly evaded and avoided the two bullies, sometimes going blocks out of my way to get to school.

This went on for about four months. Every school day I underwent the stress of trying to take a route they weren't assigned to and to avoid them in the schoolyard and the halls. They finally graduated, having made my life much more of a hell than if they had caught me!

Or at least I had made my life a hell. The ultimate retribution—a punch in the arm or a shouted threat—had nowhere near the severity of my bizarre flight scheme. The good news is that I often recall the incident—and have for forty years—to remind myself that we create our own stress through our conscious decisions and can eliminate most stress through making different decisions.

What does it take to throw an anchor out or to put a stake in the ground? The good news is that it is totally dependent on volition. The bad news is that it is totally dependent on volition. Some of us need help to recognize and respond to the threatening situations and our "automatic" behavioral response.

It may be helpful, however, to view this from both a process and a content perspective.

Process

Identify those situations that cause you the greatest stress. Don't assign blame; simply describe the situation and context. Is it when your partner stops speaking to you, or a friend nonchalantly splits a check for which he is mostly responsible, or a manager "volunteers" your services for a duty you hate?

Evaluate whether the stress is significant enough to take action. A minor matter of ten minutes is forgettable, perhaps, while a weekly occurrence at an otherwise enjoyable event may be intolerable.

Estimate what the likely result of you making a different decision might be. For example, would asking your boss to refrain from volunteering your services cause you to be fired, create a problem on your evaluation, or simply prompt your boss to choose someone else?

Select a course of action. Use an advisor, partner, or friend if you need some objective help. Don't merely decide to confront the situation or behavior, but decide *exactly how* you will do so.

Act at the next available juncture. Don't stew about it; do something in line with your chosen action. Stay the course. Don't immediately back down if the other party also "digs in."

Assess the result. Did you reverse the problem, deflect it, reduce it, or lose still more ground? What was the result of your different decision? Has it gone away or must you confront it again and, if so, with the same tactics or a different approach?

You can use an objective formula to understand and respond to the process of stressful encounters which have caused you to flee in the past, thereby resulting in still more stress. The process helps you to overcome emotions and objectively analyze your problem in dealing with the situation and enables you to involve others in the assessment if you choose.

Content

The content of these situations varies, but can usually be traced to one of the following general areas. If you know that one or more of these areas accounts for most of the stressful situations, then you can arrange for skill building or counseling to improve your ability to make new decisions.

1. *Ego.* Many people immediately enter a "fight or flight" set of choices when their egos are threatened. Either is usually a bad alternative. Overly strong egos tend to cause "fight" and overly weak egos tend to result in "flight." Healthy, secure, and appropriate ego identity usually results in neither.
2. *Precedent.* We carry far too much baggage around. While some behaviors and/or outcomes may be predictable, most are not. The variables in any situation—the performer, the other performers, the environment, the

nature of the issue, prior and proximate events, and so forth—are too numerous to allow categorical responses every time.

3. *Misperceptions.* We rarely see ourselves as others do, and more often than not tend to *undervalue* our abilities and impact. This undervaluing severely delimits our decisions and range of alternatives.

4. *Sloth.* This is the volitional aspect. We become too intellectually and emotionally lazy to deal with the stress, not appreciating the greater damage we create by living with it. The term "necessary evil" is actually one of the most unnecessary burdens in our lives.

Place your stake in the ground, and resolve that you will fight stress on that site no matter what forces it throws against you. The battle of confronting stress and attempting to manage it is never fatal. But ironically, the decision to flee it and live with its consequences often is.

CHANGING TOMORROW

The question remains: "How do I get out of a destructive stress loop and into a more productive and fulfilling cycle?"

The answer remains: "You have to begin the changes now."

In our client work, we see "deadly cycles." By that I mean a series of events, each with a causal relationship to the next, which ultimately reinforce themselves into a dizzying spiral of doom. No one seems capable of breaking the cycle; hence, we are called in as a last resort.

For example, in Figure 6.2, each component in the deadly cycle leads, inexorably, to the next. The continual self-reinforcing nature of the dynamic overcomes piecemeal attempts by management to deal with the system.

Deadly cycles arise because they are so neatly and automatically self-perpetuating. Some have happily chugged along since our adolescence, the beginning of a relationship, or start of a new endeavor. That's why it requires considerable strength to break them.

Figure 6.2. A Business Deadly Cycle

When I ask management where they would choose to break a cycle, they inevitably choose the perceived "easiest" place. In the example shown in Figure 6.2, they might select to lower the incentive standards so that inexperienced hires might have the opportunity to make more money more quickly, thereby ending the frustration causing them to leave (or the poor performance causing them to be fired).

In fact though, these cycles must be broken at those places *that will yield the most dramatic and immediate results.* In my example, I believe that to be the type of person hired. Therefore, a larger amount of available funds—even deficit financing—must be found to hire the best possible people.[4] If management will bite this bullet, the intervention will be a success and the cycle will be broken.

The same deadly cycle occurs in our lives. An example is shown in Figure 6.3.

This illustration does not show an arbitrary cycle, but rather one I've seen with hundreds of people I've counseled in the wakes of layoffs, closings, and economic downturns. The "easy" way out of this is usually considered to be increased job security or a new job altogether, or sometimes a second job or

---

4. Note that this is the best place to start because of its impact, not because it is in the "one o'clock" position.

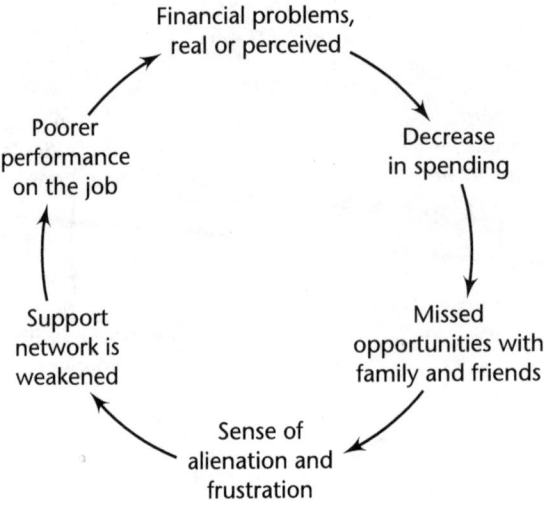

Figure 6.3. The Deadly Cycle Applied to Our Lives

loan. But the most dramatic intervention in my view is at the support network juncture. What's usually most needed is a *rapprochement* with family and friends, so that the individual has objective, loving, and well-intentioned help to break the sequence.

The best places to break in are often also the hardest places to break in, of course. It's tough to find money for better hires when there are no profits, and it's tough to approach family and friends for assistance when one is feeling isolated and even like a failure. But the remedies are not about what's *easy*, but about what's most *immediately effective*.

> Someone once said that therapy is the process of taking moderate unhappiness and turning it into stark, raging terror. Perhaps. But you can't deal with a fear unless you isolate what it truly is.

These deadly cycles must be changed immediately. I call this "changing tomorrow," not in the sense that you'll get to it tomorrow, but rather that tomorrow will be different from today. Once tomorrow is realized as being even slightly different (for example, you've reached out to just one person and received a single piece of financial advice or job counseling), the changes are underway.

If you don't believe this cycle/stress dynamic, think of the ongoing problems that many people have with losing weight, breaking an addiction (not only to harmful substances, but to video games, shopping, and so forth), ending bad relationships, avoiding abusive people, achieving new job performance, and so on. These cycles can infect our lives without our knowing it, and our immune systems are often not strong enough (aware enough) to prevent the ensuing entrenchment.

If you want to change tomorrow, break out of a deadly cycle and reduce dysfunctional stress, then follow this sequence to overcome the inertia:

1. *Identify the immediate cause of your stress.* What, exactly, is bothering you (what's the real fear)? Is it something your kids are doing (or not doing), a work issue, a relationship, a perceived lost opportunity, or something else? What is the immediate cause of the pain?
2. *Identify the sequence or cycle.* Don't stop with the proximate cause. Ask yourself what is causing it, and what effects it's having further down the line. Put a circle on a pad representing the deadly cycle sequence and sketch in the contributing factors and resulting effects. There may be three or seven, but there will be more than one.
3. *Identify the aspect which will most immediately break the cycle.* No matter how painful, whether a reconciliation with a relative, a confrontation with an acquaintance, or discipline for a child, what will begin to change things immediately? *What will change tomorrow?*
4. *Determine what help you'll need.* If it were easy, things wouldn't have come this far. The odds are that you can't break the cycle alone. Will you need family support, spiritual guidance, alliances at work, a mentor's feedback, or other assistance? You may decide that professional counseling is called for and seek therapeutic intervention.
5. *Make the changes, no matter how painful.* Get on with it and make tomorrow different. You now have *the potential for control,* but this is useless if not exercised. Understand that, no matter how painful the change techniques, the prospects of remaining in the deadly cycle are far more deleterious and

Advice from the Readers of *Balancing Act*

I had flown from Australia to New York for a psychologists' training course. The pressure was on; just to be there had been a big investment. I was about to have my "big moment," as part of the training involved a counseling session and I had just found out that mine was going to be with Albert Ellis. I couldn't believe my luck—I, along with practitioners around the world, have admired his work.

There was no doubt that my presenting question for the session had to be an important one. As I settled into the chair, I summoned up the courage to let my professional guard drop and I heard myself say, "I work so hard at trying to find a balance and it continues to elude me. If I work hard and achieve my career goals, my family and social life suffer. If I enjoy myself and catch up with family and friends, my work suffers. How can I find the balance so that I can have it all and be happy?"

During the next half hour, with expert assistance I learned that I had been setting myself up to fail—I had been searching for something that did not exist. After all, there is no universal concept of lifestyle balance. The very notion is very subjective! What may be balance for one person may be unacceptable for someone else; our values have a large part to play.

The real question was "What sort of life would make me happy?" Once I had experienced the "light-bulb moment," I could not go back to my usual way of living, as I had a new definition of what balance meant to me.

Postscript

That session took place five years ago and continues to profoundly affect my life. Upon my return, I left my job and started my own consulting business. I also met an amazing man, married him, and together we lead the life that makes us happy. Sometimes life is busy, when I work through weekends to meet deadlines; at other times, life takes on a different pace when we go overseas for a month every year or I take our Labrador for a walk instead of fighting the peak-hour traffic to get to the office.

Victoria Barsky, Barsky Consulting Pty. Ltd., Melbourne, Australia

far more lasting. "Cold turkey" is temporary, while drug addiction is for-ever. The same holds true for dysfunctional relationships, undertakings, careers, and pursuits.

> The good news is that you can change tomorrow and that there are tools for doing so. If you choose not to, however, the bad news is that you've become an active catalyst for your own deadly cycle.

Stress can help you if used productively and for a sense of urgency, pride, and accomplishment. But it can kill you, literally, if you allow it to control you and dictate your behaviors and relationships. We all have the potential for control of our lives. The only real issue is whether we intend to exercise it or not.

ALAN'S ULTIMATE LESSONS

Have you ever met people who perform at their best under pressure? They usually say that they're best when faced with a deadline or "when the chips are on the table." Bill Russell, the great former Boston Celtics center and hall-of-famer, said, "Heart in champions has to do with the depth of your motivation and how well your mind and body react to pressure. Concentration is being able to do what you do best under maximum pain and stress."

I've found that if you perform best—do your actual finest work of any kind—when the pressure is on, then you're at position #4 on my chart, and you have mastered the art of using stress productively and effectively.

Champions perform well under pressure. And we should all strive to be champions. Isn't that worth changing tomorrow for?

Balance
in Relationships

CHAPTER 7

The Other Person's Self-Interest

May I Please See Your Vacation Slides?

People are forever trying to "predict" behavior. Personality profiles and behavioral assessments are hot items, although I personally don't believe they're worth very much, and certainly not in the hands of amateurs.

Aside from some obsessive/compulsive disorders, behavior is seldom accurately predictable for these reasons:

- The environment plays a major role, and we tend to act differently at work, at home, in social situations, or with strangers.
- The other performer influences us significantly; ordinarily assertive behavior may well be subordinated in the face of even stronger assertive behavior.
- History and experience weigh heavily, so that partners of long standing may well interpret (or misinterpret) current actions in light of calcified and no longer accurate models.
- Situational factors, such as temporary pressures, personal health, and other priorities, may substantively affect behavior.

Thus, it's generally useless to define someone else in terms of "high I," "INTJ," "amiable analytic," "late adapter," or any other pop phrase.[1] *And if it's dangerous and inaccurate in the workplace, it's often calamitous and fatal in relationships.*

Our relationships are based on understanding others' behavior, separating emotion from fact, operating in the other person's best interests, and tucking away our egos. Having said all that, we're talking more art than science. And, most importantly, we're talking about the inappropriateness and inadequacy of many of the skills and techniques that we've employed in our business success.

Or to quote a classic phrase of my wife's over the years, "You're not at a client now."

INFLUENCING OTHERS IS AN ART FORM

There are basically three methods to influence others, and two of them don't work.

Power and Coercion

This is the proverbial "gun to one's head." On the job, I'm threatening you with financial pressure, job assignments, job security, and so on. In personal relationships, I'm threatening your well-being, ego, freedom to act, and so forth. With children, this may be corporal punishment or denial of a privilege (no television tonight; you can't use the car). With a spouse or partner, it can range from denial of money or favors (for example, withholding sexual relations) to physical abuse.[2] Obviously, power and coercion are not the bases for healthy relationships, yet they are used with alarming frequency, especially when you include verbal abuse and psychological games in this category.

---

1. What's even worse, of course, is that these labels and pseudo-insights are usually used to explain away behavior, not to understand it and adapt to it. We're much more likely to hear "What do you expect from such a 'driver,' who will always have a short attention span?" as we are to hear "She's very task-focused, so let's present her with the outcomes in a concise and crisp manner."

2. Physical abuse is quite common. When I served on the board of a shelter for battered women I found to my shock—despite all my psychology training and "preparation"—that spousal abuse transcends socioeconomic, racial, and ethnic lines. It's as common for a six-figure income, upper-middle-class woman to be beaten by her insurance executive husband as it is for a $35,000 household income spouse to be abused by her blue-collar, common-law husband.

Advice from the Readers of *Balancing Act*

At age thirty-nine, I have finally learned that the key to happiness is building your life around your passions, regardless of how you earn a living.

Until my mid-thirties, I continually sacrificed the things I wanted to do in favor of the things I felt I "had to do" to advance my career. I was considered successful by traditional definitions, but was not happy.

I began doing some volunteer work with the Raleigh Jaycees, a four-hundred-member community service group. I met passionate people there and became passionate about what we did. As I became increasingly disenchanted with my role in corporate America, I rose to the rank of vice president in the Jaycees and became interested in running for president, a job that took thirty hours per week and did not pay a dime. The time and travel demands of my paying job could not accommodate this. Something had to give.

I have never jumped out of an airplane, but I learned how it must feel the day I handed my boss a resignation letter. I had no plan as to how I would earn a living; I just believed it was time to put my passion first. It was exhilarating, and incredibly fulfilling.

Today, I am happier than ever before, and my motto is, "Every day is a bonus." Service to humanity is truly the best work of life, and I now feel much richer than I did when I earned more money.

Chris Wilsey, President, Raleigh Jaycees 2001 (Chairman 2002);
Managing Partner, RSR Marketing Solutions

When famed Ohio State football coach Woody Hayes was asked why he chose to run the ball on every play and never pass, he responded, "When you pass the ball, three things can happen, and two of them are bad. Why would I want to do that?"

Normative Pressure

This is peer pressure. We see it in the workplace as urgings to keep up with the "in" crowd. There might be a charity drive for which management urges "100 percent participation." We see safety slogans advertising everyone's role in continuing consecutive days of no time lost to injury.

On the societal level, we encounter "no smoking" campaigns and "say 'no' to drugs" and dire warnings about the perils of drinking and driving. While many of these may be seen as educational, they're often really blatant appeals to peer pressure. Even in areas where smoking is permitted, for instance, smokers are often looked down on, and it's difficult to be the only one to light a cigarette.

Within relationships, for children the pressure is usually heard as, "Why can't you be more like your sister (or cousin, or mother, or friend)?" A spouse might say to the partner,[3] "Why haven't you been as thoughtful about family events as your brother?" and the converse might be, "You don't support me in my profession the way other husbands/wives do."

Normative pressure doesn't work in relationships because we *don't* want to be "like the Joneses." Our families should be unique, our friendships should be distinctive, and our social and civic circles will be increasingly diverse.

Enlightened Self-Interest

The only change agent that consistently helps in influencing others and building relationships is an appeal to the other person's enlightened (or rational) self-interest.[4]

The difference between the questions, "Would you like to see my vacation slides?" and "May I see your vacation slides?" is rather momentous. In the first instance, you're asking me to invest time in what I perceive to be a boring ritual of hearing you brag about your latest exploits and imply that I don't get to see or do as much as you. In the second instance, you've reasonably requested

---

3. In case my prose doesn't always make it clear, I'm applying these situations to all types of relationships, conventional and unconventional, spouses, partners, significant others, and so forth. These elements don't really change.

4. I'm using "enlightened" and "rational" to distinguish between reasonable self-interests (for example, self-betterment, pleasure, advancement) and unethical interests (for example, advance through cheating, stealing money, avoiding a debt).

When I was hired by Mercedes to determine why some of their dealerships performed so much better than others in the wake of the onslaught by Lexus, Infiniti, and Acura, I observed an interesting phenomenon.

In the average and poorer-performing dealerships, the salespeople would highlight Mercedes' engineering and history and condescendingly dismiss the competition. Customers were expected to understand that you pay more for a Mercedes because the car is so superior, based on the intellectual argument of better design, higher standards, more proficient testing, and so on.

In the best dealerships, the salespeople encouraged the patrons to get in the cars, have their spouses or partners or family members do the same, and test drive the car without the salesperson accompanying them. The language in these dealerships was more along the lines of "You look wonderful in that car," "This car was made for you," and "Think of yourself leaving that with the valet at your favorite restaurant." The term "curb presence"—I kid you not—was often employed.

This was counterintuitive to me, but I finally understood what was happening. Cars are lifestyle purchases, and therefore most buyers are driven by emotion more than logic (particularly at luxury-car prices). You can't see engineering, but you can see the driver in the convertible alighting at the curb.

Logic makes people think, but emotion makes them act. And that is the secret of influence.

---

that I share my insights with you from my travels, which no doubt will help you make intelligent choices based on my superb commentary and excellent photos.

There is nothing at all similar about the two situations!

If you want to influence someone else—at work or at home, in social circles or political rallies—you must determine what is in the other person's self-interest and appeal to it in such a way that *both of your interests are served.*

When liquor was prohibited because a law was passed (coercion), people found a multitude of routes around the law. When the deleterious effects of tobacco were pointed out (education about one's health and longevity), the rate of smoking seriously declined. Children don't study hard when it's merely pointed out that their friends do, but they start to get quite serious when they learn they may not be able to continue with their class or get into a favored college.

Outstanding salespeople use enlightened self-interest all the time. Customers don't buy because of the features, benefits, repute, or sales temerity; they buy because of *the salutary effects for them of using the product or service.* Such behaviors tend to be self-perpetuating and long-lived, thereby lowering acquisition costs over the long term. The same phenomenon occurs in our personal choices.

Appeals to another's self-interest are almost always *emotional appeals.* The more emotional, the better. And this, too, may be counterintuitive, especially when we hear people say, "Let's look at this objectively" or "Let's shelve the emotionalism and just consider the facts." The trouble is, of course, that you can no more shelve the emotionalism than you can really expect the jury to follow the judge's orders and "disregard the last comment from the witness."

The art of influencing your closest relationships and your most distant acquaintanceships effectively and lastingly is in an appeal to the other person's self-interest on an emotional level. If I really believe I'm going to be better off, I'm going to change, barring personality disorder and aberrant behavior.

Now how do you do that so that both parties "win"?

INTELLIGENT TRADEOFFS

Life is a series of tradeoffs. That is, no one sails through reaping all the breaks, benefits, and beneficence while others experience rough rides. Nor is there some cosmic scorekeeper, with green eyeshade and pocket protector, keeping tabs on one's "balance."

You win some, you lose some, and some get rained out. But you have to suit up for them all.

Life Balance

My three favorite techniques:

Dogs—Five minutes spent roughhousing with one or both of my Labradors in the middle of the day is a fantastic way to revitalize the body and mind (yes, I primarily work from home). Taking them out for a walk, to catch a Frisbee® in the park, or to run does wonders. Watching them cavort (or cavorting with them) brings a smile to my face and to my soul. The loyalty, love, and respect feel good too. There's something special about a seventy-pound dog trying to crawl onto your lap while you're in the middle of a project. It puts things in perspective.

Get away—Whether a short trip every month (long weekend to one week) or a couple long trips (two weeks or more), along with some shorter trips, it doesn't matter. When away, I regularly check emails and messages because it negates the trip if you're overwhelmed upon return. It also impresses clients when you do so, especially if overseas (the rates are laughable, eight cents a minute from England).

Exercise—It's the best way to relieve the pressure and get the thought juices going. Too many times to count, I've returned from a run or bike ride and quickly jotted down the breakthrough ideas I came up with while panting away. Vary your routines. Depending on the season, I do running, walking, biking, weights, and Bikram's yoga. My seventeen-year-old daughter recently told me how much better she sleeps and feels when she regularly exercises. What better confirmation than from a teenager?

John Martinka, Business Resource Group, Inc.,
Kirkland, Washington

I remember the actor Tommy Lee Jones solemnly intoning, when someone commiserated with him about his lousy luck in some movie the name of which I've long since forgotten, "I'll play the hand I was dealt." That's not a bad philosophy for life and relationships, insofar as it does no good to wish we were someone else, had a different family, or had acquired different friends (although the last, at least, can be remedied).

By "tradeoffs" I mean that our relationships are about negotiations, and I use that term in a positive, not pejorative, sense. The "enlightened self-interest"

I discussed above is not usually congruent among various parties and can often be in outright, albeit healthy, opposition. (For example, your self-interest may lie in arising at 6 a.m. to work out and write, while mine is to stay in bed until at least 9 so that I can make up for my late nights.)

Perhaps the most important technique of all in negotiating within interests is the concept of "musts" and "wants." Basically, a "must" is an interest, objective, or need that meets these criteria:

- It is critical to your well-being. That is, you will be demonstrably and seriously negatively affected by its absence.
- It is reasonable. That is, taking six months off for a Tahitian vacation or being named the next governor may not be exactly rational.
- It is measurable. That is, you have to know it if you trip over it. You can't demand "comfort" or "safety" or even "beauty" without knowing what exactly fulfills the need.

If interests, objectives, and needs don't meet the "must" criteria, then they are "wants." "Wants" are desirable circumstances, but not critical for self-interest. Obviously, we have relatively few musts and a great many wants. (Otherwise, we wouldn't be able to function because so many critical needs weren't being met.[5])

Now, here's the power of the concept:

Never Negotiate Away a "Must." When you are involved in the inevitable "tradeoffs," never, ever, bargain away musts or, by their very criteria, you will be miserable. You will have "lost" the negotiation. It's one thing to cede sharing the car with a newly licensed child, but it's another entirely to surrender the approval of how and when it's used.

Try to Never Squash Someone Else's "Must." This is one of the hardest aspects to accept and may seem counterintuitive. But if you remove one of the other party's "must" objectives, you will ensure that he or she is miserable *and great-*

---

5. You must be severe about musts. I've always regarded the love of my family as a must, but the respect of colleagues as a want. I can function without the latter, but not without the former.

ly increase the likelihood that he or she will not be committed to the solution or will actually renege. Try to make yourself content to preserve your own musts and do as well as you can on the wants. But if you, for example, "win" an argument with your spouse or partner in which he or she must give up a position to suit your promotional move, you may well find yourself with no support in the new job.

Never Make a Negotiation About Ego. We discussed self-esteem earlier, and "winning" a negotiation by forcing someone else to "lose" the negotiation is not a route toward enhanced self-esteem. We don't elevate ourselves by degrading others. Such tactics actually degrade us all. The best negotiating results are "win/win," and that may mean preserving your musts while surrendering on most wants. I never try to "beat down" a salesperson on price (which may lower his commission, make him look bad with the boss, or force him to resent me, whom he will have to service in the future). Instead, I try to maximize the *value* that I can obtain. I'd much rather increase value at an existing price than jeopardize current value by obtaining a lower price. In negotiating, reciprocal value is the key, not ego and notches on one's gun belt.

> Negotiating, contrary to most viewpoints, need not be adversarial. If you're truly intent on nurturing relationships, it should be a pursuit of mutual value, even if some items are traded off or lost. Such losses should be seen as a natural result of reconciling conflicting interests *and not as a blow to one's prestige or talent.*

There is another way to view self-interest and the routes to influencing others and maintaining balance in relationships: The values, attitudes, behavior sequence.

Values are those beliefs we hold as sacrosanct.[6] A corporate value we may encounter in our work might be "We treat our employees with dignity and

---

6. Indeed, "culture" is nothing but those beliefs that govern behavior. Thus, organizational, educational, neighborhood, political, and other cultures are simply the result of the underlying belief systems that, in turn, inform people how to act in various situations.

respect and as prized assets, not expenses." A personal value could be "Under no circumstances will I ever cheat anyone out of a commitment or obligation which I owe." The company in the first example is not going to lay employees off to atone for executive mistakes; the person in the second example is not going to falsely declare bankruptcy to escape debt.

Attitudes are those positions we take based on our value systems. We may have an attitude that people who don't pay their debts are untrustworthy and manipulative, or that people who show up late and leave early have a poor work ethic. Attitudes formulate our world view, including our opinions of others and our judgment of observed behaviors.

Advice from the Readers of *Balancing Act*

I have a model that says everything we spend our time on can be put into one of three categories: family/personal, business, and community activities. Considering that our time and energy are finite, we must determine the right expenditure of time and energy for those three circles of our lives. The balance is different for each person, and it even varies for the same person at different stages of life.

For example, a young person just starting out in business may have a very large "business" circle. Because time is limited, that person's "family" and/or "community" circle will necessarily be smaller, because we are all in a box of time that circumscribes the space available to the circles of life. This may create stress because a young and growing family may demand more time of that person just when he or she feels the need to be active at work.

Over the course of one's life, the size of the circles will change relative to each other. For example, a retired person may have a larger community circle when "business" time is reduced. In addition, the circles overlap, as when a businessperson's spouse accompanies him or her to a business conference or civic dinner event.

The key to happiness is to determine the right balance of these circles for you, and then to try to maintain it, with an awareness that the balance will shift over the years.

Stub Estey, Executive Director, Shipley Center for Leadership
and Entrepreneurship, School of Business,
Clarkson University, Potsdam, New York

Behaviors are those observable actions which manifest our attitudes. We may choose to be sarcastic with someone who complains of having too much work, yet comes in late and leaves early. We may refuse to do business with people whom we believe we have reason not to trust. We may embrace people and extend proactive help—indeed, may even cede our own "musts"—when we perceive them as justifiably in need or representing a worthy cause.

Traditionally, coercion and power are focused on *behavior*. We seek to punish the manifest result of someone's attitudes. Such punishment seldom changes attitudes. In fact, despite the punishment, the attitudes usually deepen and intensify in their opposition.

Normative pressure has usually been applied in an attempt to shape attitudes and thereby control behavior: "Don't act that way, since no one else is; act this way and be a part of the mainstream or majority." Such attempts at attitudinal change have several problems: (1) they are useless if behavior itself isn't changed; (2) they are fickle, in that peer pressure can quickly take new directions and is very submissive to fads and whims; and (3) they antagonize the truly independent thinker and contrarian.

Appeals to rational self-interest, however, are aimed at the values level. People have reduced cigarette smoking not primarily because of higher taxes (punishing the behavior) or appeals to reduce second-hand smoke (peer pressure), but rather because the objective, unassailable evidence shows that their health will probably suffer (appeal to self-interest and basic values).

"The beatings will stop as soon as morale improves" has never been a philosophy that has demonstrably improved the human condition.

It's no surprise that adolescents are so difficult to persuade and negotiate with, since they tend to be unduly influenced by peer behavior and approval, even in denial of their real self-interest. (Sorry, but body piercings, spiked hair, and tattoos are not for aesthetic appeal but rather for group acceptance. And much more seriously and gravely, some African-American teenagers are claiming that they don't want to study for higher grades since they will then be perceived as "white" by their friends.) While "tough love" and punishing adverse behavior may seem like the ideal, you can't "punish" a child into studying or responsible conduct, which must be self-perpetuating.

On that note, I'll end this section by emphasizing that motivation is inherent, whether in the workplace or in the home, and that you can't motivate someone else, even a beloved family member. You can only hope to establish an environment in which the person will be more likely to become motivated.

In other words, through intelligent tradeoffs, appeals to self-interest, and "win/win" propositions, you can effectively influence others so that their behavior change is one of commitment and not merely compliance.

AVOIDING GENERALIZING SPECIFICS

Sometimes people in my mentoring program "invent" problems for themselves. Instead of visualizing a positive outcome—or at least a range of outcomes—they visualize only a negative outcome.

The process looks something like this: He was abrupt on the phone. When I see him, he'll probably immediately demand to know how I can help him. I don't like those confrontations, and we'll start off on the wrong foot. Since this is my only chance with a key buyer in this company, I'd better cancel and see if I can find someone else who's more agreeable. . . .

Of course, the correct response here is, "Great! I've got an appointment with the economic buyer!!"

In relationships we tend to invoke the same negative prophecies. "She's never liked the idea of spending money on cars, and if I ask her to go to the showroom with me she'll be very negative, so I'd better go by myself and just tell her I'm running some errands." The trip to the auto dealer is inevitably revealed, and now we have legitimate issues about lack of trust, betrayal, refusal to communicate, suspicions of what else might be hidden, and so on.

Both instances emerge from the generalization of a specific, which we've alluded to earlier. The phenomenon consists of taking a single piece of perceived evidence—it may not even be real—and utilizing it as a universal truth. This can apply either to excessive pessimism or excessive optimism, but it is overwhelmingly the former.

Here is a range, from cosmic to localized:

Universal
- He promised to call me and he hasn't yet. All men are liars.
- It wasn't what was promised. All salespeople will lie to get an order.

Generic
- She talks about her work all the time and isn't interested in mine. Every woman with a career of her own feels it should be the center point for everyone around her.
- He just loves to talk about his golf game. Have you ever met a golfer who wasn't a complete bore around everyone who isn't a golfer?

Overstated
- George borrowed something and hasn't returned it. He ignores all of his commitments.
- Harriet has been to the ladies room three times. She's so self-absorbed that she's oblivious to everyone else.

Localized
- You disagree with this great idea? You have never supported me in anything I want to try.
- You want to go out with your friends? I've never been the top priority in your life.

Since logic makes people think and emotion makes them act, we want to move *from* emotion *to* logic when trying to avoid the generalization of a specific.

When generalizing a specific, a single objective act (he didn't call; you disagree with my idea) is transmogrified into a philosophically unacceptable position (men are liars; you don't support me). Logic gives way to emotion, and emotion then shuts down all effective communication, no less than a shutoff valve stops the water in the pipes.

(The opposite is also true, in that an excessively positive generalization will lead to dangerously rosy optimism. In other words, the boss saying, "Good idea, we should have thought of that ages ago," doesn't mean that you have the inside track on the next promotion ["The boss loves my work!"]. And your partner commenting, "Perhaps we could replace the car; it's nine years old," isn't an endorsement to turn in the Jeep Cherokee for a Ferrari. Excessive optimism generated from generalizing a specific almost always leads to disappointment, recrimination, and defeat.)

The dynamic here is crucial: In trying to influence others, we should actively seek to find the emotional trigger that affects their self-interest and nudges it in the direction that is good for both of us. However, in trying to overcome the adverse effects of the generalized specific—which is raw emotion—we need to retreat back to the safe oasis of logic and objective reality.

The more intimate the relationship, the more this is vital. Acquaintances and "arm's-distance" friends usually cannot generalize a specific so quickly or painfully as a close friend, family member, or lover, because they have neither the emotional attachment nor the history. If you're late for a first meeting—or for only one meeting out of five thus far—with casual friends, they are not prone to blame you for lack of caring, disrespect, or sloth. But if you're late meeting your spouse, he or she might reply, "You've done this repeatedly to me [that is, three times out of seventy-five meetings over the past two years], you never apologize [that is, you say 'Sorry I'm late' but don't grovel on the floor and rend your garments], and it's clear that you continue to take me for granted [that is, even though you have also done this, your intent is pure and your spouse is just uncaring]."

When people are insecure or in alien territory, they will often magnify a tiny specific into a huge generality. Hence, the intense sensitivity to "disrespect" in minority communities. If we feel threatened, mistreated, unaccepted, and treated with prejudice, we will tend to see any minute sign that indicates any such mentality as proof of our entire thesis.

The closer we are emotionally (and physically) to others, the more probability that we will generalize specifics. That's because we are able to dredge up other instances *and ignore the context or the proportion* (three times in seventy-five or only once this year). Emotionalism overcomes fact and perspective. The more intimate we are, the more emotional ammunition at our disposal. (Is there a couple out there who has been together for more than five years who *hasn't*

I was casually talking to a friend while walking to the front desk of a hotel to check in. As I took a place in line, not paying much attention, I bumped into something and heard someone say, "Just pretend I'm not here."

I looked around to see I had rubbed against a woman's wheelchair. "I'm sorry," I said with a smile, "I didn't see you there."

"Right," she said sarcastically, "there's no reason for you to pay attention to me. Just barge right in. You're not very sensitive, are you?"

I realized that I had inadvertently barged into the line in front of three people, including her, but that she could have easily warned me that I was about to bump into her. No one else had said anything in the general confusion around the desk. She chose to interpret my actions as a deliberate insensitivity to her condition. She had also chosen not to warn me and to let me bump into her so she could say something.

I have no sympathy for people whose intent it is to be a permanent "victim" of the generalized specifics they invent around them.

---

heard, "There you go again! Do you remember three years ago at your cousin's anniversary when I begged you not to do this and you insisted on . . ."?)

Since generalizing specifics is far worse for close and enduring relationships, it's important to guard against them yourself and know how to deal with them from your partner and other intimate relationships.

"Ungeneralizing" Specifics

Here's how to "ungeneralize" a specific transgression, real or perceived (perception, of course, usually constituting reality):

You, Personally
- Don't look for a history, precedent, or pattern of behavior. Simply deal with the current fact: She was twenty minutes late meeting you or he didn't tell you about the phone call from your mother.

- Don't impute motive. Deal with what is (you made me late; you made me seem ungrateful) rather than a conspiracy (you're trying to undermine me; you want me to feel helpless).
- Put it in context. Will this mean the end of Western civilization? Will it threaten your health? Is it even going to spoil your morning?
- Unless it threatens a "must," rise above it and forget it. If the incident has caused you to miss a family responsibility, apologize to the affected parties. If it is just a slight inconvenience, however, tuck your ego away and forget about it.

Your Partner
- Ask what you can do immediately. Try to find a way to ameliorate the proximate incident. (Let me call and tell them it was my fault. Don't worry, I'll go pick up the kids instead.) Take away the immediate pain.
- Don't battle or argue. The emotionalism will exhaust itself *unless fueled by resistance.* You can't prove at the moment, anyway, that you really are a caring spouse or that you don't lie as a matter of course. And never enter an escalating battle as to who has been the worst offender, since that will result in a major conflagration.
- If it is singular behavior, forget about it. If it is truly repetitive behavior, either accommodate it (allot more time to meet and bring something to read) or use enlightened self-interest to change it (if you tell me when my mother calls, I can get her issues out of the way earlier and we can enjoy dinner without her interruptions).

One of the worst mistakes that we all make, particularly in intimate relationships, is to generalize specifics. Deal with what's here and now, and don't extrapolate current behaviors into universal conspiracies or deficits.

SURRENDERING THE NEED TO CONTROL

There are two primary causes of stress in the workplace and in our personal lives:

1. Not knowing what may happen tomorrow.
2. The belief that we have no control over what may happen.

Advice from the Readers of *Balancing Act*

I was writing a position paper the other day entitled: "Getting Time from Someone Who Hasn't Got Any." In summary the paper fleshes out (with examples) the concept of "You scratch my back . . ." and how to find opportunities to do this to the benefit of the other person, without pre-negotiation or stipulation that the person reciprocate. I have used this to great effect continuously in the workplace, but had never considered it for use outside the business world.

After finishing, I realized I had done this very thing for my wife the other day, and I realized how much better the last few days had been for me in business as a result. Our relationship had become stressed over the last few months, with hectic schedules and so on. But I had not realized there was an underlying tension until it was released.

Without prompting, I simply used some of my business development time and did a pile of ironing for her while she was out having dinner with friends. Needless to say, this was appreciated.

Now she is interested in how the business is developing. Now I can clearly see how she had been becoming resistive of my business expansion, because I was not showing that I understood nor cared about *her* increased workload and stresses.

As a bonus, my interactions with clients are much cleaner—and the clients are more forthcoming and responsive.

Practice what you preach, I suppose.

Stephen Cuff, Handy Managers

Hence, a traumatic event such as the terrorist attacks of September 11 generates huge and mass stress, because vulnerability, grief, and a perception of total ignorance of tomorrow's events, combined with a lack of influence over them, produces excruciating psychological conditions.

But even on a more localized and minor basis, a decision tomorrow on a promotion, your spouse's reaction to an argument last night, or not knowing whether the car will start after recent problems with it are all stress contributors.

The more things we cannot be sure about, and the less certain we are that we can influence them, the more anxious we become. Over the past decade or more, the turbulence in the workplace, including massive and irrational layoffs, combined with the sundering of traditional family ties and spiritual bonds, have created immense stress levels in general.

> Stress is caused by *not knowing* more than knowing. "Now at least we know what we're dealing with" is an accurate and intelligent antidote to amorphous stress. The more we know and the more we can tolerate ambiguity if we don't know, the more we're able to reduce stress in relationships.

The countervailing position is to try to gain control in some form, no matter how minor. Thus, at work people tend to tap into the grapevine ("Who's getting the vacant director's position?"), form alliances, over-analyze shrugs and gestures, and even create their own "artificial control," otherwise known as "bureaucracy," which is the triumph of means over ends ("You can't proceed unless you provide me with this information and keep me informed daily").

Some of these tactics may work on the job, although they tend to gum up the works. People operating on the basis of rumor are seldom accurate, and bureaucracies have never been known to enhance efficiencies. But they certainly won't work at home and/or within relationships.

The balance in a relationship lies in reciprocity—the mutual support of self-interests and well-being, even if they are skewed on occasion, because there is trust that the balance will eventually be restored.[7] Consequently, "control" is the antithesis of balanced relationships. And it is one of the greatest problems in contemporary relationships.

Consider these actual instances from my recent experience:

---

7. And "trust" is the unshakeable belief that the other person absolutely has your best interests in mind, no matter how sharp the critique or confrontational the technique.

- A woman denies her husband the right to drive "her" Mercedes because she is afraid that he will change her settings and leave debris in the car. The auto is jointly owned.
- A man scolds his wife for her personal spending, although she has a job that pays more than his and he simply chooses not to make personal expenditures.
- A woman demands of her partner that the other not disclose their relationship unless the woman approves first.
- A man is infuriated when his daughter chooses a college he doesn't approve of (although can easily afford) and threatens not to pay for her tuition unless she attends the school of his choice.

Our need to control is deep-seated and emotional and is a combination of fear of the unknown and mistrust of others' judgment. We must surrender that need and accept that we control very little.

I'm sure you can cite similar examples, perhaps uncomfortably close to home. Relationships—which should be based on trust and the understanding that control is antipodal to trust—cannot weather controlling personalities, unless one or both partners choose to be miserable, in which case I'd question the viability and quality of the relationship.

In surrendering the need to control, we are best off examining the sequence in which we find ourselves, as shown in Figure 7.1.

In the graphic, the generalized anxiety is vague and unresolvable in that state. We must reduce it to the clear fear that is generating the stress. Is it fear of a spouse's reaction to an expenditure? Is it fear that a child may be using drugs? Is it fear that you are not fulfilling your family's expectations in some way?

By determining what it "is" and what it "is not," you draw boundaries around the actual relationship threat. It "is" (for the sake of our example) your partner's silent treatment after a difficult family dinner.

You can then engage in resolution techniques. These may be:

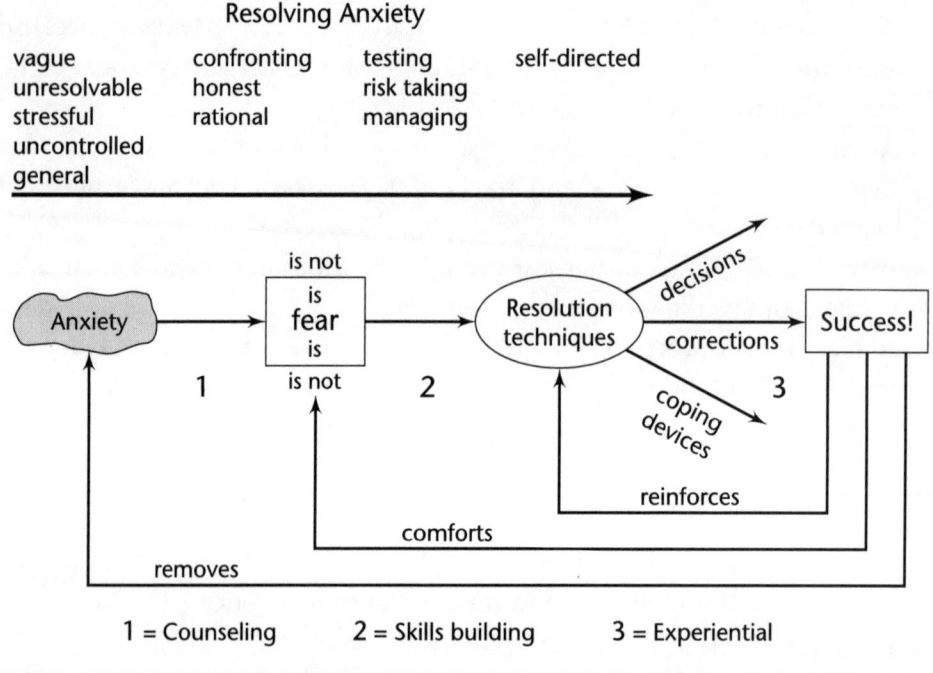

Figure 7.1. Resolving Anxiety and Relinquishing Control

- *Decisions:* I will ask my partner exactly why he or she is not speaking to me and explain that I'd like to make amends if I've done something wrong. I will not become angry at the treatment and launch counter-recriminations. I will try to explain that I can't improve unless I know what the issue is.
- *Corrections:* I know never to invite our parents to the same casual dinner again. They are unresolvably antagonistic about politics; it ruins our evening, and we all wind up inadvertently taking sides. This is impossible to control, but easy to avoid.
- *Coping:* My partner always calms down in a few hours and begins to talk things through when ready. It's best for me to endure the discomfort rather than try to prematurely end the silence, which exacerbates the unhappiness and stress.

If one or more of these three devices is successful, then the resolution techniques are reinforced, the fears are comforted, and the generalized state of stress is removed. (We now *know* what we need to know.)

> Relationships are complex and evolving dynamics. It's important to have a process to deal with the inevitable problems that arise. I've found that those with the best resolution processes are those with the most enduring and healthy relationships.

We'll discuss at length in the next chapter techniques for communication and interactions. But for now it's important to consider that

1. The unknown and lack of control of the unknown produce stress.
2. Relationships frequently generate unknowns and lack of control.
3. The conditional response to such conditions is to gain control, either deliberately or artificially.
4. Such techniques are problematic, at best, in the workplace and are lethal to relationships, which must be based on mutual trust and not unilateral attempts at control.
5. Therefore, relationships are best served by attempting to move stressful and "uncontrolled" situations through a process of reconciliation, always becoming more specific and aiming to employ resolution techniques, *not controlling techniques.*

Balance in relationships can't always equate to equal balance and *quid pro quo* dynamics. It should mean, however, a constant yin and yang which produces a long-term equilibrium of mutual trust and support. Relationships are not a zero-sum game. We both win, or we both lose.

ALAN'S ULTIMATE LESSONS

This is an age in which the family dinner table has virtually disappeared. The advent of overworked two-income families, kids' multiple extra-curricular activities, alternative forms of entertainment, one-parent households, fast food, and a much faster life pace have seriously undermined the ability of families to sit and talk for prolonged periods.

At my dinner table, which was quite modest, there were no magic answers or silver bullets. But I was able to hear my parents debate about how to pay the bills, problems at work, politics in the neighborhood, and ethical challenges (for example, Do you pay a "contribution" to get a rare and valued political job?).

The dinner table may not be making an immediate comeback. However, partners and parents—whether the relationship is two people or twelve in an extended family—must make the attempt to provide time to talk, compare notes, and exchange views on even the most mundane of issues.

When parents are unaware, for example, that their children are using drugs, possess weapons, or even who their friends are, it's not a sign of a new age. It's rather an indication of an old breakdown in communications.

CHAPTER 8

Communicating in the Light of Day

I Don't Believe You Might Have Heard What I Perceived I Thought I Meant

I can make a case that almost every problem with balance in relationships is communications driven, caused, or related. It is easy to talk, hard to listen, and often impossible to communicate. (My sophomore-year political science instructor in our international relations course informed us that "War is simply the least subtle form of communication.")

Here (Figure 8.1) is a simple but nonetheless accurate depiction of our communications processes.

All of us have background, education, acculturation, nurturing, friendships, and other unique factors that color and bias our interpretations of others' communications. From what you "mean" to what I "get" and vice versa is a torturous route. Those usually non-congruent combinations (the odds of matching the other person, even a longtime mate, are infinitesimally small) create *cognitive interference.* This is often reflected in this type of exchange:

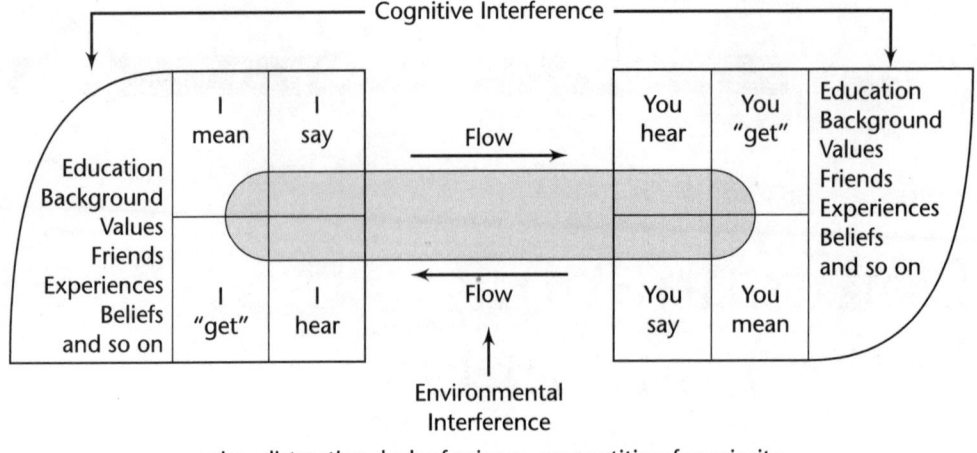

Figure 8.1. The "Communications Loop" and Opportunities for Interference

"What did you mean by that?!"

"Just what I said!"

"And what does that *mean*?"

There is also *environmental interference* caused by noise, distraction, inattention, and competition for focus. Anyone on a cell phone in a public place is only paying partial attention, no matter what he or she thinks. In a car, it's even worse. Pay too much attention to the conversation, and it could be the last call of your life.

How on earth do we manage to communicate at all?

HONESTY AND AUTHENTICITY

We hear a lot from the "gurus"[1] about "authenticity." Yet I find few of them very "authentic" and most of them little better than snake oil and patent medicine salespeople. It seems to me that "honesty," "authenticity," "candor," and related adjectives mean the following:

---

1. My definition of "guru" is someone who can say any foolish thing, no matter how outlandish and illogical, and have others say, "That's profound!" I have never understood a single useful thing, for example, that Deepak Chopra or John Gray has ever said.

The willingness and ability to reveal true feelings and emotions and to accept them from others without judgment, resentment, or retribution.

In other words, we're not communicating unless we can tell each other what we think and how we feel without fear or loathing.

Most people waste more time and invest more energy in communicating *dishonestly and disingenuously* than they would spend in being honest and straightforward. The harm we do others (and ourselves) through well-intentioned lies and obfuscations is far worse than any outright act of hostility.

Here are the key aspects of being open and honest—"authentic"—in relationships:

- Show a willingness to listen and accept opinions, feedback, and opposing views. When your kid tells you, "You have that look on your face again" as he or she is trying to explain why he or she should be able to use the car that night, you know you're not exhibiting openness.
- Admit it when you're wrong. "You're right" is a positive statement, but not a very powerful one when compared to "I was wrong." The ready admission of error will encourage others to approach you, oppose you, and try to educate you, all of which are constructive habits.
- Never deliberately support a specious argument just to salve your ego. If you chose the beach vacation too early and the water was too cold, don't go to lengths to explain that every fourth year the Gulf Stream arrives early or El Niño arrives late. Sophistry is one of the most deadly communications sins.
- Keep your mouth shut and, when you open it, do so briefly. Most people I know suffer from near-terminal prolixity. They tell you their life histories when you ask, "Where are you going?" If you think of the most powerful, trusted communicators we've ever known—Churchill, King, Roosevelt—they used relatively few words but powerful imagery: "We will fight on the beaches. . . ," "I have a dream. . . ," ". . . a day of infamy . . ."

- Don't poison the communication with history, biases, and precedent. "The last time she brought this up she wanted me to send the kids money" is not a helpful aid in interpreting the current conversation.
- Admit it when you don't understand something, you misstated a position, or there was other confusion. I've seen people lost in conversations when they didn't understand a word and were too stubborn or proud to ask for a definition, or they just plain missed something and were too arrogant to think that they couldn't infer it later. Conversations are like buildings, and a weak foundation will doom the upper floors.

I have great respect for someone who stops another and says, "Sorry, but I don't know what that word means." That person is an honest communicator. I have the most respect for those people who then learn the word for use themselves.

One would think that years of living together would make partners much more powerful in accurate and authentic communications. Actually, it makes us worse if we aren't attentive. When people are merely dating—and trying to impress each other—they tend to hang on every word with the intent of finding a route to favor, flattery, and finesse. We have to listen to understand the "stranger's" interests and attitudes.

When we're inured to someone over years, we tend to assume and infer far more than is healthy. Thinking, "I've heard her talk about this a hundred times" causes us to tune out the actual words and meaning of the current discussion. "He's always been intransigent on this subject" precludes understanding what's actually on his mind today.

The great situation comedies of television—"I Love Lucy," "The Honeymooners," "All in the Family"—featured people who knew what the other was saying before they said it, which accurately reflected long-term relationships. If you wonder why people interrupt and cut off others' sentences so often, *it's primarily because the listener at the moment viscerally believes that he or she absolutely knows what will follow, so there's no need to listen to it.*

What does it take to get us to talk on an honest, unimpeded, and direct basis? It takes meta-talk.

A teacher of mine related this fabulous story to us.

He had to call his brother, whom he spoke to only a few times a year. The teacher lived in New York, his brother in Baltimore. The teacher had heard from a cousin that his brother's wife was ill.

The teacher called and the two exchanged pleasantries for several minutes. You know the kind:

"How are you?"

"How are the kids?"

"Are you working hard?"

"Have you chosen a vacation spot this year?"

After about ten minutes, the teacher reluctantly finally asked about his brother's wife. The response was, "I have no idea. I haven't seen her in years, as you know, and I don't care if the bitch is dead."

It turned out that the teacher had dialed a wrong number, and each party assumed he was talking to a relative he knew. This lasted for ten minutes, and could easily have gone longer.

Any other questions about "authenticity"? Do you think people really care when they bump into you somewhere and say, "How are you doing?"

META-TALK

Meta-talk is "talk about talk." Therapists often use this device, especially in marriage counseling, when partners don't really understand that they may be talking but not communicating.

Meta-talk is a process aimed at reviewing, analyzing, and deciphering how you talk to each other. (I'm using "each other" because this technique applies especially to partnerships.) It means that you jointly investigate the language that you use, how you use it, when you use it, and why you use it.

For example, "talking about talk" might involve the following:

If you want to know whether or not your life is in balance, listen to your body. Through observation and personal experience, I have come to the conviction that no matter how much you tell yourself mentally that you are coping with a stressful situation, your body will always tell you the absolute truth.

A friend of mine was going through a court proceeding in relation to an abusive relationship she had been in. She knew she was doing what she had to do and was remaining strong for all intents and purposes. One day there was a break in the proceedings and she went to the bathroom; when she started brushing her hair, it came out of her head in fists-full. To this day, she wears a wig.

Several years ago, my husband and I were involved in a difficult business partnership. We were working and living two hours away from the business when a situation arose that required that we recommence hands-on management. We had our regular lives on Monday to Friday; then we would leave work on a Friday to travel to this business to put in long hours all weekend to return in time for work on Monday morning. This in itself was stressful. Additionally, my husband had been keeping the true, disastrous financial state of the business from me when I noticed him losing weight rapidly and becoming increasingly sick.

Your body is your best friend. Your body knows when you are placing demands on yourself that are too high. If you do not listen to your body to check that it is in balance, it will stop you dead in your tracks. It will not be ignored, nor should it be. Remember: You are a sum of your parts and your physical being is a huge part of the sum.

Therese Watson-Weir, Life Coach,
Buddina, Queensland, Australia

The Timing of Talk

"We never talk early in the morning, and we start our day as housemates, not lovers," might be one conclusion. Or "We watch TV and read at night, and we talk only enough to say 'Good night' and 'Did you lock the back door?'"

Talk that's hurried, rote, or without meaning is useless, yet you may engage in it more often than you care to admit. If you put aside time for meetings, kids' activities, and church, why not put it aside for quality talk?

Have you ever heard two or more people blithely talking at once, without losing a beat? That's because the talk is empty and meaningless to the other speakers. In that case, are we really talking? If a tree falls and no one hears it, is there a sound?

The Location of Talk

Meaningful and useful talk ought to occur in unimpeded space. If you look at the chart in Figure 8.1, that means minimizing environmental interference. Talk is undermined in crowds, during other activities that demand attention, in uncomfortable settings, and so on. You wouldn't play softball in the living room or cut your toenails in the neighbor's house (I hope), and you probably shouldn't attempt to talk about certain matters in the car or while watching a dance recital.

The Use of Language

Psychology texts often mention "scientific language" and "magical language." Scientific language accurately reflects exactly what it refers to. An "elephant" is that large mammal with the long trunk and tusks, and a "leaky faucet" is that tap in the house from which water is spilling unacceptably. Magic language has certain connotations which transcend the words themselves. "Gay" is not used much any more in its "scientific" meaning of light and frivolous, since it's been co-opted to denote homosexual individuals. The "elephant in the room" isn't really a pachyderm, but rather an issue that people refuse to acknowledge, and a "leaky faucet" may be someone on the team who can't keep a secret.[2]

Meta-talk should focus on the nature of the above factors so that two people can maximize the ability to communicate. Here are some examples:

- "When you begin a sentence with, 'You've done it again,' I don't hear what comes after that."

---

2. I'm talking about interactive and interpersonal oral communication. Written communication, especially in email, obviously has its own problems, since it doesn't reflect intonation, inflection, or volume. "What a result!" could range, in writing, from unqualified happiness to vituperous sarcasm.

- "You tell me whenever I've done something wrong in your estimation, but you never mention when you've done something wrong or I've done something right."
- "You talk to the kids, but never listen to them. Sometimes you just grunt and never look up from the paper."
- "You're at your best when you explain exactly why I hurt your feelings so that I know what I've said and can avoid it in the future."
- "I really enjoy it when you put down whatever it is you're doing, ask about my day, and comment on what I say to show me that you've heard it and care."
- "I appreciate your counsel, especially when it's contrary to what I want to hear, but expressed so lovingly that I know I'd better consider a different viewpoint."

Meta-talk should take place periodically. Otherwise we tend to fall into language ruts and depressions. We can never take our communications for granted, because that means we're taking our relationships for granted.

Communications Test

Meta-talk opens the drapes and ensures that we're communicating in the light of day. Most couples who run into serious relationship problems have long since ceased communicating effectively.

Here's a quick test to help you assess your own degree of open communication and involvement with meta-talk. Apply this to your partner, spouse, family, work colleague, or anyone who is close to you. (But do this one person at a time. It's not unusual to be far more effective communicating with some people—good friends, spouse—than with others—children, in-laws.)

1. Do you find yourself consistently misunderstood or misinterpreted?
2. Do you often agree in person and then find the two of you nevertheless pursuing different courses of action?

3. Do your (or the other person's) eyes roll up and other facial expressions occur when discussion begins?
4. Do certain phrases you use immediately spark a violent reaction, even if prior conversation had been calm?
5. Do you frequently break into someone else's speech and/or does the person break into yours?
6. Are you frequently asked to repeat something or explain what you've said in other ways?
7. Do you find that you often don't get around to sharing something until it's too late or long after the fact?
8. Are you often in the position of having forgotten what you were told, or uncertain about instructions you were given?
9. Do you find yourself instantly disagreeing with the other's points even before giving the person an objective hearing?
10. Have you been told that you're a poor listener?

If you said "yes" to four or more items, you've got some communication problems and you haven't been engaged in much meta-talk with your significant other or companion. (If four seems low, bear in mind that we're talking about communications with lovers, family, and intimate others, so this is a "pass/fail" test, not a graded one.)

Some of the worst "communicators" I know are nonetheless excellent speakers. That is, politicians, business executives, professors, keynoters, and others who make their living by speaking aren't always adept at communicating honestly (and, in some cases, actually make their living communicating *dishonestly* at times). Speakers and orators aren't generally engaged in two-way conversation and seldom involve themselves with meta-talk.

It's ironic that communication is the key to so much of our existence—and, most notably, partnerships—yet we spend so little time understanding its nature. We know more about our car's radio system and our VCR's programming than we know about our efficacy in communicating with others.

I've been in situations in which people have emailed business colleagues sitting several desks away rather than getting up to speak to them, thereby diminishing their communications by all the dynamics lost in that decision. As much as we laugh at that foible, we also tend to leave a note or shortcut a conversation or merely hint at something, rather than really discuss it with a valued other. You wouldn't email your spouse from the kitchen to the bedroom, and you might find the notion absurd.

So then why commit the same type of error without the computer?

CAUSE VS. BLAME

We are critical people. We tend to find fault. There is relish in finding someone to "blame," since we by implication then absolve ourselves: "If it was *his* fault then it couldn't be *my* fault." "*We* did *our* part."

This is dysfunctional enough in the workplace or among friends, but it's absolutely devastating between couples or within families. A cause may or may not involve individual culpability, but that's neither here nor there because we should always seek a cause of a problem, anomaly, errant decision, or other difficulty for these reasons:

- We arrive at the cause faster. Once blame is suggested, people will try to deflect and defer it and will obscure or distort facts in an attempt to escape culpability.
- We enlist others' help in reconciling the issue. If it's "us against them," "them" will resist. If we're all in this together, then we have a decent chance of a supported and committed resolution.
- We avoid retribution, retaliation, and reprisal. Once we affix blame, you can bet that the other party is going to lie in wait for a chance to reverse the tables. (You know this is the case when you say accusingly, "You forgot to turn out the lights," and the immediate, visceral response is, "And *you* didn't turn out the lights; what's your point?")
- We provide a mutually supportive atmosphere that carries over to other aspects of our relationships. The refusal to assign blame in favor of finding a cause and eliminating it affects our communications, sharing, physical intimacy, and mutual support ("benefit of the doubt") in the future.

A multi-million-dollar Mars landing craft was lost, crashing to the planet's surface, as a result of an apparent equipment malfunction. Upon investigation, it was learned that two teams working on the project in different locations had used different measurement criteria. One had used inches, and the other centimeters. The landing craft never had a chance, programmed with incompatible commands.

In many relationships, we use dissimilar and contradictory talk and never get together to examine its efficacy, similar to those two teams never actually talking about their measurement standards. We sail through our lives together assuming we are speaking and listening along the same wavelengths, but in fact, we're using incongruent talk.

Meta-talk can straighten out the dissimilar communication, just as an interactive team meeting and talk about the standards would have saved those Mars programmers and engineers. If we don't do this, we'll never have a chance, programmed with talk that makes us incompatible.

It's easy to assign blame. It's difficult to remove it. And it's impossible to eliminate the blemish you've created for yourself by resorting to that tactic to begin with.

Among partnerships and families, blame can become pre-emptive. In other words, anything your mother-in-law says you know is meant to undermine you, so you know you're going to blame her for a divisive comment, unhelpful suggestion, or gratuitous insult even before she articulates her thought. If you blame your child for not heeding your advice and wasting her life and your money, you're apt to disregard any suggestion she has to improve communications or launch a career.

Cause is different from blame in that it is the element or combination of elements that caused the problem. Some causes are solely human error, some are solely process or equipment malfunction, and some are a combination of all of the above.

How to Focus on Cause

Here's how to defuse hunts for blame and truly search for cause, either alone or with others:

1. Describe the effect, symptom, or discomfort objectively and dispassionately. For example, if you're about to take your car to a meeting and find a tire is flat, don't immediately scream at your spouse, who was the last to use it, "How could you park the car this way?!" The point is that you have a flat tire and the car can't be driven in this condition, and the effect is that you may be late for an important meeting.

2. Review your alternatives to ameliorate or correct the immediate condition. It's premature to search for cause. Can you use another car? Can you call a cab? Can you call AAA? Can someone drive you? Can you call the local service station? Can you call to inform your colleagues that you may be late? Can you change the meeting time or reschedule it? Can you put on a spare tire? There are eight—eight!!—quick alternatives to deal with the current condition. Usually, you have more choices to reduce the suffering than you immediately think.[3]

3. *After* you've successfully dealt with your immediate discomfort, find the cause of your problem. (You can't eliminate a problem unless you find the cause and remove it. Otherwise, you are merely adapting to it. A cab gets you to the meeting but doesn't fix the tire.) Are you picking up nails in your driveway? Is the tire old and worn? Have your kids been fiddling with the tire valve? Was there vandalism in the mall that created a slow leak?

4. Understand that rarely is someone "out to get you," particularly a loved one. These things happen. If we only had good luck and smooth rides, life would be quite boring.

5. If someone could have been responsible, or at least could have eased the pain, then raise it in light of the above. In other words, show your spouse what happened and suggest that both of you need to be more vigilant about the car's tire pressure, gas level, and overall maintenance, especially when both of you are using it. Make it a joint effort.

6. Fix it or learn to live with it. You can fix a flat tire, but you may choose to live with a balky air conditioner rather than spend a fortune to fix it. You can't live with your kid flunking out of school, but you may be able to live with clothing you'd never have chosen for him.

---

3. Interestingly, while there is usually a single "cause" at work and a single person you want to "blame," there are usually a multitude of interim and/or adaptive actions you can take to ameliorate your immediate discomfort.

In the vast majority of cases, no one is deliberately trying to ruin your life or even discomfort your day. Others may cause you pain, but it's usually inadvertent. If you go around assigning blame to every misfortune you endure—whether it be your spouse, kids, colleagues, family, or the fates in general—you're eventually going to become a neurotic puddle of antagonism.

All of this may seem rather clinical and mechanistic, and flat tires are hardly the warp and woof of interpersonal breakdowns. So allow me to put this in more realistic and gut-level terms.

A husband takes a message for his wife while watching television. He writes it down, but leaves it on a pile of magazines and forgets about it. He doesn't tell his wife when she returns home, and she only finds out when she gets a call from her boss asking why she isn't at the emergency meeting being held that evening to save a major client.

The wife's normal reaction may be to scream at her husband: "How could you?! Why are my calls less important than yours, which I dutifully record on the phone pad and leave on top of the phone so you can't miss them? You have never taken my career seriously, and this is another example of undermining my professional life. You've resented my success from the beginning. . . ."

Everything goes downhill from here as the husband points to his innocent mistake and his lack of evil intent, and proceeds to dredge up chapter and verse of examples of his wife's lack of support for his business, his travel requirements, his nights with clients, and so forth.

Here's a different scenario, using cause and not blame:

1. The wife realizes her boss is upset and she's missing a key meeting at which her expertise and experience are badly needed.
2. She asks the boss whether she can still get there and be useful. Can she prepare a written analysis? Can she participate immediately by phone? Can she come in early tomorrow and brief him one-on-one? Can the meeting be adjourned until she gets there? The boss agrees that they'll put her on the speaker phone so as not to lose time.

3. After the phone call—and perhaps a day or two later so as to allow emotions to give way to objectivity—the wife and husband sit down together to design a new phone message system. They agree to put a cork board above the downstairs, kitchen phone, and Post-it® Notes near the other phones so that messages can be attached right to the phone itself. They both agree that the new "system" will help them both and avoid the unintended but serious problems in not forwarding messages.

My first scenario, replete with recrimination and invective, is by far the more common, and we've all engaged in it much too often. But the latter scenario is eminently realistic, is engaged in by healthy couples, and needs to be your first reaction.

Ergo, cause, not blame.

SELECTIVE OPENNESS AND RECEPTIVITY

Before we get too carried away with communicating at warp speed, I want to sound one alarm that needs to be heeded. Marshall McLuhan, the originator of the phrase "the medium is the message" and the identifier of "hot" and "cool" media, observed once, "The price of eternal vigilance is indifference."

By that he meant that we can't remain on a constantly high and uniform state of alert because the condition will lead to ennui and inevitable lapses— errors of omission and lassitude. A sentry who is constantly on duty with no variation or threats stands a large risk of missing a true threat when it eventually rears its head in an otherwise similarly bland and predictable night.

> There is no ethical, moral, legal, or social imperative that says all feedback, regardless of source and timing, is valid, valuable, and verified. You pick and choose your fights if you're smart. And you'll pick and choose your feedback sources and openness to them as well.

What does this have to do with relationships and life balance? If we're truly to remain open and constructive in our most important relationships, then

Advice from the Readers of *Balancing Act*

I was in a meeting in St Petersburg, Florida, when the call came. "Mom had a stroke," my sister's trembling voice relayed. "She's in the hospital." I could hardly think. My only clear thought was how to get back to Dallas/Fort Worth. It was a natural reaction, but it was strange, nonetheless. After all, I had been in Ohio when my only daughter had called to announce she was pregnant with my first grandchild. I had been in California when my grandchild was born. I had never felt quite this compulsion, to get up and go home.

Consulting is a commitment to the client relationship and to the project. I understood this very well and had worked hard to develop a strong client base. My travel schedule was grueling. I traveled an average of forty-nine weeks a year. I cancelled vacations, missed birthdays and anniversaries, but this was different. Suddenly, everything was changed. All I could think of was getting home! Hugging my dad, holding mom's hand, supporting my siblings.

Consulting is a great vocation. I love it, always have. I can't think of anything I would rather do to support myself. Consulting was suddenly just that, a vocation; just a few moments before it had been a "life."

Fortunately, mom survived the assault. She never fully recovered, but we didn't lose her. Her stroke changed my life. I refocused on what was really important. I vowed never to let my vocation interfere with my life again.

Since that time I have cut my travel time to fewer than thirty weeks a year. I have always taken at least one month a year off, with one two-week block to spend time with family. I was present for the birth of my second grandchild! When home, I will shut down the office in the evening to watch old movies with my husband of thirty plus years.

I find it sad that my mom had to have a stroke to wake me. But I'm sure thankful that I woke up before it was my own stroke.

Leslie Furlow, Ph.D., AchieveMentors, Inc.

we have to set some priorities on our open communications with others. To put it another way and in McLuhan-esque terms: If we are open and accepting to everyone and anyone (eternally vigilant), we're soon going to grow bored, calloused, and immune to *all* feedback, irrespective of the source (indifference).

It may be useful to view this phenomenon and how to manage it in terms of degrees.

Unlimited Acceptance and Access[4]: Immediate Family and/or Significant Others

This feedback and these discussions should require the most careful restraint and sensitivity. Even if "wrongly accused" or offered gratuitous advice, we must assume that the other party has our own best interests in mind.

Identifying characteristic: Willingness to listen and drop all else if the other person deems it urgent. A child's trauma at school should take precedence over a project for work, and your spouse's feedback that your stories aren't as funny as you think they are should influence your behavior at the next social gathering.

Careful Consideration and Ready Access: Close Friends and Esteemed Colleagues

These sources also can be presumed to have your best interests in mind and deserve a high place in your priority list and a wise investment of your time (and subordination of your ego). If "wrongly accused" or offered gratuitous advice, you may objectively and dispassionately demur and ask for further evidence and proof.

Identifying characteristic: Willingness to listen at appropriate times and even "accept" suspect feedback (you don't argue, but don't act on it either) for the sake of preserving the relationship. You reciprocate not on a case-by-case (tit-for-tat) basis, but rather as your honest evaluation dictates. A friend telling you that your jokes aren't funny may be overruled by others telling you they are, and a colleague who thinks you're too harsh with subordinates may be

---

4. As much as we can ever be totally accepting and control the "blame vs. cause" phenomenon. We'll all have our lapses, but the idea is to minimize them.

excused because her own philosophy is strongly consensus, neither right nor wrong, but different from your own.

Little Consideration and Tightly Controlled Access: Acquaintances and Strangers

In these cases the feedback is virtually always on behalf of the senders. They are usually playing one-upmanship, trying to elevate themselves by denigrating your performance (you did well, but I still found something wrong with it—gotcha!). Unless unequivocally accurate ("You cited the wrong precedent in that report; here's the right one"), you may choose to aggressively ignore these sources.

Identifying characteristic: You state politely but firmly that you are not interested in the feedback because you don't believe it's accurate, you don't need it, you have no relationship, and so on. Someone who tells you you're sexist or racist (or any other "ist") because of a tortured and inaccurate interpretation of something you said can and should be safely told that you don't agree and you feel no compunction about having to defend your position.

Being selective about your receptivity to feedback and its sources is a major life balance component for at least two reasons: First, you reduce your overall stress level caused by infuriating and often specious feedback. Second, you are able to concentrate your attention and receptivity on those who are closest and most important to you.

These categories obviously have overlap and are intended to provide some guidance and alleviate some stress. There may be times when a family member provides egregiously inaccurate and self-serving feedback or a remote acquaintance or even a stranger points out something immensely useful.

Feedback Checklist

Here's how I assess the utility of feedback in general:

- Does the individual have a history of honestly and truly helping me? Obviously, these favor people you know and with whom you have a trusting relationship.
- Is the feedback specific, timely, and useful, rather than vague, late, and/or impossible to do anything about? For example, the suggestion that you're unwittingly talking so loud in the theater that people around you are being

disturbed is specific, in "real time," and can produce an immediate improvement. But the feedback that "You seem to be always two beats behind, and last week you didn't appreciate a single story that Harry told at the party" is of dubious accuracy or value.

- Does the feedback contain evidence or supposition? "You have been a dropout of our foursome three of the last four weeks, causing us a problem to get our game together" is evidentiary (if true) and a stated fact. The judgment, "Your refusal to attend our multi-level marketing workshop demonstrates that you're aloof, elitist, and feel you're superior" is arrant nonsense, since there are much more plebian and obvious reasons for not going to such an event.

- Is there a major issue involved? The safety of our driving, the love of our children, the support for a philanthropy, the impression on a prospective employer, and so forth are major issues (at least in my book) deserving serious consideration if we're making an error or missing an opportunity. But the way we use the television remote, the style of our cursive writing, or the pattern of a blouse or tie I deem to be unworthy of serious discussion. This is a personal decision for all of us, certainly, since I play racquetball strictly for the pleasure and don't want to hear about how to improve my serve, and you may play to be competitive and would regard legitimate help on your serve to be highly important. But the key is that neither of us can afford to consider *all* issues major, and therefore *all* feedback legitimate. If we allow the latter, then we're back with McLuhan.

We spend more time listening to vague, invalid, and poorly intentioned feedback—and actually expending energy on considering it and even acting on it—than we do re-creating or developing our skills. The good news is that we control this totally and can stop doing it tomorrow. And we should.

- Does it fit in with the other priorities in your life at the moment? Just because the feedback might meet the other criteria doesn't mean that there is currently "room for it." If you're concerned about a sick child, improving

Advice from the Readers of *Balancing Act*

01/01/01: What an auspicious date for a new beginning! I became a consultant on 1 January 2001, having spent eight years as chief executive of a government agency in the education field. As well as embarking on a new career, I moved to a new home in a new city with a new partner.

In the first year of my new life, balance has been greatly enhanced by following much of the excellent advice in Alan Weiss's book, *Getting Started in Consulting*. I have found the advice on writing proposals and setting value-based fees to be particularly helpful.

Working from home as a sole practitioner, I have been able to minimize many of the things that really skewed the balance and allowed work to dominate my life. Things like commuting time, unfocused meetings, unproductive travel, work-related social functions, dealing with interpersonal issues among staff. Result: less stress, more control over how I use my time.

Things were not all rosy at the start, however. I was not prepared for suddenly feeling de-skilled in my new role. Many of the things I was good at were now of no use to me, while some of the skills I needed were absent or underdeveloped. I had to adapt to a new pace of work and change my expectations of how much I could achieve in one day!

The very best thing I have done to improve my life balance is to hang a bird feeder from a branch outside my office window. And to take the time to notice the birds!

Cynthia Deane, Options Consulting,
Carrigard, Kilcoolishal, Glounthaune, County Cork, Ireland

your sales presentation might not be an important issue at the time. If your partner indicates that you may not be able to take a long-planned vacation because of an unforeseen development, you're not going to be in the mood (or shouldn't be, at least) to hear about your kids' feeling deprived about not having your attention about a new toy.

Communicating in the light of day often means having to create and shine our own light.

ALAN'S ULTIMATE LESSONS

There are times to be rude. And one of those occasions is when someone is playing "gotcha" with uninvited and egoistic feedback. Otherwise, you begin to waste too much of your time and energy debating and contesting the feedback. Such feedback doesn't merit the attempt at legitimate response from you.

Whenever I step off the keynote platform, complete a successful consulting assignment, or have published a major article or book, I tell would-be "critiquers" that I'm not interested and walk away, literally or figuratively. *The worst thing you can do to these people—and, consequently, the sweetest "revenge"—is to ignore them.*

One particular wise guy sent me a scribbled fax informing me of several typos in a new book (the publisher's problem, not mine) and told me that he would hesitate before buying another of my books, even though they are otherwise quite valuable (his problem, not mine). He was clearly anticipating either a free book or a spirited debate, and he got neither: I threw away the fax and knew he would be incensed. I can live with one less book purchaser if it means one less pest as well.

More recently, a reader of my *free* electronic newsletter, *Balancing Act*™, sought to chastise me for being "verbose." I replied to his email by telling him he was free to cancel his free subscription, but I was not going to respond to, or even read, any further emails on that topic.

These are the small actions that can vastly improve your day and make you much more receptive to legitimate and well-intentioned feedback from friends and loved ones.

Synthesis

CHAPTER 9

Self-Possession and Control of One's Fate

Was Maslow Wrong All Along?

Maslow's hierarchy of needs has been cited ad infinitum by amateur psychologists, consultants, and workplace gurus as the logical progression of motivation and human needs over one's life and career. For those of you somehow mystically spared from the catechism, it looks like Figure 9.1.

I know of no research, studies, or articles in serious journals that have ever validated that Abraham Maslow's hierarchy was of even vague utility in managing people or in helping to establish one's life goals and, presumably, balance. I don't think it's a progression at all, but merely a description of important needs which ebb and flow, influenced by a myriad of confluent events in a person's life, work, and relationships. The pyramidal progression is really a convenient construct within which to view these needs, but not one that necessarily describes their logical relationships.

Our needs are diverse and interrelated. Moreover, any concession to a predetermined hierarchy or natural order co-opts our own ability to influence and control our destiny. (In other words, the model implies or seems to ask, "How can we pursue

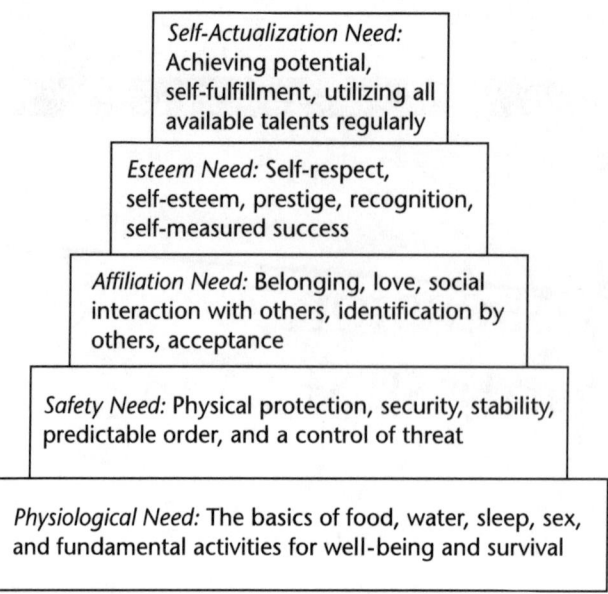

Figure 9.1. Maslow's Hierarchy of Needs

affiliation needs if we still have physical security concerns?" And forget about self-actualizing until we've attained security!) I know a lot of people who self-actualize effectively, but are still craving love and affection. I know of loners who need no affiliations, but are quite healthy and successful nonetheless.

Our lives don't (and shouldn't) work in hierarchical response to needs. Just as we were circumscribed in our thinking by the Ptolemaic view of the universe, with the sun revolving around the earth, we may be constrained by the sanctity with which Maslow (and/or countless derivations or other "sequences") has been accepted by the unschooled and non-critical. The church threatened to excommunicate Copernicus when he stipulated that the earth actually revolved around the sun, but he was nonetheless right, no matter how threatened the contemporary guardians of sanctity and correctness.

So I ask you: What if we have the revolutions backward or confused? How has our otherwise unresisting fealty to such arbitrary life and relationship priorities removed our abilities to master our own fate and set our own course?

What if Maslow was wrong all along?

> To balance our lives we need to situationally and frequently reinforce and renew our "tethers" to various levels of need. It's quite possible to be self-actualizing all over the landscape while we simultaneously require a need to improve our physical well-being or security.

THE INVIDIOUS NATURE OF GUILT

In my observation, the great dampener of talent and frustrator of potential is guilt.[1] In our private lives, work lives, and relationships, we tend to berate ourselves for failing and chastise ourselves for succeeding.

The guilt in our lives is usually rooted in one or more of the following fertile grounds:

1. Our cultural/nurturing/spiritual upbringing or surroundings inculcated us with a sense of overarching humility and sense of not deserving what we achieve. Some cultures, of course, are overt and sincere in this philosophy: The Amish disdain modern conveniences, and the Catholic priesthood accepts a vow of poverty. However, it's the unconscious and subliminal delivery in many families that is all the more pernicious. I know many otherwise highly successful people whose parents instilled in them a perverted belief that, no matter what they accomplished, they hadn't succeeded enough, and it haunts them (and affects their behavior) to this day. It's the silver medal recipient whose father says, "If you had prepared better you would have had the gold," and the sales leader whose boss says, "You look good because your competition is so bad."

2. We feel responsible, rightly or wrongly, for some act or result. You missed the key shot that cost the team the championship. You were inattentive while baby sitting, and your younger sibling broke a leg which never

---

1. I'm Jewish and my wife is Catholic, and I heard a comedian point out one evening that "The Jews, of course, invented guilt, but the Catholics perfected it."

properly healed. You missed the kids' field trip because you went on a business trip that really could have been postponed. You made a bad investment, placing your family's future in jeopardy. This kind of guilt seeps through cracks and oozes through tiny openings and is never confined to the specific issue that generated it. Instead, the guilt pervades and permeates all aspects of our lives. (Your spouse may say, "If you had been here for the kids at times, I would have a career right now," and you may say, "If I had been here for the kids, they wouldn't be hanging out with such a horrible crowd.")

Guilt is like a poor-fitting pair of shoes. Your feet begin to hurt after a while, and you don't realize that you're perpetuating the pain by wearing the shoes every day. (Or worse, you understand the cause of the pain but feel you can't stop wearing the shoes.)

3. Our self-esteem is so low that we sincerely believe we deserve our misfortune but are lucky to gain any good fortune. We have a history of suspect results or poor performance or outrageous good luck, which undermines our ability to see ourselves as successful contributors.[2] This attitude is reflected by the individual who sees someone else's promotion or successful marriage as a tribute to that person's talents, traits, and temperament, but who sees his or her own similar successes as factors of a mentor at work, an exceptional spouse, a favor from others, or other external sources. When someone else trips, it's because another person thoughtlessly left a briefcase on the floor. When they themselves trip, they are clumsy.

2. Understand within the context of this "Ultimate Consultant Series" that one may appear highly successful on the surface and in the eyes of others, but be firmly convinced that one is an impostor and undeserving personally. Some star athletes, high-level politicians, and powerful business executives have all admitted to feeling rather worthless and pathetic, despite public accolades and the accoutrements of success.

It's imperative that, when my life gets out of balance, I add one more activity—one more calculated activity. One that enflames my imagination and adds energy to my existing mix of activities and interactions. This one little extra brings a balance to the whole and strengthens my resolve. It "changes everything" just by being present. It may seem contradictory to add fuel to the fire when it is burning fast and furiously, but the catalyst I'm talking about is totally different from any of the activities that, together, overwhelm me.

Usually, when so much is going on, it all fits in the category of "lots of little details that are boring me to death, although they're all very necessary." So the catalyst I add is something very creative or hobby-oriented: writing a poem, redecorating my office, or repotting some plants. These extras put me in a completely different mind frame that has absolutely *nothing* to do with the other activities. And that little break—thinking about the new activity ahead of time, getting together what I need for it, then actually completing it—is all that's needed to "reset" my pressure valve.

Learning what works for me came from a few well-timed experiments. It's made me much happier, because I practice giving myself opportunities for wholeness regularly. Some people comment that they can't believe I'm doing "that too!" but they never argue with what I'm able to accomplish.

Harmony Tenney, International Business Empowerment Consultants, Staunton, Virginia

Guilt effectively can prevent the fulfillment of any of the hierarchy of needs, not because they are unachieved but because they are *unenjoyed*. Guilt exacerbates the nadir and blunts the apogee. It is a profligate consumer of energy, imitative, time, and focus.

Guilt Trip Tips

How does one deal with guilt so as to create synthesis and balance in life, work, and relationships? My suggestions:

1. Recognize Guilt for What It Is.   Identify the anthropomorphic guy whispering in your ear that you "shouldn't" and "don't deserve" and "really ought to. . . ."

That is the guilt guy you have created for yourself. Flick him off your shoulder, stomp on his body, and refuse to listen any longer. When you find yourself saying, "Oh, I really couldn't . . ." or "I don't deserve this . . ." or "Someone else should receive this. . . ," understand that this is neither humility nor humanity, but self-imposed guilt.

2. Separate Guilt from Culpability and Responsibility. There are times when you've erred, caused a problem, and/or even been the catalyst for a crisis. In these cases you are *culpable,* in that you are the causal factor, and you are *responsible* when you accept the culpability and participate in the remediation if possible. It is accurate to assign yourself culpability when appropriate and healthy to accept responsibility for the results and correction. This is different from wallowing in guilt. The former is a constructive and healthy endeavor, and the latter is a damaging and deleterious behavior. (I met a woman once who felt guilty about not having emotional connections to her mother and then felt guilty about *that* since it indicated to her that she was too weak to be an independent adult. There's the double whammy of all guilt.)

3. Allow Yourself Temporary Emotional Guilt, Then Go to Pragmatic Zero-Tolerance. If you've vastly disappointed your partner, blown the big sale through unpreparedness, or forgotten your kids' birthdays, by all means allow yourself the luxury of wallowing in your malfeasance, selfishness, or neglect. Then get over it and make things right. Guilt can be a useful catharsis short-term (for a couple of hours), but it then should give way to constructive recovery (for the rest of your life).

4. If You Can't Perform Steps #1 Through #3, Get Therapeutic Help. Guilt, like depression, is nothing to fool around with. If these self-recognition and action steps prove to be impossible, seek out a good therapist. (Ask your regular doctor for recommendations if you've never been through therapy.) Deep-seated guilt not only may be impossible to alleviate on your own, but it is also insidiously self-reinforcing, so that it becomes calcified in your psyche. If you recognize the guilt symptoms and can't break out of the cycle, engage a learned other.

THE COURAGE TO STAND ALONE

Almost by definition, "ultimate" success means you're in rarified air with few peers around you. As the sage frog Kermit put it, "It's not easy being green." This is a world where intense peer pressure and an almost perverse drive to bring everyone down to the lowest common denominator are exerting extreme "g-forces" every day to haul you back into the mainstream.

Life balance is about choice, and when you have the resources that a successful career generates, those choices are not only more plentiful, but they are also more complex and individualistic. The desire and ability to travel, become a benefactor to charity, support an extended family, live in an expensive home, drive an exotic car, become active in politics, and other personal options create a unique persona.

Many people take refuge in a crowd and solace in the anonymity. This will always mean that you're driven by the herd mentality. True life balance is about individual choice, not for its own sake, but for your own values and beliefs. Don't believe that "no man is an island." At a certain level of success, *every person* is an island.

The courage to stand alone is a self-fulfilling, positive reinforcement. I'm not talking about selfishness nor about isolation from your family, but rather about individualistic values and pursuits, such as the following:

- *Opposing a popular movement because it's wrong.* Not too long ago parents in a Rhode Island community argued that students receiving a "D" grade— which traditionally barred them from athletics—be allowed to play football. This was because so many of them were receiving D's and the team had a chance to win a championship if everyone could play. The administration successfully withstood the pressure when a relatively few parents stood behind it. On a larger basis, the rate of graduation of athletes at major universities is so low that it's a humiliation (often less than 50 percent of football and basketball players), yet the faculty, parents, and administration allow the sham to continue.

- *Pursuing unique fulfillment.* Life is short and our society offers us a variety of choices to fulfill our quest for learning, recreation, and growth. Learning to fly, climbing a mountain, owning a horse, racing a car, and a plethora of other alternatives are available to those who have the resources and inclination. If one's life includes contributions to worthy causes, why can't it include personal enjoyment? Once guilt is removed (see above) then the courage to stand alone—and to enjoy oneself—is greatly facilitated.

- *Prudent risk taking in a conservative world.* As our success grows, we are enabled to take intelligent risk—in investing, running our businesses, supporting new endeavors, testing our talents. When you're winning at the casino, this is called gambling with "house money," since you're using your winnings. I'm not suggesting gambling, but I am saying that successful people can and should

  - Use credit and loans intelligently, since the capacity to repay is well-established, especially for signal events (for example, kids' education, a world tour, supporting a new business venture).

  - Put their egos on the line and explore a new interest or publicly test an existing one (for example, play in a band, hold an exhibit, cater a banquet). Earlier in the book is the case study of a successful boutique owner who held her own opera recital.

  - Reinvent themselves. Change your "brands" in your business. Change your look or image (makeup, hair, clothing). Become active in a new charitable cause or launch one. Reconcile old animosities and establish new friendships.

  - Constantly innovate. We become so adept at "fixing" things that we are constantly in danger of merely restoring past performance. Raise the bar. Set new standards. Maybe you're so "good" because the competition is so "bad," and it's time to compete with yourself and your own past.

The toughest issue, perhaps, about being "successfully alone" is that you're never sure whether you're doing well enough to be better than the herd or whether you're really excelling. The way to escape that trap is to constantly set new heights for your own ascent.

My wife has taught me that balance is about intelligent choices, and not political positions, despite the mainstream. Her greatest example is the feminist movement.

The idea that a woman is "unfulfilled" without a career is an arbitrary and rather biased position. A woman should have the option of a career without prejudicial treatment and with the guarantee of equal opportunity in the workplace. But a woman who chooses *not* to have a professional career, but rather to remain at home and be a full-time parent, is no less a liberated woman than one who becomes vice president of an insurance company or who founds her own realty firm.

Liberation—and balance—are about personal choice, not group dictate. Several studies have drawn correlations between women's rising numbers in the workforce and the amount of failed marriages and/or troubled children. A woman's choice to pursue work, pursue family, or combine both is entirely hers, and fulfillment is in the eye of the individual, as is her ability to manage, blend, and balance her life goals.

When women respect each other's choices in those areas as equally valid, then true liberation will have been attained.

An example of the courage to be alone is the practice of "tough love." We have to be confident and courageous enough to help the ones we love, even though they may feel our actions aren't in their best interests at the moment.

When my son was graduated from the drama conservatory at the University of Miami, he returned home to explore his options. Six months later he was still exploring—with his own room, his own vehicle, two pools, his meals prepared, his laundry tended to, and financial support for his entertainment. I knew that I was going to throttle him sooner or later, but that he had no real reason to hurry his decision under the circumstances.

I told him that he could move to New York or Los Angeles—after all, that's where the acting jobs are—and we would subsidize his entire move and help him get established. When he asked how long he had to decide, I told him twenty-four hours, since a carpenter was arriving to turn his room into a huge train layout for my new hobby.

My son has lived in New York for the past five years, has begun his own production company, and has acted in dozens of off-off-Broadway plays. We happily continue to subsidize him. In retrospect, he realizes he needed the shove.

That wasn't easy to do, but my wife and I knew it was for his (and our!) best interests. You must be able to make such decisions independent of your friends' and family's opinions and reactions. The courage to stand alone isn't an "in your face" contrarian position, but rather a confident assessment that successful people can achieve independent of peer pressure and societal norms.

Life balance is about being able to make the right decisions without fear.

THE FALLACY OF PERCEPTION (IT'S *NOT* REALITY)

Every wag and amateur psychologist will remark periodically, just like those airport announcements warning you not to park in the loading zones or leave baggage unattended, that "perception is reality." They will then generally bask in the glow of their erudition and await the bestowal of a MacArthur Foundation Prize.

I ask you now to tell me what the logical reason is for the sequence of the numbers below. By logical reason, I mean it is not my phone number or Social Security number, nor is it random. Logic should tell any reader of this book why the sequence exists as it does:

8 5 4 9 1 7 6 3 2 0

I did not get the answer to this when first confronted. Like many of you, I began on the left and assumed some kind of interval, but was thrown by the 9 and 1. Then I began on the right, but the 7 fouled me up. The people who are the very worst at this are accountants, mathematicians, and bankers. My son's high school math teacher gave up after two days.

The numbers are in *alphabetical order* (8 begins with "e" and zero with "z"). This is not a numbers or math problem at all, but rather a linguistic or verbal one. (Non-native English speakers may be excused.) If you treat this as a math

My work calendar, like everyone's, is quick to fill up with meetings, events, and activities that can potentially keep me from being a part of my family's life. To keep my family time in balance with my work time, my wife and I established a "family calendar" several years ago. It is a large paper calendar with sheet-type magnets taped to the back. It lives on our refrigerator door. I place annual leave, office holidays, and work-related overnight travel on the family calendar.

But more importantly, I regularly transfer family events/activities from the family calendar to my work calendar. I do this as soon as the activity or event is written on the family calendar. Once I have blocked out family time on my work calendar, nothing erases it. If I am asked to attend a meeting or work event that has a family conflict, I am not ashamed to admit that I am already committed to a family activity. If a family activity conflicts with an already scheduled work event, I will do everything I can to reschedule the work event.

Over the years, I have found that if I simply put family things on the work calendar early, I am much more focused on what is really important in my life. And my wife, children, and grandchildren can count on me to "be there" when it's important to them.

Keith Niemann, Director of Extension Human Resources,
University of Nebraska, Lincoln, Nebraska

problem, there is no answer that I've ever seen. If you treat it as a language problem, the answer readily occurs. About one person in twenty gets the right answer within five minutes, and they invariably tell me the same thing when I ask how they did it: They simply let their minds wander once they couldn't do the math!

One of the fundamental premises for gaining control of our own fate is that perception *is not* necessarily reality. Perception is perception. There is often a greater reality to which everyone else responds.

Perception is not synonymous with reality. The idea that we act on our perceptions, so that those perceptions become our reality, is a flawed position. Our "private realities" cannot be divorced from a greater reality, by which I mean "those conditions to which most other reasonable people ascribe their existence."

Why is this important? Because we can't control our destiny unless we understand where and when—and to what degree—our own perceptions might be incongruent or even antithetical to those around us, whether a loved one, a colleague, or most of humankind.

We've all seen the woman or man who enters a room and creates the immediate whispered reaction, "How can she wear that at her age?" or "How can he dress like that at his weight?" The truth is that no one dresses to be gawked at or to be the subject of ridicule, so those people's perceptions are that they look just fine, thank you very much. The problem occurs when *the reality* is that they are less effective, less accepted, and less able to influence others because of the more accurate, shared reality of the viewers. The same thing occurs at work ("How can he manage that way?") or in social encounters ("Why does she talk so much?") or within families ("Why does Dad always kid around when I'm asking a serious question?").

We need to constantly test our perceptions. Otherwise, our destiny becomes controlled by a pernicious belief in our own mental "press clippings" and the often disingenuous feedback from others seeking favor. Because at the Ultimate Consultant level of success, we become intimidating without trying to be and begin to suffer the same fate that a top executive, celebrity, or politician does: We lose touch with the greater reality.

There are small indicators of this "detachment" every day. When my daughter was young, we were waiting for the valet to bring our car around after dining at a favorite restaurant. The couple ahead of us stepped into their Lincoln, and my daughter said that the car had the same name as a President. "That's true," I said, "and can you think of another car that has the same name as a President?" (thinking Ford).

She thought long and hard and finally asked, "Mercedes was a President?"

I've cautioned earlier about listening to (and, worse, heeding) unsolicited feedback, which is always provided for the sender, not recipient. I'm now suggesting that we do need *solicited feedback* from trusted and respected sources, so that we can calibrate our perceptions with the greater reality.

Ironically, control of our fate requires that we surrender control to the extent that others whom we select can provide us with the feedback necessary to evaluate our own attachment to reality. The more successful we become, the more danger that we construct an artificial reality and act in accordance with it.

We all have the long-understood "baggage" from our youth and nurturing, which may have driven us to and shied us away from certain pursuits and interests. As we mature, we should become more and more successful at rooting out such baggage and dumping it, since few things that applied during our growth apply in our current position of success. (In fact, for many of us, our current level of success has turned earlier baggage and perceptions upside down, and good riddance.)

However, we seldom realize that we are constantly creating new baggage, which can become just as dysfunctional and damaging as the old stuff we finally discarded. "New baggage" constitutes flawed perceptions of ourselves, our lives, and our relationships, which are formed through strong perceptions—routinely reinforced—detached from the greater reality around us.

Some examples of that "new baggage" might include

- *A belief that our judgment is never flawed and can be relied on, even against the facts with which we're presented.* There is a difference between using judgment to decide among several good options and using "gut feel" to decide based on pure emotion and in contempt of the facts.
- *A belief that we are "charmed," or "lucky," or simply "above the fray."* This is narcissism unabated. President Clinton clearly thought he could get away with things in his personal life that others wouldn't dare. John F. Kennedy, Jr., took an inordinate risk in flying an airplane in conditions for which he was not qualified, losing his life (and the lives of others) as a result.
- *A belief in our omniscience.* I've heard successful entrepreneurs spout all kinds of "facts" that have basis only in their own prejudices, misheard communications, or misunderstood reading. Just because we fervently believe something doesn't mean it's correct.

The first indication that the direction of my life needed changing was the unexpected death of my sister-in-law in July 1999 from melanoma and the effect this had on my extended family. This was closely followed by severe job losses in my local community, which ultimately led to the dissolution of my long-term professional partnership due to stress and the lack of trust involved.

Although I listened to these events and recognized that changes were required, the necessity to restructure my business and complete an extensive home renovation overshadowed any good intentions.

Nature then took control in July 2001 and I developed pneumonia, which required hospitalization. It was apparent I was no longer bullet-proof and it made me realize I had not achieved life balance. Since then I have rearranged my priorities, commenced an exit strategy from my business, and developed a program to achieve life balance.

This includes improving relationships with family and friends, rediscovering a passion for hobbies, contributing to others on a voluntary basis, seeking other ways to use my professional skills, personal growth, and restoring my health. In addition, over the last few months I have reread several articles and books that reinforced that only I can make the changes required to meet these goals.

However, my very supportive, loving family, my beautiful dog Lilly, and the sanctuary we have created for our retirement have made the journey easier. Fortunately, I have been given a chance to rediscover myself and enjoy a life which gives me time to "smell the roses."

Syd Donaldson, Eden, New South Wales, Australia

- *A belief in the hand of fate.* "I've been through these business cycles before and something has always come up" is an accurate historical description, but hardly a recipe for alleviating current conditions. Variables change and the relief of the past may have been just that.
- *Sclerotic arrogance.* Most of us exhibit high degrees of confidence to achieve our success and to maintain it. But there is a thin line between confidence (the belief that we can help others and can provide value commensurate with high fees) and arrogance (the belief that we, ourselves, have nothing

left to learn). Arrogance precludes growth and bars learning. It is the great wasting disease of successful entrepreneurs.

> The stronger our personal perceptions become, the more dangerous they are if they are not borne out by the greater reality around us. This is a double-edged sword. Strong beliefs are important for success, but strong beliefs that are wrongly held are usually fatal.

Taking control of our own fate and synthesizing our balance in life, work, and relationships means ceding control in critical areas. We need to be receptive to solicited feedback, which can calibrate our perceptions against others' realities. We need to be willing to suspend long-held beliefs to the extent that they can be tested and continually proved (or disproved). We need to recognize that success doesn't necessarily mean more accurate perceptions or even better judgment.

In fact, there is evidence to the contrary about judgment and performance naturally improving. Many successful start-up entrepreneurs prove to be incapable of effectively running the businesses they've begun, and they end up losing control to disgruntled investors, family members, or acquirers. Many consultants fail to transfer their impressive expertise to even closely related areas and lose their momentum as their narrow niche is exploited or falls under heavy competition. The divorce rate among second marriages is higher than among first marriages, and that for third marriages is even higher than for second marriages! This is counterintuitive, in that you'd think the partners would have learned from the mistakes of the first relationship, but apparently the flawed judgment and bad decisions just get worse (or are reinforced and perpetuated).

Success itself does not breed success, contrary to still another bromide. But the factors behind our success—continual learning, hard work, openness to change, prudent risk, admission of error, bouncing back from defeat, and so forth—are the factors that, if allowed to continue to flourish, will account for continual success.

We can control our fate if we allow ourselves to step out from behind our own success long enough to do so.

THE PLATINUM ASSET: INTELLECTUAL BREADTH

I want to close the discussion about life balance, synthesis, and control of one's fate with what I believe is the platinum asset for achieving our life goals: intellectual breadth. This is a standard that has been debased, abused, and undermined. As an example of a growing revolt against "pseudo-intellect" and artificial achievement, Harvard University's faculty has recently voted to change the grading system so that *the current rate of 60+ percent* of graduates no longer so easily receive "honors."

In a society that has constantly "dumbed down," intellectual force is the most valuable weapon in your arsenal. The "dumbing down" of society has occurred through the confluence of these pernicious reasons:

- The "entitlement" mentality, which has prompted groups to lobby for perquisites and advantages irrespective of merit and accomplishment.
- The "victimization" mentality, which has encouraged groups to claim prized status in compensation for some perceived slights (from fragrance allergies to physical handicaps).
- The "political correctness" mentality, which has discouraged honest debate and open communication and has instead raised the specter of racism or anti-Semitism or bias against the obese in the place of honest and factual criticism.
- The politicization of education, which has led to "new math," "open classrooms," justification of poor grammar as culturally driven, and other drivel, diminishing actual classroom learning.
- The decline in the status and competency of the teaching profession. Abysmally low pay has finally created a primary and secondary cadre that is often itself marginally educated.[3] At the university level, we've excused the presumed true scholars from teaching any but the most elite courses; books on popular music are accepted as "scholarship"; and political agendas are more in evidence than lesson plans.

---

3. Challenge the English teacher to name the eight parts of speech or the history teacher to define the role of Robespierre in the French Revolution, or try to find a geography teacher. It's not a pretty sight.

- A popular culture and wealthy society that provide inexpensive luxuries and access to recreation for the masses, often at discounted prices. An excellent job—and the education required to claim it—are not as critical in terms of a nice car, home entertainment system, or vacation in Florida.

When all around you decline, you tend to stand out. When you choose to continue to grow while all around you decline, you are like a giant in the landscape. Fortunately or unfortunately, this is a lot easier than it sounds.

My observation is that truly outstanding, happy, and balanced people rely strongly on their intellect. This may pass as intelligence, "street smarts," "gut reactions," or other cognomens, but they are all part and parcel of being learned and articulate. In interviewing thousands of people over a quarter of a century, I've learned that you can identify high intellect through three synergistic traits:

1. *A wide and well-developed vocabulary.* The researcher Johnson O'Connor actually has written that he can demonstrate an increase in I.Q. scores as individuals build their vocabularies.
2. *A well-defined sense of humor.* People who can effectively employ humor—especially self-effacing humor—tend to maintain perspective, reduce stress, and invigorate others.
3. *The frequent use of metaphors and examples.* People who can paint verbal pictures and bring richness and depth to their speech are superb communicators who usually are easily able to influence others and win debates.

Intellectual depth is the rallying point and underlying resilience for most successful people (and perhaps for the most successful people). We've all seen people who can generate a following and provide direction merely by indicating a preference, since those listening are fully confident that an intellectual force is behind the choice, and that force, once felt, doesn't require constant expression. When used capriciously, this is a manipulative and nefarious trait, but so are most positive traits when used dishonestly. But when used sincerely and judiciously, intellectual force and its accoutrements—tight arguments, perspective, confidence building, and clear direction—are unmatched in their power.

> Watch the person who gets the most done with the fewest words, and you'll find a person capable of many words, but who doesn't need to work that hard. Synthesis is about realizing your goals with the least work and most effectiveness. That's what intellect is about. Being smart is helpful, and being clever is advantageous, but being wise is the ultimate asset.

In my estimation, Maslow was wrong, in that we are constantly "dipping" among his levels, searching for more physical security, new affiliations, more tests of our talents, and ongoing self-actualization. That is the nature of the Ultimate Consultant and the success that accrues to such a station in life.

Intellect is the fuel that enables us to engage in such concurrent actions successfully. And we can build our intellectual armamentaria at any time in these dimensions:

- *Read voraciously*. Read fiction and non-fiction; classics and contemporary; science and biographies. Stretch your mind.
- *Build your vocabulary*. Whenever you read a word you don't know, note it, look it up later, make a note of its definition, and use it in your own future communications.
- *Deliberately develop the ability to use examples, metaphors, analogies, and other verbal devices*. Listen to others who do this well and consider the occasions under which they employ them.
- *Teach a course*. Teach it at a university, community college, trade school, learning annex, or service club. Teaching forces you to both thoroughly understand a subject and to place it in a context that helps others to understand it.
- *Write*. Even in a personal journal. Put your thoughts on paper and force yourself to interpret your conceptualization into concrete terms and exam-

Advice from the Readers of *Balancing Act*

My four children have all been involved in ski racing, a hugely time-consuming sport that requires waking up early in the morning, driving for several hours, and standing in the cold. Ski racing is standing in front of a fan in a meat freezer, tearing up fifty-dollar bills.

So what is the advantage? Hours of talk with your kids. Discussions of how to cope with triumph and disaster and treat them the same. The difference between first place and tenth place may be a couple of seconds. Did we win? Probably not. Did we have fun? Oh, yes.

The best "coaching" I have ever given my kids is "go fast and have fun." Just as they step up to the start gate, I whisper that mantra. Not bad advice for my own life either.

Now my daughter is involved in competition soccer. Lots of intense young girls with pony tails, running with all their hearts up and down the field. Again, hours spent driving to tournaments, but hours of talk, socializing, and bonding. What are her hopes, fears, dilemmas? What is happening with her friends? How does she handle her enemies at school? What great insights does she have from her teachers? Without those hours of driving to the tournaments, how much would I have come to learn? How could we ever be as close?

Joy comes from rejoicing in those triumphs and disasters with those you love. Go fast, my friends. Go fast . . . and have fun.

Lynn D. Johnson, Ph.D., Solutions Consulting Group, Inc.,
Salt Lake City, Utah

ples. You don't have to write *War and Peace*. You simply have to write what you mean.

- *Search for deeper interpretations and related events.* Don't accept the bland causal relationships that we too often blindly ingest (people don't like change). Look for novel and/or contravening explanations (for example, people change every day, finding new routes to work around traffic jams, getting repair people for the appliances, searching for new sources of entertainment). Try to be innovative and original, not derivative and emulative.

The primary reason that there is nothing stopping you from achieving synthesis and life balance is that there is nothing stopping you from developing your intellect. Laziness and sloth will undermine those attempts. If sitting in front of mindless television shows, or playing the umpteenth round of unrewarding golf, or simply following the herd is your instinct, then you're not going to develop anything but a physical and mental paunch.

Ultimate Consultants, however, did not get to where they are through sloth. They've been innovative and bold, scrupulous and disciplined. Now that the money is literally in the bank and the opportunity arises to enjoy life all along Maslow's scale, why abandon those gifts?

Are you happier today than you were last year? If not, what do you intend to do about it? If so, what are your plans to be happier still next year? You can't help anyone else unless you're helping yourself.

ALAN'S ULTIMATE LESSONS

There isn't a room I can't command or a conversation I can't influence with a few pithy comments, dramatic examples, shared humor, or precise interpretation. Once this has been demonstrated, it need not be repeated with equal drama in the future if the same people are present. They will, instead, read Gnostic wisdom into even your prosaic and plebian commentary.

I developed these skills no less than someone else would develop a vegetable garden or stock portfolio—I paid careful attention, took nothing for granted, and constantly built on the positive results. It never cost me a nickel (which is fortunate since, when I needed these talents the most early in my career, I didn't have many nickels).

I'm still growing, and still building my talents. I'm self-actualizing all over the landscape. Maslow would be proud.

CHAPTER 10

Essays on Life Balance

*Periodic Refreshment
and Reinforcement for a Better Life*

GUILT

The greatest inhibitor of performance, enjoyment, and freedom that I know of is guilt. Guilt is virtually entirely self-imposed in that, despite the actions and words of others, only you can invoke your own guilt.

I know this because the converse is so true. I've seen people respectfully and solemnly sit in a church and perform all of their obeisances and rituals. They are, for the hour, moved by the spirit of their religious beliefs. Yet no sooner than driving out of the parking lot at the end of the service, these same pious people are cursing and gesticulating as other drivers forge ahead of them.

If guilt can be so easily shunted aside, it can be just as readily claimed.

I've always felt that a key to eliminating guilt as much as possible resides in the fact that life is about success, not about perfection. (I learned that from therapy years ago, and it was worth the price of admission.) If we make ourselves feel bad, low, or worthless every time we're not perfect, we're going to lead a guilt-ridden life. But if we recognize our imperfection, vow to do better next time, and strive to do our best in all conditions, success will likely be ours when we deserve it and guilt should be avoidable.

Those who should feel guilty (criminals, betrayers, cheaters) seldom do, so guilt doesn't play a role for those for whom it should and plays far too great a role for those for whom it should not. One of the textbook definitions of a psychotic, for example, is that he or she feels absolutely no guilt.

The best ways to avoid and/or confront guilt:

1. Don't insist on perfection, but simply do your best to succeed against clearly defined goals. I once heard a professional speaker say that "fine isn't good enough; I have to be great." That's not a burden I want to carry.
2. Examine the "shoulds" we all carry around. Is it really a crime not to call your mother every week, to allow the kids to do their homework by themselves, and to forego contributing to the United Way campaign because money is tight?
3. Find a reliable sounding board. Tell your spouse, friend, or significant other that you're beginning to feel guilty about something, and let that person help you analyze it.
4. Separate your feelings from your actions. Acknowledge that you might be feeling guilty about something, but don't necessarily act on it. We tend to get into trouble when we act strictly on our emotions without allowing logic to creep in.
5. Get over it. Excuse yourself. Allow yourself the same grace you would allow someone else. If you broke a friend's favorite old record, apologize and offer to make amends. Search the Internet for a replacement or buy something equally sentimental. But don't beat yourself up. Accidents, poor judgment, and sloppiness happen. It won't be the last time.

There's great drama on the television law shows when the jury is asked to read a verdict—"guilty" or "innocent." You are your own jury. Cut a deal with the prosecutor before the jury reconvenes.

ZEST

There are those among us who would rather light candles than curse the darkness. I've always liked to be counted in their ranks.

As opposed to the energy suckers, the zest merchants infuse us with a sense of well-being and joy. They are infectious and ingratiating. They are not necessarily pranksters, jokesters, or even humorous, although they may be all that. Primarily, they love life, are objects of interest themselves, and create an energy field around them. The equation, therefore, is to surround ourselves with far more energy merchants than sappers.

Why are some people such ready purveyors of happiness and purpose, and how do they get that way? I'm not sure of the causes, but I have observed a thing or two about the traits they generally possess:

- *Positive self-image.* These are people who feel good about themselves, so there is no "loss" for them in helping others feel good about themselves.
- *Fantasia.* Energy merchants tend to be dreamers, with bold visions and unorthodox views. They see life from viewpoints and dimensions that others do not. They serve the same purpose as those glasses that enable us to see 3-D movies.
- *Ability to rebound.* Defeats are acknowledged and dealt with (or forgotten), and life moves on for them. They can't be derailed or deterred for very long.
- *Empathy.* They don't sympathize (feel what others feel) so much as empathize (understand what others feel), which enables them to commiserate but also provide fresh air and new options without descending into bathos.
- *Appreciation.* Energy providers appreciate each new day, every new experience, and all new relationships. They realize that life is a privilege, and act accordingly.

Want more zest in your life? Even better, want to be a zest merchant? The key to being an upbeat and positive individual, I believe, lies in perspective. We need to remind ourselves that rarely, if ever, are we engaged in a battle to save civilization as we know it. In fact, we're usually upset, discouraged, and thrown off balance by the trivial, the mundane, and the miniscule. Yet dealing with perspective takes a lot more than simply the banal admonition: "Don't sweat the small stuff."

We have to be thankful for each new day and each new opportunity. Just as my dogs are revitalized by the fact that the yard awaits them each morning, seemingly unchanged to me but offering a new world of opportunities to them, we should be re-energized by the options and possibilities of each new day. Failure is seldom fatal, and success is never final. It's courage that counts.

If you're in a job, a situation, a relationship, or a dynamic that is painful, stressful, and debilitating, do something about it. Confrontation isn't nearly as painful as a wasted life, lost time, and lack of zest.

Light candles. When you curse the darkness, you'll only hear the echo of your own sorrowful shouting.

FEAR OF AMBIGUITY

I'm drolly amused by people who need everything wrapped up in a tight bow with instructions taped to the side. A Supreme Court justice once commented that he didn't need to define pornography because he knew it when he saw it. I like that confidence in a jurist. There is an old Roman saying: De minimis non curat praetor. (The magistrate does not consider trifles.) Exactly so.

Lower-level people in clients are forever asking me "What are the deliverables?" and "How much time will you spend?" and "What will be the costs?" Higher-level executives are usually more focused on "Okay, these are the goals; let's exceed them!"

In our personal lives, there are those who say, "Let's play it by ear," and others who officiously pontificate, "You can't win without a plan." Another cosmic-sized banality is, "If you can't measure it, it's not worth doing." Well, it's tough to measure happiness exactly, or love specifically, but I know it when I feel it. De minimis non curat Alan.

My son told me once that he refused to go into a dark room. My wife and I assured him that he needn't be afraid of the dark. "I'm not," he stated firmly, "I'm afraid of what might be in the dark."

Fair enough, that's why they sell flashlights. It's one thing to have a tangible fear, whether of leaving a small, comfortable pond in which you're a big fish, standing in front of an audience, or dealing with a call in the middle of the night.

Rational, discrete fears can be dealt with, through either resolution or coping. But it's another thing entirely to fear the outside world, other people, or the night itself.

Religious beliefs—of any type—help to provide a feeling of centering and safety in a universe about which we actually know shockingly little. We construct mythologies, stories, and belief systems in order to help us deal with the basically unknowable and incomprehensible. (I've heard more than my share of atheists and agnostics say, "Thank God!" on traumatic occasions.)

It doesn't make sense to fear the ambiguous in the course of our daily affairs, which largely are knowable and comprehensible. There's no sense getting anxious about meeting a new boss, visiting a new city, or trying a new vegetable. (A dinner companion told me the other night that she would not, under any conditions, eat sushi. "Can you imagine where that comes from?" she asked, warily eyeing an aggressive piece of uni. "Can you imagine where the eggs you had for breakfast come from?" I wondered.)

Let's stop worrying about the dark or about what may be lurking in it. And let's stop creating additional fears about the unknown in a world that guarantees we can never know enough. Franklin Roosevelt said that the only thing we have to fear is fear itself, and he said that after the country had been rocked by surprise attack.

Uni, anyone?

ZEALOTRY

Reader and buddy Dan Coughlin took a chance and sent me a book he thought I'd like. It's called *When Pride Still Mattered,* and it's the biography of Vince Lombardi, the man credited with leading the Green Bay Packers to football immortality, and who purportedly said, "Winning isn't everything. It's the only thing."

Lombardi, always cited as one of the greatest of the football coaches in high school, college, and professionally, is a depressing character. His single-minded devotion to the game effectively circumscribed the rest of his life. His relationships with his wife, children, and friends were dysfunctional. In fact, he wasn't a very interesting man to be around, unless you wanted to chart plays or talk draft selections.

My *Webster's* says that a zealot is "full of zeal; a fanatic." There's an old phrase that says, "There's no zealot like the converted," meaning that those who come to a cause late often take it up with a fervor that the originators neither intended nor embraced.

Extremism is always dangerous. (Barry Goldwater said once that "extremism in the defense of liberty is no vice" and promptly lost a presidential election in a landslide.) Passion is often beautiful, but it's most rewarding when tempered with perspective and respect for others' views. Deeply religious sentiments are universally respected, but proselytizing is not.

Worse, zealotry replaces pragmatic reason with perfervid emotion. Elian Gonzalez, the Cuban boy saved from the sea only to be drowned in a whirlpool of politics, was a victim of zealotry from all sides. The spectacle of crowds in the streets, round-the-clock press conferences, armed rescue teams, and media frenzy over a single child's fate is fascinating when viewed in contrast to abused, starving, and sick children all over the world, for whom people don't provide a moment's thought, nor the media even a monthly broadcast.

On the invisible but omnipresent continuum of our behaviors, we need zeal, but not zealotry; vigor, but not obstinacy; assertiveness, but not belligerence. Our moral "rudder" has to steer us toward those behaviors which enable us to best interact with our loved ones and acquaintances. To sacrifice or moderate our objectives for the moment is an act of compassion, a gesture of good will, an effort toward tolerance. To hold our own no matter what harm we do to others, because we are zealous in our beliefs and committed to our own "true" cause, is the height of self-absorption, sanctimony, and narcissism.

Lombardi was not a great coach. He was a coach who won. Life is not about winning. It's about success. There's a difference. You can win by yourself. But you can only succeed through others.

IRRATIONALITY

One of the most frustrating situations we encounter is when we try to deal rationally with someone who resists every cerebral and analytical approach we undertake. We soon become agitated (or worse) and demand how it is that the other party can't see our entirely sequential, perfectly aligned arguments. Unfortunately, this often happens with loved ones and partners.

The reason for the disconnect is that you cannot deal logically with someone who is emotionally paralyzed in a given position. When someone complains, "Why can't they understand that they're wrong in not inviting our cousins to the wedding?" it's not a matter of what they understand; it's a matter of what they FEEL. Logic makes people think; emotion makes them act. Debates are logical and civil. Arguments are loud and unruly.

The key to dealing with someone who is blinded by emotion is in finding out what other emotions will tend to influence their judgment. That's right . . . you have to tap into the very source of the fire in order to extinguish it. Confronting emotional certainty with logic may be frustrating, but confronting it with equivalent and antithetical emotional certainty can be downright dangerous. There's a reason why those in favor of and opposing abortion, or animal experimentation, or the 2000 vote count in Florida can't talk civilly. It's called moral certainty, and it's volatile stuff.

Someone who is acting purely on the basis of emotion is not mentally disturbed, obstinate, or fractious, at least not in his or her intent. He or she is merely being driven by a fundamental emotional fuel that doesn't readily exhaust itself.

Find out what the emotional need being served is, and find other ways (more productive for you and conducive to cooperation) that may induce change at the visceral level. If someone is adamant about not spending money on a particular item or opportunity, find out why, and don't make a huge pitch for the wisdom of the expenditure and his or her blindness in not seeing it. Find out why there is such resistance to spending the money. The probability is that there is a fear of not having sufficient funds for something else deemed much more basic or urgent (tuition, retirement, health care). Agree with the priority; then demonstrate how the more basic financial needs are absolutely safeguarded and have adequate reserves.

Any attempt to settle this on the wisdom of the new investment fails. Only an attempt to satisfy the emotional need for safety will allow the investment to be considered.

We all try too hard to be good salespeople, selling our alternatives, instead of collaborators and partners, trying to understand the other person's real needs. Worse, we often become emotional when our choices are threatened or critiqued, at which point communication breaks down entirely.

There may be no such thing as irrationality, short of actual clinical personality disorders. What we really have is cerebral and visceral decision criteria, and both are equally important. You can't override one with the other.

If you don't believe that, try forgetting your partner's birthday and then convincing him or her that there were logical reasons for your inability to remember it.

EGOCENTRICITY

So a guy calls me the other day and says, no kidding, "I've heard about you and your mentor program. I'd like to consider being a part of it. I'm calling to get five references to see if you're really any good. Also, although I've never read any of your books, this concept of value pricing you're credited with makes no sense to me, and I don't see how it can work. What's your reaction?"

"How long have you been in consulting?" I asked, already knowing the answer.

"Oh, I'm just retiring from my job and am entering the profession. But, hey, you're not going to tell me that just because you've been doing it longer you're smarter than I am, are you?"

I wasn't, but only because I hung up.

Most people trip through life because their egos are hanging down around their ankles, getting in the way of their feet. I think that a healthy ego is important to success and emotional well-being, but I think egocentricity is a form of self-absorption that borders on implosion.

We need to understand that *confidence* is based on the belief that we can help others to learn; *arrogance* is based on the belief that we have nothing left to learn ourselves; and *smugness* on the belief that we don't need to learn. Egocentricity is smugness raised to an art form.

The people most intent on preserving delicate egos are, perforce, the most insecure. Any slight, intended or inadvertent, can puncture the delicate fabric of their well-being. Consequently, they tend to excel at offense, because defense is so dangerous. (I believe that here is where you'll find most passive-aggressives lurking—that most hateful of all personality disorders.)

We see egocentricity in one-upmanship: "You were in Rio? Ah, but you missed Carnival, which is why we went when we did." We see it in volume over logic: The jerk who continually breaks in on our conversation, too busy telling us why we're wrong to listen to what we're actually saying. We see it in gamesmanship: Asking questions of dubious worth to throw the other party off track and off the subject. And we see it in the "ignorant expert": The person lecturing us on wine who doesn't realize that someone at the table really does know about wine and that sniffing the cork does absolutely nothing other than make you look like a stunned Labrador retriever.

Here's what you do with egocentricity: Call the bet. That's right, just like in poker when you suspect a bluff, you match the last raise and you ask to see the cards. Unlike poker, when the other party might not have been bluffing, the egocentrics are never holding anything above a nine of diamonds. Ask where she got her information. Tell him that he's wrong, and that volume makes it even a louder wrong. Tell her that the comment about your child going to a "backup" school is worse than inaccurate, it's an attempt to cause pain, and you wonder why she feels the need to do that. You will repel all boarders, who will quickly attempt to jump back into their little rowboats.

Don't ignore the behavior, which only enables it. Egocentrics thrive on a lack of resistance (remember that they're always on the offensive), and they become bigger and bigger in their self-promotion. They can become so big that the rest of us can't breathe. Puncture the gas bag.

SELF-EFFACEMENT

Humor is rooted in pain. If you want to use humor deliberately and most effectively, make it your own pain. Hence, the utility of self-effacing humor.

Someone paid me a great compliment the other day, which was probably an overstatement of vast proportion, but she said, "When you cite success, you use someone else as the example, but when you cite failure, you use yourself. That's tremendously endearing."

Now, "endearing" is not a term applied to me very often (okay, hardly ever). But her observation was astute, since I deliberately employ that technique.

When much younger, I was a "put down" artist of rare achievement. I could slam, debase, deride, scorn, undermine, and deflate almost anyone or anything on a moment's notice. I was often funny, but seldom likeable. I usually made people laugh, but couldn't make them stay.

Whether in a business or social setting, a self-effacing demeanor is an advantage if your objective is to influence others, develop relationships, and build friendships. Yet self-effacing doesn't mean self-demeaning or self-defeating. The irony, perhaps, is that it takes confidence, self-possession, and great perspective to be self-effacing.

The reason, I believe, is that confidence allows you to be self-effacing without damaging your self-image or identity. Chicken impresario Frank Perdue made a fortune telling people, "It takes a tough man to make a tender chicken." Well, it probably also takes a well-balanced individual to engage in self-ridicule.

The people I've warmed to fastest are those who tell me how they hit a golf shot that damaged two homes, scared three animals, and took four shots to recover from a moving garbage truck. The ones I not-so-subtly walk away from are those who regale me with the backspin they placed on their six iron to achieve an "impossible" birdie on a tough hole. (I am using golf because I find it truly one of the most boring of activities a non-player must ever listen to, but that's a topic for another day.)

Is the opposite of "one-upmanship" something like "one-downmanship"? I don't know. But I do know that I love the person who tells me how the cop gave her a ticket for claiming that the speed limit was higher than it was much more than the one who tells me how he used his connections to escape the summons.

That doesn't mean that we shouldn't rejoice in our great experiences or feel good about our achievements. It does mean that we need to remember that the route to victory is lined with failure, and that we learn as much from the one as from the other.

If you want to make people laugh, share your foibles and your pain. If you're at all like me, you're a pretty funny person!

CONTEXT

Having earned a Ph.D. and spent a quarter century in the consulting profession, I can talk about "context." But when I was much younger, battling for my breathing space in Union City, New Jersey, we had a more pithy term: Pick your fights.

I'm astonished at the relentless pursuit of the trivial. Not long ago a visitor to my website contacted me and told me in no uncertain terms that I probably want to change the photo of me in a sailboat (one of my favorites, since I can't sail at all) because my "PFD wasn't zipped."

Well, this alarmed me, to say the least, since my site is quite popular and no one ever told me that my PFD was unzipped for all to see. Just to make sure I didn't repeat the error, I asked for help locating my PFD and learned that it was my "personal flotation device." Knowing what it would take to make me float, I realized that he was talking about my life vest, duly being worn but, alas, clearly unzipped.

I told him I didn't see the need to remove the photo for this small transgression, and he proceeded to tell me that I was leaving myself open to legal problems and setting a poor example for children. (Gads, what would be the reaction if I also held the rudder with the improper grip?)

Now, I'm all for boating safety and believe in good examples. But a publicity close-up of me with a life vest unzipped on a page that children never visit is hardly a clarion call to action, demanding that the villagers ascend my driveway with torches and pitchforks. I mean, come on.

But we see this kind of behavior every day, people not knowing where to pick their fights or when to put their backs up against the wall and get bloody for a worthy cause, versus dismissing a perceived transgression as a trifle. People ought to use their directional signals, shouldn't cut into a ticket line, ought not play music in public that drowns out a train wreck, and really need to clean those airplane basins after use. But what the hey, it doesn't ruin my life when they don't.

My day is ruined, though, when someone tries to cheat me of my good name, attacks my family, threatens my career, or tries to impose a morality on me that I don't embrace. So I fight back at the voting booth, through an attorney, in a letter to the editor, or by whatever means are appropriate at the time. I find I don't need to do this very often. Basically, I'm just not threatened at that level very often. Nor should you be. (Where is Maslow when you need him?)

So my advice to you is not to consider trifles and to adhere to Jefferson's great admonition: "In matters of principle, stand like a rock; in matters of taste, swim with the current." In less profound oratory, Get Some Context.

And when you do sail, consider either zipping up your PFD or prohibiting photos taken with it open. There may be children watching.

SOLITUDE

My wife and I recently returned from Nantucket, where we adjourn every year for a brief time to enjoy one of the last unspoiled pieces of America. We take one of the convertibles on the ferry, breeze around the island, eat our way through the place in true Japanese horror movie style, stay at a favorite resort, and hit the beach.

Except this time. For the first time during any of our beach vacations anywhere, we were shut out. It rained every day, and even the determined (and lovely) Maria was afraid to go near the water lest she be swept to sea. (Seeing the movie *The Perfect Storm* didn't help.) So we made do with driving around, shopping, exploring, treating ourselves well, and reading voraciously.

On the ferry coming home I realized that we had had an awfully good time. Just getting away is wonderful. We could have read the same books back at the house, had equally good meals in our favorite restaurants, and explored in the same way, I guess. But changing one's environment and creating some forced solitude is an elixir.

We are, all of us, rather conscientious beings, which is a polite way of saying we carry a lot of baggage, along with a little guy on our shoulder who keeps whispering, "You don't deserve this" and "You really oughta. . . ." Consequently, we don't take the time to create solitude for ourselves and/or with our significant others. But solitude—that is, being away from the normal environment of repair people, supermarkets, neighbors, and the vicissitudes of communal life—provides for contemplation, perspective, and renewal.

Now I'm not talking monk-like privation or isolation. I could never disappear into the wilderness for a few weeks, and I only lasted twenty minutes out of a paid-for forty-five in an isolation tank that my sister once bizarrely thought was a great gift. But changing the daily regimen of one's life on a vacation of any sort is cathartic.

I've watched friends and colleagues who are never alone. They awake to a family breakfast, join friends at a health club, endure the forced socialization of the office, engage in meetings, have dinner, share family time (if they're lucky), work at home, and another day has evanesced. When they do go out, it's with friends or at parties. And work on the computer is not solitude. It's simply membership in an unseen but greatly felt wider community.

We all need solitude at regular intervals if we're to take stock, to regard ourselves from a greater height, and to look toward the horizon. A great deal of the aberrant behavior I must deal with, personally and professionally, is the result of people who can't imagine they're acting irregularly, because they never take the opportunity to think about themselves or their behaviors.

Most philosophers and psychologists regard humans as sentient because they exhibit self-awareness, supposedly alone among all animals (which I doubt). But is there sentience when that self-awareness is sacrificed in the scurry of constant motion, achievement, and competition? Margaret Wheatley in her book *Leadership and the New Science* posits that the ability to process information is a sign of consciousness. So a dog is more conscious than a snail, because a dog can process much more information than a snail.

Doesn't that also mean that some people are more conscious than others, because some take the time to gather more information about themselves and their impact on their environment? It would certainly explain a lot in terms of differences in human capability.

Solitude is great for one's mental health. Sometimes you get rained out. But that doesn't mean you lose the game.

CULPABILITY

In the wake of trauma, we often engage in an introspective culpability in which we search for ways in which we, ourselves, contributed to our own predicament. Aside from a terrorist attack, this can occur with an alienated child, a co-worker who is fired, someone else's choice that was not favorable to us, and so forth, dozens of times a day. The outrage or hurt is generally so deep that we seem to want to believe that we had to be at fault personally, ergo, we can control it the next time by simply changing our own behaviors.

But life isn't that simple. There are unspeakable and completely unjustified acts of evil. There are children or spouses who become self-destructive or abusive without any assistance from us. There are adverse conditions at work that are completely divorced from our performance and behavior.

Part of one's balance is the perspective that we are not always involved in a cause-and-effect dynamic. Things happen. The key is what we decide to do about them. Personal equilibrium is restored when we can proceed with healthy and constructive actions untainted by presumed guilt and unburdened by the amorphous baggage of responsibility we often automatically assume.

When my wife is unhappy with me, sometimes it's my fault and sometimes it's not. When I'm late because of heavy traffic, sometimes I made a bad choice of routes but sometimes I made what should have been the best choice. When a client is unhappy with my findings, sometimes I might have been more tactful and sometimes it has nothing to do with tact and everything to do with the client. I'm not perfect at separating the two possibilities, but I've become much better at it as I've grown older and as I've realized that a great deal of adversity that I must deal with (as must we all) is simply not my fault, not my doing, not my creation.

I served for several years on the board of a shelter for battered women. Despite my psychology background, I was nonetheless shocked by two facts: First, battering occurs across all economic, educational, and other demographic slices; second, the battered woman often enables the batterer by refusing to leave. I'm not saying that it's her fault that she's battered, only that, by not leaving, the battering is allowed to continue. What I found in the course of my work is that there is a high proportion of these women who don't leave because they feel that somehow what's happening is their fault, and that the roots of the behavior lie in their own past actions. Once I understood that, I had more insight into why they didn't leave.

Similarly, many of us tolerate and even exacerbate poor treatment, harsh conditions, and inappropriate behavior because we believe—subliminally or consciously—that somehow we are at fault, responsible for the condition existing in the first place. In many (most?) cases, this is simply false.

This country has done nothing to merit the slaughter of nearly three thousand innocent civilians on that September 11th. Battered women have done nothing to justify the terror heaped upon them. And most of us, in most cases, are not culpable for the problems, injustices, and suffering about us. That's not to say we shouldn't take an active and aggressive role in solving the problems, removing the injustices, and alleviating the suffering. But it is to say that those constructive actions are almost always more effective, more sincere, and more long-lived when we take them because they are the right thing to do, rather than when we take them out of guilt for presumed sins.

FREEDOM FROM FAILURE

Driving cross-country in the aftermath of September 11, the client with whom I was sharing the driving told me that he had lost a good friend in the World Trade Center. He told me that his friend, a financial executive, was utterly self-assured, instilled confidence in those around him, and generally provided a sense of direction, calm, and trust in all those with whom he came into contact.

"I can cite only a few people like that," he reflected, "and you're probably one of them, as well. What's responsible for that degree of confidence and self-worth?"

Although I had another 1,500 miles or so during which to expound, the response only required a few seconds: "Being unafraid of failure," I said. Truly confident people, from business leaders to politicians, from teachers to lawyers, simply aren't intimidated by the possibility of failure. They do fail, as all bold and innovative people will, but they don't allow their actions to be altered by that possibility.

I met my client again the other day, and he mentioned to me that he had repeated my definition to a multitude of people, and all of them thought that it was a valuable observation, one that they probably hadn't fully considered. I'll let you be the judge of that, but I do want to expand on that premise a bit here.

Outstanding public speakers get "butterflies" before they mount the stage, which is actually a feeling of great anticipation and an eagerness to begin what, for them, is a thrilling and energizing experience. Poor speakers get stage fright, not to be confused with those premonitory butterflies. Stage fright is a near-paralyzing sensation generated by the fear of failure, of being seen as foolish, of not fulfilling expectations. This difference is more than a nuance. It's the difference between greatness and mediocrity.

Many people I've met are not trying to win, they're trying not to lose; they aren't trying to succeed, they're desperately trying not to fail. That is a sure route to nowhere. I'd rather be going somewhere, even if I fail to get there, than assuredly going nowhere.

Once we remove the fear of failure from our behaviors, our lexicon, and our frame of reference, we free ourselves to innovate, to explore, to experiment, and to fail in a good cause. There is nothing humiliating about failure, since it's seldom fatal. If you don't believe that, I suggest you read the biographies of Lincoln, Edison, Gandhi, Jackie Robinson, and Golda Meir, to name a few.

How do we remove that fear of failure? My recipe is simple. Ask yourself these two questions: (1) What is the worst that can happen? and (2) Can I live with that outcome? If you're honest and tuck your ego away, in almost every case you can tolerate the setback. And failure in a good cause, of course, is always superior to success in an ignoble one.

How do some of us manage to stand out in a crowd every time? We don't care what the crowd is thinking.

CONSPIRACIES

There are still people spending more time than I can comprehend on who killed John F. Kennedy: Cuban operatives, Russians, our own CIA, the Mafia, little green men, or Bill Gates. Call me naïve, but I've concluded it was a single demented nut case with a rifle.

A few years ago, a man died in Scotland. He was the man who had taken the most convincing photo of "Nessie," the fabled Loch Ness Monster, with neck and head fully extended from the lake. The significance of this event was that, on his deathbed, he produced incontrovertible evidence of the props he had used to fake the photo. Most people had long suspected the fraud, and he decided that setting the record straight before dying might just be an asset in the afterlife.

I wrote to a San Francisco man—a member of Mensa, no less—who was the chair of the Bay Area Loch Ness Monster Committee, or some such thing, and asked if he would now disband. (Hey, it was a slow day.) His answer was that the props were a fake, and that the dying man wanted to hide the secret of the real monster.

Now, why hadn't I thought of that?

People engage in conspiracy theory with great fervor and frequency. I've had planes cancelled under me—with mechanics clearly crawling around the innards—when a fellow passenger would point out in low tones, "United always does this when there aren't many passengers and they won't make much money on the flight." The fact that United still had to accommodate those people, needed that equipment at some other site, and was thrown off its own schedule seemed to be incidental to the conspiracy.

Why is so much time and energy spent on theories that fly in the face of fact? (If there's a Sasquatch in the woods or a Yeti in the Himalayas being hidden from public view, why has one never died and left its carcass? And don't they ever have to relieve themselves, leaving some evidence?) I think it's because these theories, no matter how convoluted, provide us with some control over an otherwise inexplicable set of circumstances.

How could a loner like Lee Harvey Oswald have killed a well-protected President? Why do our flights cancel when others don't? What accounts for people reporting strange sightings? We need some way of organizing the long shots, random events, and unpredictable nature of our lives. I don't think I've ever instituted a major survey for a company without someone, somewhere, claiming that there were hidden codes that would identify the respondent so that the company could retaliate if necessary. I used to tediously explain why that would be detrimental to the company and to me. Now I simply tell them to get over it. (The more effort you expend trying to explain, the more calcified their belief in a conspiracy becomes.)

A conspiracy implies that there is some agent or intelligent planning at work that can explain the inexplicable. That's why, evidently, the Air Force is holding the bodies of some dead aliens in Hangar 54 in Roswell, New Mexico, along with the remnants of their spacecraft. My favorite recent example (and this, too, is very popular in Mensa, so go figure) is that we never really landed on the moon, but have been hoodwinked by our government with trick photos and special effects. (The fact that the same government can't protect its own nuclear secrets and would require unprecedented secrecy and cooperation from hundreds of people is conveniently ignored.)

Teapot Dome was a conspiracy, as was the South Seas bubble, as are almost all network and pyramid marketing schemes, in which late entrants can't possibly make money. But random events are nothing more than random events. We do have an urge to try to explain why they occurred when they did and where they did, and that urge would rather create hidden schemes than go unfulfilled.

But life's not a conspiracy. It's what we make it.

TRUST

Someone asked me the other day how I defined "trust." I told him that people who trusted each other shared vulnerabilities, felt confident to critique and question each other, and relied on each other without qualification.

"Well, those are attributes and traits," he agreed, "but what really constitutes trust?"

Good question. And I determined, upon due reflection, that trust is really the underlying conviction in any relationship that the other person has your own best interests in mind. That's why we can accept adverse critiques and even anger from those we trust: We know, deep down, that they are just trying to help us.

Advice from the Readers of *Balancing Act*

My usual routine of traveling down Southington Mountain from Waterbury was interrupted one spring day by a mother duck and five ducklings meandering up the left lane of the I-84 overpass. She seemed to be oblivious of the fact that it was morning rush hour and people had to get to work. As I slowly approached, staying to the far right, the woman in the car behind me also noticed the sight and slid in behind me to marvel at a brief encounter of nature.

Suddenly I heard the sound of a car horn blaring and as I looked out the side mirror I saw an older man barreling up the left lane in an ancient Pontiac trying to shoo the ducks out of the way. This seemed to confuse the mom and she really didn't have anywhere to go other than in front of my car. As soon as they were out of the way, the man stepped on the gas like a teenager and hurried off to some unknown destination.

The road ahead offered several traffic lights and I had the opportunity to get a good look at the aggressive driver. He was well past retirement age and I chose to not do or say anything to antagonize the situation. My thoughts for most of the day kept returning to the morning incident and I wanted to believe that the man thought the ducks were actually pigeons that could be shooed away easily. It was difficult for me to think that a person could be so close to the end of his life and still not have learned tolerance.

Kevin McDermott

Trust is an interesting quality, because in my experience, while it's tough to gain, it's even tougher to recapture if it's been gained and lost. Many a relationship has gasped its last breath on the words, "I just don't trust you any more." At best, the absence of trust creates indifference, but at worst that vacuum is also often filled by cynicism, the antithesis of trust. And misplaced trust is often cataclysmic, whether in the tragedy of Jonestown or the abandonment of a friend.

We become cynical about our government, or our news sources, or our schools, or our family when we no longer believe that their actions—on a continuing basis—are truly intended to support our own best interests. And it's ironic that "tough love" and harsh penalties may often be more of a sign of respect and support—and, hence, trust—than sycophancy, blind adherence, unqualified support, and persiflage.

Early in a relationship a young person will often try to gain advantage with a partner by demanding, "Don't you trust me?" In reality, the question actually being asked is, "Why won't you give in to me?" That same dynamic occurs in more subtle forms throughout our lives. Unquestioned fealty isn't a sign of trust. It's a sign of avoiding conflict, even if the other's interests are sacrificed by your own silence and obedience.

Many wedding vows archaically speak of "love, honor, and obey." I wonder, though, if in any relationship we shouldn't be most concerned about trust and the difficult forms of feedback, communication, resistance, and pain that it may often demand. I dimly remember reading somewhere that acts of kindness aren't determined by what one, out of affection, does for someone else, but rather what one, out of greater affection, refrains from doing.

"Whom Do You Trust?" was the television quiz show that launched the career of Johnny Carson, later of "Tonight Show" fame. It should also be the question we use to determine how seriously we accept others' feedback, how comfortable we are reciprocating kindness, and how proactively we extend help and comfort.

I don't see how we can go through life, grow, and be productive without relationships of mutual trust that we recognize as such. And if that trust doesn't exist within our own families and inner circles, we are all the poorer for it.

Whom DO you trust?

NOT GIVING UP

I was playing poker once at a remote corporate compound in northern Minnesota with my CEO client and his four top officers. It was after a day of strategy work, a huge dinner, and fine wine. The "pot" never exceeded about $20, so little damage could be done.

During one hand, the CEO and I were the only ones left, and I belatedly realized that I had a pair of fours, since I wasn't paying close attention (or the wine was even better than I had thought). This is not exactly a power hand. But in for a dime, in for a dollar, and I kept raising the ante. The pot grew to $25 and

I raised still again. The CEO considered for a long time and dropped out. As he folded his hand I saw that he had three tens. Neither of us ever said a word about that hand.

I don't recommend charging through life with two fours, but I do believe that we should stay in the game as long as we possibly can. Too many of us drop out too fast.

Salespeople often give up too early, at the least sign of resistance (or what they perceive to be resistance); mediocre athletes give less than 100 percent for the entire game; otherwise determined people will bend in the face of opposition at the school board, zoning committee, or Little League meeting; sometimes just one more bid would have secured that hotly contested item at an auction.

I won the greatest chess game I ever played after my opponent had captured my queen, ordinarily a fatal development. He asked if I wanted to resign, and I said, "Are you crazy? I still have all my other pieces!" I launched a relentless attack, never letting up, and checkmated him in a game most people wouldn't have bothered trying to finish. I've come from behind more than a few times in my life, usually because of two dynamics: My perseverance and others' belief that I was done for.

I don't mind being bested by someone else, so long as I've given my best. The other person deserves credit, and I've probably learned something. But I hate giving up, because that is within my control. Even more importantly, how many of us give up too early on relationships, passions, self-development, and recovery?

John Paul Jones, in the rebuilt French merchant ship Bon Homme Richard, engaged and defeated the larger, heavier armed British war ship Serapis. When Jones's ship had a hole in its side "large enough to drive a coach and four through," as one observer noted, the British asked if he would like to surrender. "Surrender?" shouted Jones in one of the most famous of all battle replies, "I have not yet begun to fight!"

When the British finally pulled down the colors, Jones had to transfer his command to the captured ship because his own literally had sunk beneath him. But he won the battle because he refused to give up.

The ship might be taking on water, but that's no reason to give up. "It's not over until it's over," said the sage, Yogi Berra, and it's usually up to us when we deem it over. Life is short.

Don't give up.

BAD DAYS AND GOOD

I'm intrigued when two people engaged in the same endeavor or occupation provide entirely different responses to helping others. I'm not talking about the "bad day" we all experience, but rather a behaviorally consistent response (or the equivalent of every day being a bad day).

One hotel desk clerk will greet you with, "Welcome to the hotel. How may I help you?" while another demands, "Next!" One telephone operator goes an extra nine yards and says, "The listing wasn't in Princeton, but I did a state-wide search and found it in Morristown," while another states, "No listing with that name," and cuts the connection.

(The other day I called the cable company to have a line moved, expecting the worst. A service woman gave me my choice of times and told me that if their repair person was not on site between 8:30 and 10:30 as promised, they would fix the problem for free and give me a $50 credit. "Who are you?!" I asked, amazed, and thinking I had called FedEx by mistake. "We are the Cox Cable Company," she said, "and we intend to give you excellent service even if it kills you!" I hit the floor, hysterical. These people are intent on ending the cable company's poor repute.)

So why does one mail clerk smile, say "Hello," and take pains to find a better way to ship your strange package, while another orders, "Go over there and fill out those forms; then get back in line"?

I think it has less to do with the boss, the family, the environment, hormones, television, ornery customers, UFOs, and Bill Gates than we think. I suspect it's actually about one's world view.

I've found that some people are viscerally cynical, with deep-seated convictions that life is, in reality, a slow, deadly march through enemy territory. You can tell who they are because they have that attitude as soon as they arise, before there's any chance that something or someone has adversely affected them, and the new sunrise, the chirping bird, and the kids playing ball in the street are not nature's signs of renewal and redemption but are rather intrusions and annoyances, endangering one's defenses. These are the true misanthropes, who feel that their jobs would be better if it weren't for the customers and life would be sweeter if there weren't so much, well, life.

As the economists say, "On the other hand," we have those people who see their awakening each morning, no matter what their condition, as better than the worst alternative, and who believe that existence demands mutual supportiveness and civility. This has nothing to do with profession and everything to do with outlook. I've found nurses who were unsympathetic and needlessly cruel, and police officers in riot gear who were unfailingly polite and respectful.

Californians and the English share a peculiar idiosyncrasy. If a visitor complains about the weather, the local person will immediately apologize, accepting full responsibility for nature's unreliability. (In fact, Californians are often pre-emptive, apologizing for the weather before you even say "Hello," on the assumption that you have as much right to climatic perfection in the Golden State as you do to sand on a beach.) As I've considered that behavior, I've realized that it's eminently logical: The apology costs nothing, and if it makes me and them feel better, why not?

If you feel the world is out to get you, it probably will. But if you believe that existence is largely what you make it, you'll probably make out just fine. And if you manage to help someone else make out well along the way, that's money in the bank of life.

150 Techniques for Balance

*Remember, Improve
by Just 1 Percent a Day,
and in Seventy Days
You're Twice as Good . . .*

1. One of the worst mistakes I've ever made was to "compartmentalize" my life. It dawned on me a few years ago that I don't have a "personal life" and a "business life," but simply A LIFE. Consequently, I do things when they feel right, which might include writing an article or taking care of client work on a Saturday morning and sitting at the pool on a Tuesday afternoon.

2. Time is the great equalizer, since we all have the same amount of it available. When we say that we don't have the time to help a spouse, watch our children perform, fix things around the house, or improve ourselves, we really mean that we don't consider it a priority. We actually do have the time.

3. When you receive reading material that you may or may not want to review, place it in an obvious pile where you'll

see it every day. Whatever you haven't read after two weeks, simply throw out. It's not urgent and you don't need it.

4. People often make the mistake of allotting time for various aspects of their life each week, thinking that the technique provides balance (two hours a day with the pets, an hour every other day exercising, a weekend day with a significant other). But this meting out of hours only provides quantity, not quality. The real test is in the intensity, fulfillment, and enjoyment of the time, not the mere expenditure of it.

5. Most anger is actually self-directed anger that is transferred to others in order to achieve self-preservation. If you're angry a lot of the time, don't assume you've met a rash of incompetent people on the phone, at work, among customers, and in social settings. Find out why you're really angry with yourself.

6. A certain amount of stress—eustress—is healthy because it keeps the adrenaline flowing and provides for a sense of urgency. We've all heard others (and/or ourselves) say, "I work best under pressure and approaching deadlines." Don't try to eliminate stress, but do try to manage it so that it creates energy but stops short of anxiety and paralysis.

7. Most people I've worked with place an inordinate emphasis on correcting weakness and do very little about building on strength. No one excels by correcting weaknesses (which simply serves to maintain the status quo a little more easily). Find out what your real strengths are (many people are totally unaware of some of them) and make plans to exploit them in work and at play.

8. Always have a book and a pad and pen next to your bed, even when traveling. If you can't sleep, read the book. If you suddenly have a bright idea, write it down. I find that many people lose their best ideas because they don't capture them quickly after thinking of them.

9. Balance in life and work is not about equal distribution. It is about variety, diversity, and establishing the correct priorities for yourself. I don't care if I never manage people again, because it's an activity that I loathed. But I get skittish if I don't have a book to read at any given moment when I have the urge to do so.

10. The "success trap" occurs when you are rewarded and lauded for something that you're good at but actually dislike. This is how jobs get in the

way of careers and how necessary evils come to impede our lives. Let your internal gyroscope tell you what's right for you, not external influences.

11. Every year (Is that too much to ask?) set a goal to do something you've never done before. Smoke a cigar. Sky dive. Buy a $500 bottle of wine. Go to a spa. Attend the opera (I don't blame you if you avoid Wagner, though). You get the idea. After a few years, you've added immeasurably to your life.

12. Put a stereo unit or boom box or something that can produce music in your work area. Cue up the music that you can't get enough of, no matter what your taste. Arrange things so that you can simply hit a button—or better still, a remote—to start your music. Turn it on whenever you're working on something that is enhanced (or merely not interfered with) by background music. I try to regularly go through all my Sinatra, Billy Joel, and Bobby Caldwell. (Hold your critique; I'm a romantic at heart.)

13. Find a book on the basics of something in which you're deficient—art, music, theater, architecture, whatever—and then create an experience to match your new learning. Go to a museum or exhibit, attend a symphony or opera, visit the theater, go on a walking tour. I learned something about architecture in Barcelona, of all places, using this technique.

14. Surprise someone who means a lot to you. Forget about significant, recognized occasions. Buy a gift, write a note, send some flowers, provide a compliment—completely out of the blue. Has anyone ever done that for you? If so, how did it feel? If not, how would it feel?

15. Pull off your beaten track and drive up a road that you've never traveled before. See what's up there.

16. Don't be afraid to vent. Stress is either internalized (making you ill) or externalized (making someone else ill). My wife tells me I'm a carrier. Nevertheless, if you're upset with service, quality, responsiveness, or results, speak now or slightly later, but don't forever hold your peace. It's unhealthy. Let it out, and then let it alone and move on. Nothing makes me crazier than people who go around informing me, "What I should have said was. . . ."

17. Find a competitive activity and throw yourself into it. Hear me out before you send me nasty emails. If you want to be physically active, choose tennis or racquetball or something like it; if not, try chess, or bridge or some board game. Healthy and cordial competition gets the juices flowing, exorcises

hostility, and provides the opportunity for some passion. Life's not about winning, per se, but about joyously entering the fray and engaging with our best effort, win or lose.

18. Do not be lulled by these "models" that have you plot out the various components of your life on some wheel and spoke system and then ask how much attention you're paying to each. The implication is that you should "balance" your time commitment quantitatively, which is nonsense. (You heard it here.) The point is really to balance your interests *qualitatively*. A lot of useless time with the kids doesn't measure up to an hour spent at their recital or soccer game, and spending hours speechlessly sitting next to your significant other doesn't hold a candle to the two seconds it takes to say, "I love you." (I see a lot of people having breakfast with their families at restaurants, with husband and wife both hidden behind the morning paper while the kids play with the silverware. Quality, anyone?)

19. Decide on something selfish you're going to spend a few hours a week on. Make that time inviolate (you may shift the schedule but not the commitment). Whether it's a hobby, volunteer work, fixing up the abode, or sitting on a rock contemplating the universe, make it your sacrosanct time. It's not what you concentrate on, but the quality and passion of your concentration that counts.

20. Sit down and list six things that you hate doing, or that get on your nerves, or that generally make you crazy. Eliminate three of them. (This includes relatives.) Stop suffering the "necessary evils." Take control of the stuff sapping your energy. Here's a silly but effective example. I know a terribly bright and rather charming guy who was driven to distraction by the staples that his dry cleaner utilized to attach the identification tags to his clothing. He'd struggle with these in the early morning while trying to catch a plane or keep an appointment. He went to the cleaner and said, "Find another way or you'll lose my business!" The cleaner now painstakingly puts his tags in with easily removed safety pins (and affords him a wide berth when he enters the store). He's ecstatic at having removed one of the thorns in the side of his life. So am I.

21. Be very polite to the people in service jobs who often verge on the invisible: airline counter clerks, receptionists, wait staff, and others. I find that "pre-emptive politeness" accomplishes two objectives: It provides better service, even if the person's having a bad day, and it eliminates the stress

involved in having to deal with someone treating you rudely because he or she is having a bad day.

22. If you have a hard time saying "no," provide options. "No, I can't meet with you today because I have to leave at noon, but I can meet with you tomorrow or the next day, talk on the phone this afternoon, or respond by email before this evening. Which is best for you?" This defuses a confrontation over "no" and turns it into an examination of which "yes" is best.

23. Don't look on a long airplane trip as an ordeal, but as an opportunity. I write articles, read the "tough" books, watch a movie I missed, make some calls, listen to music I might not otherwise (even country and western, to my shock), and think about my goals. Those of you who talk to other passengers have even more options at your command. I usually finish a flight with a great sense of accomplishment.

24. Arguments with a loved one are not threats to the relationship, nor are they tests of fidelity or commitment. They are merely temporary disagreements, which grow worse only if we attach too much import to them. Holding a grudge against a loved one over a trivial matter is like refusing to use your legs because you bumped your knee.

25. Don't ask your kids IF they liked or disliked a movie, a dinner, a vacation or any other experience. Ask them WHY they liked or disliked it. This helps you understand their reasoning, biases, and premises, and occasionally teaches you something that you missed the first time around. (Doesn't hurt with an adult, either!)

26. You're going to write me nasty letters about this, but if you want to buy a special gift for a loved one, buy yourself something as well. It gets you in the mood, provides a bit of a reward, and makes it more of a joint venture.

27. Recently, we took a three-day mini-vacation in Boston (one hour from our home) and walked the Freedom Trail. I know people in New York who have never been to the Statue of Liberty or the Empire State Building. Don't miss what's in the backyard. (We went to Paul Revere's home, and I discovered he was different from what I had imagined or been taught forty years ago.)

28. If you want people to listen to you in a group setting, no matter how informal, simply practice this technique: Speak loudly and firmly, use a recent example, and look people in the eye. For example, "I thought that *Sixth Sense* was a good movie with a surprise ending" is better posed as, "*Sixth*

Sense reminded me of Hitchcock at his best, and the ending created a silence in our theater that lasted while people walked out."

29. Create a time of the week—we like Sunday afternoons—when you get in the car and drive for at least an hour to have dinner, or just to take in the scenery and explore a new place. It's a great tradition to share, even if you have few other interests in common.

30. Don't get caught in the war of the bromides. "Don't sweat the small stuff" is offset by "For want of a nail. . ." and "Haste makes waste" creates a conflict with "Time waits for no one." For every aphorism, there is an equal an opposite aphorism, which is Alan's Fourth Law of Thermodynamics. Live your life according to what's right, not what someone has memorialized (and trivialized).

31. Gifts are an expression of regard for another person. Yet gift selection is often an odious chore. Perhaps this time they can be true expressions of affection.

32. Don't waste your time telling spammers to remove you from their email lists, or junk faxers to remove you, or overbearing catalog companies to stop mailing ponderous tomes. They won't do it, or they'll stop only temporarily, or they'll be happy that they have your accurate address and increase their onslaught. Simply throw the stuff out or delete it and get on with your life.

33. If you want to communicate with your loved ones, never generalize a specific. In other words, don't tell your child that he has no respect if he abruptly interrupts you. Simply point out that he shouldn't interrupt without saying "excuse me" (unless the house is on fire). Once you say to a spouse, "There you go again with the same old. . ." (fill in the blank), you might as well go to a movie by yourself, because rational conversation is over.

34. One of the greatest lines I ever heard was spoken by actor Dudley Moore playing the title role of "Arthur" when he drunkenly says to his long-suffering valet (Sir John Gielgud, no less), "Don't you wish you were me? I know I do." Hey, shouldn't we all feel so good about our lives that we aspire to be us?

35. The bromide is that we should read slowly for business and professional purposes and speed read for recreation. I don't think so. Most professional stuff I can race through, but I love to savor a well-written book I'm reading for pleasure. We've got that one all reversed.

36. Around the holidays, I've sometimes gone to the town welfare people to ask which families really need help desperately. I then leave an anonymous gift in their mailbox with what I estimate is enough money to take them through a month or so. It assures me that the help goes directly and completely to those who need it the most. I call (from a public phone, now that caller I.D. is so prevalent) to make sure that they know it's there.

37. It may be imprudent to treat every day as if it may be the last, but it's not difficult to treat each holiday family gathering as if it's the last. Special occasions should be joyous and forgiving. I've seen too many despondent people who say, "If I had only known it would be our last holiday/anniversary/birthday together."

38. Tell someone flat out when they're confusing you, are wrong, or obnoxious. I received a call recently from a woman who wanted my free help to set up a self-aggrandizing position that she was totally unsuited for. I told her so. She got angry. Better her than me.

39. Before you die, visit the following: Hong Kong, Rome, London, and Paris. See a great play on Broadway from tenth row center. Share a corner table in a fabulous restaurant. Write a short story. Take a cruise and get the best stateroom you can afford. Give your kids a completely unexpected gift. Learn to dance well (I'm still working on that one). Make the winning bid in an auction. Get into the ocean and let a wave wallop you. Sing with exultation, if only in your own shower.

40. If you can arise at 6:30 in the morning and feel rested, I guarantee that you will increase your productivity by at least 50 percent. You'll get to all those things you thought you would never have time for.

41. Make a contribution to an animal shelter, pound, or animal rescue league. There are dedicated, unselfish, sacrificing people trying to do humane work, and even a $10 donation goes a long way toward food and boarding. Do the right thing.

42. Tell your spouse, partner, significant other, and/or lover (political correctness is exhausting, isn't it?) that you've set aside an entire day just for him or her. Provide for their most sybaritic, educational, or fantastic day. (If you make this offer with a reciprocal date in mind, it sort of loses the effect, you know?)

43. Trace your family tree as specifically as possible while the elders are still with you, as a gift to the young. You really can't appreciate where you are unless and until you know where you've been.

44. The next time you're REALLY ANGRY, remember that virtually all such rage is actually self-anger being transferred elsewhere. Take the time to find out why you're so unhappy with yourself.

45. Attend a sports event in person and root like a crazy person. Don't worry about winning; just have a wild time. When I was an undergraduate, our "fight song" was, "Nobody ever dies for dear old Rutgers."

46. If you have kids, next time you need advice about something, ask them for their advice and see what happens. You'll establish a great respect for their opinions, and you might just learn something.

47. Joseph Heller recently died, and *Catch 22* remains one of the great anti-war books of all time. If you've never read it, now's a good time.

48. Listen very closely to the words of our modern troubadour, Billy Joel, on "Shades of Grey," a song on his "River of Dreams" CD. Tom Stoppard wrote once that "Age is such a high price to pay for maturity." "Shades of Grey" is a lyric reminder of the sagacity of simply living long enough.

49. Get an hour-long massage, and make it a weekly treat.

50. If your head tells you one thing and your gut tells you another, go with your gut. Analytic and cerebral processes can objectively tell you a great deal, but emotion, not logic, is at the root of effective action. If you don't feel it, don't do it.

51. Become sensitive to the positive nature of interactions around you. We're too prone to focus only on the negative. For example, a surgeon of great renown recently operated on my dislocated finger to improve it aesthetically. The surgery was a failure. After reviewing the results, he said to me, "Well, Alan, I'm sorry to tell you that I've gotten a lot more out of our relationship than you have." I thought it was a classic response, and I realized that a slightly bent finger should be the worst thing that ever happens to me. I was energized by his humility and candid admission of "failure."

52. Don't hesitate to write a letter of complaint. I call this "positive venting." (My wife calls it "constant whining," but let her develop her own devices.) I find that when a corporate monolith or supercilious individual causes me grief or stress, I'm much better off immediately venting the frustration. About two-thirds of the time I get an apology (often with a refund or freebie of some kind) and about one-third of the time I'm ignored. But 100 percent of the time that I do this, I feel better.

53. I've had some inquiries about how best to volunteer talent and time. Given the age we're in, I've found these sources on the web that accommodate online volunteerism. I'm sure there are a hundred others. So here's some online volunteering for the time challenged:
   - New York Cares, 212-228-5000, www.ny.cares.org
   - ImpactOnline, 650-327-1389, www.impactonline.org
   - Points of Light Foundation, 202-729-8000, www.pointsoflight.org

54. Here's an interesting new self-published book on a little-acknowledged stress factor in the workplace: *Mobbing: Emotional Abuse in the American Workplace,* by Noa Davenport, Ph.D., et al. (Bookmasters, Inc., Box 388, Ashland, OH 44805, 800-247–6553, noadnz@iastate.edu). It talks about how co-workers advertently and inadvertently "gang up" on a victim and what can be done about it.

55. Read the music liner notes. I've just purchased a Sammy Davis, Jr., boxed CD set, and the voluminous liner notes are incredible in terms of educating me about why certain phrases, accompaniments, and instrumentation make a difference, which I can then listen to with some intelligence.

56. Buy an art book on an aspect you know nothing about (which for me includes almost everything) and then visit a museum that features that school or style. All of a sudden, you will become conversant.

57. If you find yourself beset with "road rage," quickly ask yourself if the perceived transgression is worth losing your life over. The answer is: NEVER. Recently, one non-violent woman shot and killed another non-violent woman in such a confrontation, while a minister killed another motorist with a cross-bow in still another. Stay in your car and count to ten, then count your blessings. It ain't worth it.

58. There are some classic books out (see authors Milton Cross and Karl Kohrs) which describe the great operas in detail. They allow me to understand what otherwise, I have to admit, would be indecipherable. (There were times when I rooted for Tosca to throw herself off the roof quickly and put us all out of our misery.)

59. Find an inn or bed and breakfast out of season, and stay there overnight. It's peaceful, the service will be great, and you'll get a real bargain.

60. If you want to laugh very hard, watch the old "Roadrunner" cartoons. Wile E. Coyote's dealings with the Acme Co. for his rocket sleds, huge

spring skates, and other devices of mayhem (which never work and always backfire) knock me out. What really kills me is that the coyote has such an outstanding credit rating.

61. "Counting to ten" actually works very well. If you are enraged or deeply hurt, count off the numbers before replying. This is PARTICULARLY true before you hit the email "reply" button!

62. Every study on the subject I've ever read says that a glass or two of wine at dinner is healthy and poses no harm if you are otherwise healthy. Most wine, including red, can be kept in the fridge for a few days, although the quality declines rapidly.

63. Go see the movie *Topsy Turvy*, about the efforts of Gilbert and Sullivan to launch *The Mikado*.

64. I'm asked a lot how I handle the pressures of keynoting in front of high-powered groups. It's simple: I show up on time, do my very best, and then go home. My being and esteem are not wrapped up in that sixty minutes, nor should yours be in whatever the temporary activity happens to be.

65. Your parents are often wrong and your kids are often right. If you don't resign yourself to this fact, you're in for very rough sledding.

66. I hate to admit this, but the absolute best way to quickly end unwanted solicitations is to say, "Sorry, but I just don't need any. Thanks for calling and good luck," and hang up.

67. If you want terrific background music that is soothing and timeless, think about the Baroque school and Vivaldi in particular. Find his lesser works, not *The Four Seasons*, which has been overdone. Other good candidates: Telemann and Pachelbel.

68. So I'm in this client's office the other day and he's looking in the dictionary muttering, "iatrogenic, iatrogenic." I responded, "Illness caused by the hospital or caregivers themselves." He looked at me with wonderment. Now tell me that you don't think it's worthwhile to improve your vocabulary every week, which costs precisely nothing.

69. Compliment someone when you meet him or her. About anything. You'll find that the conversation is much easier after that. (Men are even more susceptible than women; don't kid yourself.)

70. Always tip 20 percent if the service is decent in a restaurant, and treat cab drivers and bell people well. The extra tip is a minor amount, they make their living that way, and most of all, you'll feel better about yourself. I find

a lot of grumpy people agonizing over the fact that they paid $2 too much or left too much as a tip. In the course of things, it doesn't matter.

71. As much as I loathe personality profiling, there is a neat place on the web that doesn't take itself too seriously. Emode.com has a wide variety of self-testing psychological instruments, including "What Breed of Dog are You?" I advise all readers to take that one, and we'll see just what this kennel looks like.

72. If you're uncertain of wines but find yourself in the position of having to select one at an important event, here are some easy selections. For expensive occasions ($100 and above), order any French Montrachet as a white, or any Opus or Far Niente (both from California) as a red, and discerning people will fall on the floor in admiration. For inexpensive occasions, Glen Ellen (California) makes a quite acceptable white and any recent French Beaujolais will be fine. (If I've offended your wine sensibilities, please send your email to our complaint department.)

73. One evening a week volunteering—which is less than 2 percent of your time—will make you feel 200 percent better about your life and yourself. Not a bad return on investment.

74. I'm skeptical about online universities and learning, even though several sites carry courses based on my books. Learning is largely reliant on interaction, and you're better off creating a "mastermind" group, or a book club, or a learning dynamic of some kind with friends. Hint: Make sure your group includes people from whom you want to learn and whose opinions you respect.

75. For all its power, a continued caution on email. I instigated an email fight the other day with a friend who had sent me what I thought was an obnoxious note about how wrong I was on a point we were debating. It turns out that he was kidding me and being sarcastic. (Can you imagine, me missing sarcasm? But there you have it.) We finally ironed things out, but after some damage was done. Even among friends, email can't denote inflection, intonation, volume, and body language. Caveat scribum.

76. Isn't it interesting how an unexpected small gift always carries more affection and provides greater impact than a large, expected one? A single rose, unannounced, trumps two dozen that are awaited impatiently. When is the last time you surprised someone?

How do we retain balance in the wake of such horrific acts? The answer is, we don't. At least not in the short term. We have to take time to realize that the world is inevitably altered. Our sense of security, complacency, and invulnerability has been shaken, and will never quite return to the original position.

There are no wise words or philosophic principles that can wash away the sickness we all feel. We have all been brutalized.

It occurs to me that one of the emotions that emerges in the aftermath of the shock is great clarity, an utter crispness about what is important. New Yorkers have conducted themselves with a unity and control which is not only beyond what could have been imagined, but is also an example of bravery so immense that one has to think of wartime London for a comparison. The country at large has responded with a singularity of purpose. People who can hardly wait for a traffic light to change have calmly waited in three-hour lines to donate blood.

On a larger scale, I'm receiving emails from all over the world, and we see public displays from Ireland to Australia expressing outrage, support, and sympathy. Cataclysm erases the superficial and drives our attention to what is ultimately important.

I was in Los Angeles. When it became evident that it might be impossible to return for a week, I knew that my place was to be beside my wife in Rhode

77. Self-talk is, I believe, effective therapy. Sid Caesar, in his autobiography, claimed that he cured himself of serious depression through an audiocassette journal which he faithfully recorded and replayed daily. Writing is a form of self-talk as well. When you're confused or uncertain, record or write your thoughts, feelings, and observations. Then play them back or reread them. You just might find that you have the resolution within your own questions.

78. Have you ever driven in a convertible on a spring day? Why not? I never did until 1990. I've let the wind clear out my head ever since.

79. Combat stress aggressively, don't endure it. If you know you'll have to wait in a doctor's office or at the division of motor vehicles, don't go there and stew about it. Take a book. Bring your laptop. Read the article you've

Island. Both of our kids work in New York. Mercifully, they were spared, but the horror had come too close.

A client from the East Coast and I agreed that we had to control our fate. In just two days, we drove from Los Angeles to Charleston, West Virginia. On the third day, yesterday, I drove twelve hours, non-stop, to get home. It never occurred to me that it wasn't possible to drive 3,000 miles in three days.

It's very clear to me: My family is my root, my base, and my strength. The only consideration was to be together.

Our lives have all been changed. Many have lost loved ones, and that loss can never be eased. All of us have lost our balance. But these times have brought out the very best in many, and serve to provide the clarity that may have been missing from our lives.

What is the most important thing in your life? It surely isn't money, or a job, or a house. That real core is what must be valued and treasured. Perhaps many of us are now being refocused on what is our essence.

My sympathies to any of you who lost loved ones in this tragedy. My best to all of you to overcome the challenges of these times.

Alan Weiss

always been meaning to get around to. Listen to your Walkman®. If someone is stepping on your foot, you don't remain where you are. If the situation is stressful, change it to your liking. We control more of our lives than we think.

80. Put a bird feeder somewhere you can see it frequently. Don't fret about the squirrels. They have to eat, too.

81. If you need some good sources for financial planning to put your mind at ease about your future, try these:
   - Certified Financial Planner Board of Standards, 888-237-6275, www.cfp-board.org
   - Financial Planning Association, 800-282-7526, www.fpanet.org

- National Association of Personal Financial Advisors, 888-333-6659, www.fee-only.org

82. There are quite a few offers available (for example, American Express Platinum Card) wherein you can purchase one first class or business class ticket and receive an accompanying ticket for free. That's right, for free. These are wonderful opportunities to take your spouse or partner on a fabulous trip.

83. I'm increasingly convinced that most people are most stressed by time demands. Learning how to intelligently invest your time is one of the best "balancing acts" you can perform. Hint: Most of us are doing things each day because we think we should, not because we actually need to.

84. While it may be true that "no one can intimidate us, we allow ourselves to be intimidated," this is not a blanket guilt trip. If someone talks in the audience during a theatrical performance, we're certainly not "allowing ourselves to be interrupted." We have to tell them to stop if our night isn't going to be ruined, or else we enable the boorish behavior (such as cell phones ringing during speeches). The balance is in where to draw the line: If someone who is seated later is served before us in a restaurant, that's a minor inconvenience. If someone constantly interrupts our family time, that's something else entirely.

85. Here's a fact about "secrets": It's as bad to hear them as it is to tell them, because you're often caught in a moral vice once you've heard compromising information. When someone offers a "secret," especially at work, tell her that you can't guarantee confidentiality because it may be information you'd have to reveal in order to prevent pain or harm to someone else. You'll usually be told anyway, and you'll at least have recourse to divulge the information if you deem it necessary to do so.

86. When someone suggests something that he's sure you'll enjoy, and you're positive it would fling you into a homicidal rage, don't agree out of courtesy. Instead, say something like, "Why is it you found the bagpipe concert so engrossing?" Get the person talking to avoid having to refuse generosity or submitting yourself to excruciating pain.

87. When you call someone, introduce yourself first and then make your request: "Hello, this is Alan Weiss calling for Ms. Jones" or "Hello, this is Alan Weiss. May I speak with Tom Clark, please?" It's more professional, more assertive, and often gets by the gatekeeper nicely. Coincidentally, it helps with restaurant reservations because the person on the other end

often assumes that you're a regular or someone who should be recognized, and therefore manages to find a good table.

88. If you're interested in an MBA in about three hundred pages, read *The Capitalist Philosophers* by Andrea Gabor. It's a comprehensive but highly readable study and analysis of most of the outstanding management thinkers, including Frederick Winslow Taylor, Mary Parker Follet, Elton Mayo, Peter Drucker, and many others.

89. Get a speaker phone for your home phone, and every time you're placed on "hold" by a catalog firm, repair operation, government agency, or any other annoying source, place them on the speaker and go about your business by opening mail, reading a book, playing with the dog, or watching television. This removes all the frustration and keeps you focused on your goals, not the wasted time.

90. If you'd like to travel with your pet, here's a source for pet-acceptable lodgings: www.petswelcome.com.

91. Make a list of those movies you never got around to seeing because your partner didn't want to or they weren't appropriate for the kids or your local theater wouldn't show them, and rent them one by one to watch at your leisure with some hot popcorn and a bottle of champagne.

92. Find a dealer who has the car you've always wanted to drive and arrange for a test drive. (It's best to act confident and not smirk or giggle while you do this.)

93. When's the last time you went to a museum? Do you realize that they've changed the names and positions of a lot of the dinosaurs because of findings over the last few years? Are they more modern than you are?

94. I can't think of a school that would reject a request by a professional to volunteer some time with one of the classes. Are you teaching anybody anything lately?

95. Determine the issue that is completely in your control and is driving you the craziest, and allot two hours to eliminate it this coming weekend, be it an overrun garage, a broken appliance, a letter unanswered, or an article that needs to be written. The two-hour investment will gain you weeks of freedom from stress.

96. Scan Amazon.com for a subject in which you've always wanted to improve and order a book. Don't order the most profound work, just something to gently begin the process.

97. When is the last time you told a chef, a flight attendant, a repair person, a postal employee, or phone order taker that he or she had done a really fine job for you?

98. I met a guy once who collected photos of old streetcars. He had thousands. People contacted him from around the world, because he was such an acclaimed expert on them. I met another guy a year ago who specialized in bridges that opened to let boats through. Eccentric? Maybe. But they sure seemed like vigorous people to me. What's your passion? Where is your fuel source?

99. If you haven't read John Irving's *The Hotel New Hampshire,* you really ought to before you die. It is one of the four or five funniest, yet most poignant, works I've ever read by one of our great writers. There's a rather wonderful dog in it called Sorrow.

100. Remember that there is no such phenomenon as "I just don't have the time." If you're missing significant variety, joy, learning, sharing—or LOVE—in your life, then make time for it. The time is yours, and so is the intent.

101. When a relationship is troubled, focus on observable behavior, not psychobabble. "You interrupted me three times during dinner before I could finish my thought" is much easier to talk about than "Your trouble is that you have no respect for anyone else's opinion."

102. Break tension through a nice, minor gesture. Offer a drink, a kind word, a pleasant mutual memory.

103. Try to describe breakdowns as mutual difficulties or challenges, not as something inflicted upon you by your partner.

104. Let silences reign at times. They can be healthy periods for reflection and aren't necessarily meant to infuriate you. Nine times out of ten you will fill a silence with something you regret if you speak too soon.

105. If the sight of the other person or sound of his or her voice triggers a visceral reaction, start with a note. Don't type it—write it.

106. Never universalize a specific. In other words, if the other person acted rudely last night, that doesn't make the person an ogre for his or her entire life.

107. Remember that most anger expressed maliciously at others is actually self-anger that is being transferred to protect your own self-image and efficacy.

108. Be honest about your emotions and don't try to camouflage them. It's healthy to say "You really hurt me by that comment" or "I felt betrayed."

109. Remember that what you feel and what you think are two different things. Logic makes people think, but emotion makes them act. You have to communicate on both levels.

110. Seek third-party help if you're at an impasse. Therapy has a bad name only because people choose bad therapists. Ask for referrals and wait to find one with whom you both feel comfortable sharing and communicating. I'm convinced that 50 percent of the potential effectiveness of therapy is in simply being patient and diligent enough to find the right resource.

111. Do not take yourself all that seriously. Every time I think I'm walking on water I look down to find my knees wet. Nothing we do daily affects the course of Western Civilization. Lighten up.

112. Use humor as a release. When people yell at me I often reply, "Don't repress, tell me how you really feel." This makes me laugh at their discomfort, and often makes them laugh, as well.

113. Create a familiar "anger buster." Whenever you feel anger building, especially if it threatens to be uncontrollable, resort to a common behavior or setting. For example, you might take out a picture of your kids to calm yourself, or start humming a favorite tune, or recite a short poem. The familiar sequence will tend to take you out of your approaching anger mode.

114. Discuss what bugs you at the time and don't allow stress to accrete. When the New York police cracked down on petty crooks, they also immediately reduced major crimes. Discuss small annoyances as they occur to vent the pressure.

115. Ask loved ones or friends to help. Give them permission, when they see certain signs (your speech pattern, volume, making fists, etc.) to "break" the mood by saying, "I'm asking you to pause here, because you asked me to help you at this point."

116. Work it out. Physical activity dissipates stress. Go to the gym, work in the garden, play ball with the kids, wash the car, paint the hall (assuming it needs it). Make the endorphins gush.

117. Focus on observed behavior and evidence, and not what you think the other person is thinking or plotting. (I saw a woman become enraged once because she was convinced that someone was going to steal her best material, although there wasn't a shred of evidence, behavior, or history to support that fear.)

118. Don't drink, even in moderation, prior to, during, or after a stressful meeting or interaction. Alcohol lowers inhibitions and greatly increases the odds that you'll say or do something to exacerbate the anger.

119. Acknowledge your anger. There's nothing wrong with the emotion, but there's a lot wrong with behaviors that are based on it. It's the height of health and balance to say to yourself, "I'm angry, and with good reason. Now what are the options that are rational and best for me?"

120. Get help. If you're angry daily, you have a problem that is psychological or emotional in nature. Find a good therapist. If you think that therapy is painful, humiliating, and/or expensive, it often is. But think what is happening to you, your loved ones, and those with whom you come in contact when you're hostile, volatile, and unpredictable. No contest.

121. Never act on the basis of your immediate emotions. Remember, all emotions are legitimate, but all behaviors that follow may not be. Acknowledge your immediate emotions, but then decide what your behaviors should be.

122. Use a piece of music, a favorite memory, a poem, or a fish tank to provide some solace as a constant device to place you in a state of calm. I'm told that some aromas can do this, and it seems probable that any of the sensory mechanisms can serve this purpose.

123. Ask yourself if your future is actually in jeopardy, or only your ego. No one can tell what your ego is feeling or what state it's in, so the only "embarrassment" may be completely internal. The worst decisions are invariably those based solely on ego need.

124. Have a buddy. When I worked on a suicide hotline we had a system whereby we could turn to other volunteers to vent, particularly when we found we'd been "had" by someone playing a practical joke, which is emotionally crushing (only about 10 percent of callers were really at risk, but the point is to find out which ones). Use a trusted other who serves the purpose of allowing you to blow off steam and talk through your issues.

125. Walk away from the stressor. Physically remove yourself from the phone, the letter, the meeting, the event. Proximity, or lack of it, is everything. If there is a constant irritant at work, explore changing your work space or location. If the train whistle annoys you, stop cursing the train and move away from the tracks.

126. Find a hobby. A passion is always comforting. I always feel better after doing something I like. Don't deny yourself your pleasures because you're anxious, because you'll only be delaying the calm.

127. Get a pet. Animals produce great calm if you allow yourself to enjoy them and don't see them as another chore or challenge. I'm especially partial to dogs, since they seem to have a sense of our moods and a great gift for play. Most "dog psychologists" are convinced that dogs have reached the apotheosis of happiness when they're sitting around doing precisely nothing. If that's not calm, I don't know what is.

128. Get some sleep. When we're tired, ragged around the edges, and cranky it's tough to stay calm. A broken potato chip, in those circumstances, can be a traumatic event.

129. Get in the water. Water is quite soothing. Take a swim, go out in the boat, sit by the pond, take a bath. I have a friend who can sit on a sailboat for hours. He's one of the calmest people I know. (Which is quite important, since I insist on steering and I refuse to take lessons.)

130. Learn from your mistakes. If you "blew the calm" yesterday, reflect on what that was and what you can do to prevent it in the future. The only thing worse, perhaps, than losing our calm is not learning anything from it.

131. Virtually all humor is based on pain, yours or someone else's. It is a form of stress relief and "belonging." Slipping on a banana peel is the classic painful scenario, but I've also heard hilarious stuff from someone who's just lost a bundle in the market. I'm convinced that humor evolved so that we didn't all become clinically depressed as a condition of life.

132. Someone listening to me once said that "Your stories of success are largely about others, and your stories of mishap are generally about yourself." The safest humor is self-effacing. Others will like you all the more for it, and it prevents your ego from becoming a float in the Rose Bowl Parade (or is that now the Weed Whacker/Alpo/Roto Rooter Parade?).

133. Irony is the mother lode of humor, in my opinion, from Voltaire and Swift to Seinfeld and Sahl. When ousted from Emmy nomination by Michael J. Fox's portrayal of a political operative, Seinfeld, playing the title role in his own series at the time, observed, "Evidently the academy members feel that Michael J. Fox is better at playing a fictitious person than I am at portraying myself." It brought the house down.

134. The difference between discipline and obsession is that the former allows you an intelligent and prudent break or deviation (as from a diet or regimen) and the latter affords you no such leeway or mercy. Be disciplined, but not obsessed.

135. Humor is less effective, somehow, if you break yourself up. That's why I find Dennis Miller smug and not terribly funny. He's too in love with his own wit.

136. Timing is everything. Jack Benny used to simply pause, and the laughter would escalate. After a robber had to ask him three times, "Your money or your life?!" Benny, a notorious tightwad, finally yelled, "I'm thinking about it!"

137. The funniest stories are absolutely true. "Jokes" and artificial contrivances are seldom really humorous and are seen as deliberate attempts at mirth. Consider what happens to you every day for side-splitting, funny reminiscences. What has happened to me in immigration, sailing, and, most recently, nearly wedging a Mercedes between two buildings in an alley in Spain, are classics that I could never invent.

138. People learn best when relaxed, and humor is relaxing. If you want to accomplish an objective, influence someone else, or make progress with your own plan, try to remember to lighten up. I don't know about you, but I haven't been in the position lately to change the course of Western Civilization. I'm constantly trying to determine, "Do I have the proper perspective here?"

139. Allowing others to engage in humor is as good as using it ourselves. Laugh at others' stories, even if you have a better one. Don't engage in one-upmanship. (Sorry, but "one-up-personship" just doesn't work for me.) It's the laugh, not the source, that's important.

140. Allow yourself to laugh. I kid you not (as Jack Paar used to say). I drive my wife crazy by laughing out loud at books I'm reading while sitting on an airplane. One time, someone approached me at a resort and said, "What on earth are you reading, and how can I get it?" (It was a great book called *Abbreviating Ernie*.) Don't be selfish about laughter. Share it.

141. Make some priorities. If everything is a priority, nothing is a priority. Choose three things to resolve or accomplish quickly. (It actually doesn't matter what they are, just get three things done.)

142. Focus on the solvable. You can't resolve a personal loss or change government policy. Don't let that inability stop you from confronting the things you can change.

143. Delegate. The odds are that you've taken on too much. Can subordinates at work handle some projects? Can your partner and/or kids help? What about your friends? There is no shame in asking for help. You probably got in this mess because several people asked for your help and you couldn't refuse.

144. Miss a deadline. That's right, it's not the end of the world. The key is to tell the other party that the deadline or commitment will be missed, so that there are no unpleasant surprises at the last minute. The sun still rises the next morning.

145. Listen with your heart, then act with your head. In other words, choose accountabilities that your gut tells you should be attended to, then figure out a way to achieve them practically and efficiently.

146. When you're 80 percent ready, move. Most people find themselves under a pile because they believe they have to be 100 percent prepared in order to move forward. In fact, we can never be 100 percent prepared and the additional work in trying to move from 80 percent to 100 percent is dysfunctional (most people don't appreciate any qualitative difference, despite our efforts).

147. Question WHY you're doing (or procrastinating about doing) every single item that is part of your overwhelm. We tend to do things out of habit, not logic, and you may well be able to chuck half of them as really unnecessary. I stopped reading a slew of magazines that showed up every week without bettering my life in any way. I haven't missed one of them.

148. Tend to daily needs immediately. Go through the mail. Do the shopping. Answer phone messages. It's more efficient to do these things in "real time" than to allow them to pile up.

149. Keep a speed dial list of help, and use it. Call the plumber, then let the leak be his problem. Call the insurance agent and tell her to attend to the incorrect cancellation notice. Call the restaurant and have dinner prepared and delivered. Call the kids and tell them to stop charging things to your account or you'll stop paying their rent (this actually works immediately).

150. Remember: Life is about success, not perfection.

Index

A

AchieveMentors, Inc., 174

Acid reflux disease, 121n.2

Adaptive action, 42*fig*, 43, 45

Ade, G., 92

Advisory boards, 12–13

Alan's ultimate lessons: on balance in relationships, 157–158; on ignoring unsolicited feedback, 66–67; on leveraging, 45; on maintaining sense of humor, 24; on rewarding oneself, 112; on self-possession/control, 202; on stamp collecting/spontaneous pleasures, 90; on uninvited/egoistic feedback, 179

Anchor positions (stake in the ground): content perspective on taking, 127–128; overview of, 122–126; process perspective on taking, 126–127

Andersen, 25

Anxiety: resolving, 156*fig*; stress vs., 115

Archimedes, 29

Aristotle, 53

Arm & Hammer, 60

Asking "Why?," 28*fig*

Atlas Shrugged (Rand), 91

Attitudes, 146–147

Authenticity: case study on relationships and, 163; defining, 107; honesty and, 160–162

B

Bad Days and Good (life-balance essay), 223–224

Bailey, M., 94

Balancing Act: Blending Life, Work, and Relationships (newsletter), 4nl2

Balancing Act reader advice: on balancing life circles, 146; on being involved with your children, 201; on benefits of creative activities, 187; on building life around passions, 139; on changing negative into positive, 96; on contributions, 4; on diversity of life as life balance, 89; on fallacy of perception, 196; on "family calendar" benefits, 193; on having quiet moments, 41; on increasing life balance, 9, 14, 23, 35, 57; on integrating work and life, 78; on junk mail, 94; on letting vocation interfere with life, 174; on life balance as touching others, 75; on life balance and stress, 117; on listening to your body, 164; on managing too many interests, 82; on navigational fixes, 63; on NO MEANS MAYBE principle, 170; on organizational life balance, 108; on reducing stress in relationships, 153; on reward of taking risks, 50; on rewards based on personal values, 103; on satisfaction of owning business, 30; on stress, 52, 117, 118, 125, 132; on three favorite life-balance techniques, 143; on tolerance (mother duck/ducklings), 220; on travel hobbies, 27; on volunteer work benefits, 118

Bandura, A., 76

Bardwalk, J., 48

Barsky Consulting Pty. Ltd., 132

Barsky, V., 132

Battered women, 138n.2, 216

Bay Area Loch Ness Monster Committee, 218

Behavior: the art of influencing others, 138, 139–142; attitudes and, 146–147; avoiding generalizing specifics on, 148–151; case study on emotion as motivation behind, 141; case study on "victim," 151; difficulties in predicting, 137–138; egocentricity, 210–211; enlightened self-interest to influence, 140–142, 143–145, 147; normative pressure to influence, 140, 147; power and coercion to influence, 138, 147; role of motivation on, 148; surrendering need to control and, 152–157; ungeneralizing specifics, 151–152

Berra, Y., 222

Best Laid Plans: Turning Strategy into Action Throughout Your Organization (Weiss), 20n.4

Beyond perfection, 32–36, 33*fig*

Blame: cause vs., 169–170; defusing hunts for, 170–173; difficulty in eliminating blemish of, 169; focusing on cause instead of, 168–173

Blanchard, K., 170

The Blob (film), 6

The Book of Agreement (Levine), 4

Bromfield, A., 89

Burnout signs, 119–120

Business deadly cycle, 129*fig*

Business life: advisory boards and, 12–13; business plans/strategies and, 10–11; case study on, 12; office and/or staff and, 11–12; working too hard and, 30–36, 33*fig*. *See also* Consulting

Business Resource Group, Inc., 143

Buyer deliverables, 19

C

"Carriers," 122

Carson, J., 221

Case studies: on authenticity and relationships, 163; on changing alignment of our lives, 86; on courage to stand alone, 191; on critiquing, 74; on the "deliverables" prison, 16; on emotion as behavior motivation, 141; on estate planning vs. life balance, 87; on "failed" sales call lesson, 64;

on gathering information, 31; on measuring contributions, 5; on reaching your dreams, 105; on reducing work according to Occam's Razor, 26; on reinventing oneself, 60; on rewarding oneself, 97, 98; on self-doubt, 84; on small victories, 110; on stress, 116, 123, 126; on successfully avoiding "deliverables," 17; on taking risks, 49, 80; on testing the envelope, 54; on "victim" behavior, 151

Cause: benefits of focusing on, 168–169; blame vs., 169–170; how to focus on, 170–173

Chopra, D., 160n.1

Churchill, W., 9

Clance, P., 82

Clients: example of how to avoid "deliverables" prison with, 15–18; techniques to reduce deliverables problem with, 18–19; unhealthy interest in "deliverables" by, 14–15, 16

CML Consulting, 118

Cognitive interference, 159–160

Communication: Alan's ultimate lessons on uninvited/egoistic, 179; cause vs. blame focus during, 168–173; honesty and authenticity in, 160–162; meta-talk and, 163–168; opportunities for interference in, 159–160*fig*; selective openness/receptivity during, 173, 175–178; waste of dishonest, 161; written/email, 165n.2. *See also* Feedback

"Communications Loop," 160*fig*

Communications test, 166–168

Con Ed, 16

Conspiracies (life-balance essay), 218–219

Consulting: avoiding the "deliverables" prison, 13–19; importance of timing in, 63; measuring real contributions, 3–19; reducing complex to basics, 28*fig*–29; working smart and not hard/seeking perfection, 30–36, 33*fig*. *See also* Business life; Life balance

Context (life-balance essay), 212–213

Contingent action, 42*fig*, 44, 45

Contributions: *Balancing Act* newsletter readers on, 4; business life and relationship to, 10–13; case study on, 5; how to identify, 3–5; input/output rule on, 5–8; prison of "deliverables" and, 13–19

Control. *See* Self-possession/control
Corrective action, 42*fig*–43, 45
Coughlin, D., 9, 207
Courage to stand alone: case study on, 191; examples of, 189–190; making the choice for, 189; taking risks and, 190; "tough love" practice as, 191–192
Cuff, S., 153
Culpability (life-balance essay), 215–216

D

Danger in the Comfort Zone (Bardwalk), 48
Daring/daring feats, 79–80
Deadly cycles: applied to our lives, 130*fig*; business, 129*fig*; changing to break, 129–131, 134; described, 128
Dean, D., 48
Deane, C., 178
Delegating, 39–40
"Deliverables" prison: case study on client interest in, 16; case study on successfully avoiding, 17; described, 13; focus group example of avoiding the, 15–18; guaranteed techniques to dramatically reduce, 18–19; unhealthy interest in the, 14–15; value vs., 18
Dierickx, C. R., 35
Discretionary time, 92–93
Dodo birds, 37
Donaldson, S., 196
Dreams: case study on reaching your, 105; continuing to dream bigger, 106; instantiating your, 101–102, 104; making them come true, 104–106

E

Echelon Management Institute, 125
"Ed Sullivan Show" performers, 45
Egocentricity (life-balance essay), 210–211
Ellis, A., 132
Email communication, 165n.2
Emotion: actions based purely on, 209; as motivation behind behavior, 141
Enlightened self-interest approach: healthy opposition aspect of, 143–144; to influencing behavior, 140–142, 147; "musts" vs. "wants" in, 144–145

Enron scandal, 25
Entrepreneur risk taking: areas of, 51; *Balancing Act* reader advice on, 50, 57; building on success/not correcting weakness, 62–66; case study on, 49; case study on taking personal risks, 80; mid-flight test of, 55–58; reinventing yourself for, 58–61; "success trap" and, 58*fig*; testing the envelope and, 53–54; willingness for, 48, 50, 52
Environmental interference, 160
Estey, S., 146
Eustress, 113
Evans, P., 23
Evers, J., 50
Extension Human Resources (University of Nebraska), 193
External locus for growth, 76–77

F

"Failed" sales call lesson, 64
Fallacy of perception: *Balancing Act* reader advice on, 196; creating "new baggage" and, 195–197; importance of overcoming, 194; recognizing and overcoming, 192–193
Family: *Balancing Act* reader advice on being involved with children, 201; *Balancing Act* reader advice on family calendar for, 193; benefits of the family dinner table for, 157–158; domestic violence/battered women in, 138n.2, 216; relationship openness/receptivity with, 175; taking the time for vacations with, 87, 93. *See also* Relationships
Faust, M., 125
Fear of Ambiguity (life-balance essay), 206–207
Fear factor, 115
Feedback: benefits of solicited, 194; ignoring uninvited/egoistic, 179; ignoring unsolicited, 66–67; utility for assessing relationship openness/receptivity, 176–178. *See also* Communication
Fight-or-flight choices: case study on, 126; content perspective on, 127–128; process perspective on, 126–127; situations which generate, 124–125
Financial tithing, 95–96
Focus groups, 15–16

beyond perfection as, 32–36, 33*fig*; effective time usage as, 36–41; four types of actions for increasing, 42*fig*–45; as getting most accomplished with least input, 41; as removing problem causes, 44; solo practitioners and, 25–26; "why," observable behavior, and seeking evidence for, 28*fig*–29; working smart and not hard as, 30–32

Levine, S., 4

Life balance: case study on changing alignment of our lives and, 86; case study on estate planning vs. life balance, 87; courage to stand alone and, 189–192; "deliverables" concept as threat to, 15; intelligent trade-offs and, 142–148; making better use of time for, 36–41; movement as key to professional, 57; 150 techniques for, 225–245; relationship openness/receptivity and, 173–178; sense of humor and, 24; strategic vs. tactical standpoint and, 20–24; testing the envelope and, 53–54; working too hard vs., 32–36, 33*fig*. *See also* Consulting

Life balance *Balancing Act* reader advice: on balancing life circles, 146; on benefits of creative activities, 187; on building life around passions, 139; on diversity of life benefits, 89; on "family calendar" benefits, 193; on how to manage too many interests, 82; on increasing life balance, 9, 14, 23, 35, 57; on integrating work with life balance, 78; on letting vocation interfere with life, 174; on organizational life balance, 108; on stress and life balance, 117, 132; on three favorite life-balance techniques, 143; on tolerance (mother duck/ducklings), 220; on touching others as life balance, 75

Life-balance essays: Bad Days and Good, 223–224; Conspiracies, 218–219; Context, 212–213; Culpability, 215–216; Egocentricity, 210–211; Fear of Ambiguity, 206–207; Freedom from Failure, 216–217; Guilt, 203–204; Irrationality, 208–209; Not Giving Up, 221–222; Self-Effacement, 211–212; Solitude, 213–215; Trust, 219–221; Zealotry, 207–208; Zest, 204–206

Life-balance techniques, 225–245

Lincoln, A., 6

Linking Visions Consulting, 30

Loch Ness Monster, 218

Lombardi, V., 207, 208

The Los Angeles Times, 5

Lynch, L., 78

M

Magical language, 165

Making It Work (Weiss), 20n.4

Market Navigation, Inc., 27

Martinka, J., 143

Maslow, A., 200, 202, 213

Maslow's Hierarchy of Needs, 183, 184*fig*

McDermott, K., 220

McLuhan, M., 173, 177

McQueen, S., 6

Mensa, 4, 218, 219

Mercedes, 141

Meta-talk: as communications test, 166–168; described, 163; language use during, 165–166; location of, 165; timing of, 164

Momentum/habit of learning, 72–74

Moral certainty, 209

Motivation: behavior and, 148; case study on emotion as, 141

Multi-tasking, 40n.2

"Musts" vs. "wants" interests, 144–145

N

National Speakers' Association, 66

Navigational fixes, 63

Needs: diverse/interrelated nature of, 183–184; guilt and, 185–188; Maslow's Hierarchy of Needs on, 183, 184*fig*

Negotiating, 145

"Nessie" (Loch Ness Monster) photo, 218

Neurosis and Growth: The Struggle Toward Self-Realization (Horney), 77n.2

"New baggage," 195–197

New York Tri-State Chapter (National Speakers' Association), 66

Niemann, K., 193

NO MEANS MAYBE principle, 170

Normative pressure approach, 140, 147

Not Giving Up (life-balance essay), 221–222

O

Occam's Razor: described, 26; four choices for action and, 42*fig*–45; reducing deliverables and, 19; reducing work by, 26, 28–29

O'Connor, J., 199

Offices, 11–12

"One o'clock" position, 129n.4

Organizational life-balance, 108

Ornish, D., 4

Oswald, L. H., 218

P

Peer pressure, 140, 147

Penn, W., 51

Perdue, F., 211

The Perfect Storm (film), 214

Perfection seeking, 32–36, 33*fig*

Personal actions, 6, 7

Personal challenges: to exceed prior performance, 77–78; to master something, 78–79; to try something daring, 79–82; to try something new, 79

Personal space/spirituality, 93–95

"Playing it safe," 48

Playing to win: *Balancing Act* reader advice on diversity in life and, 89; *Balancing Act* reader advice on life balance vs., 75; *Balancing Act* reader advice on managing interests and, 82; competition and, 71–72; creating personal challenges and, 77–82; external locus for growth and, 76–77; ignoring the score/rewarding the effort and, 86–88, 90; momentum/habit of learning and, 72–74; the rational child and, 82–86; self-esteem and, 74–76*fig*

Playing to win case studies: on changing alignment of our lives, 86; on critiquing, 74; on estate planning vs. life balance, 87; on self-doubt, 84; on taking risk, 80

Positive self-talk, 112

Post, B., 14

Power/coercion approach, 138, 147

Preventive actions, 42*fig*, 43–44, 45

"Pride position": arriving/maintaining, 117–119; stress and, 116–117

ProScribe Medical Communications, 117

Q

Quiet moments, 41

R

Raleigh Jaycees, 139

Rand, A., 91

Rational child: described, 82–84; freeing the, 85–86

Reciprocity, 154–155

Reducing complex to basics: asking for evidence, 29; asking for objective information, 28–29; asking "why?" to, 28*fig*

Reinventing yourself, 58–61

Relationship openness/receptivity: access to close friends/esteemed colleagues, 175–176; life balance and, 173–175; tightly controlled access to acquaintances/strangers, 176; unlimited acceptance/access for family/significant others, 175; utility of feedback checklist for assessing, 176–178

Relationships: Alan's ultimate lessons on, 157–158; avoiding generalizing specifics in, 148–151; *Balancing Act* reader advice on reducing stress in, 153; case study on lack of authenticity in, 163; complex and evolving dynamics of, 157; determining what generates stress in, 155; enlightened self-interest approach to, 140–142; key aspects of honest/authentic in, 161–162; negotiating and nurturing, 145; NO MEANS MAYBE principle and, 170; normative pressure approach to, 140; power/coercion approach to, 138; reciprocity and balance in, 154–155; resolution techniques for, 155–157; resolving anxiety/relinquishing control in, 156*fig*; selective openness/receptivity in, 173, 175–178; surrendering need to control and, 152–157; trust in, 154n.7; "ungeneralizing" specifics in, 151–152. *See also* Family

Reorganizing your life, 122

Resolution techniques, 155–157

Rewarding oneself: Alan's ultimate lesson on, 112; *Balancing Act* reader advice on changing negative into positive, 96; *Balancing Act* reader advice on junk mail, 94; *Balanc-*

37–38; *Balancing Act* reader advice on, 41; combining downtime with uptime, 40; delegating for better, 39–40; discretionary, 92–93; eliminating the nonessential to increase, 38; flexibility in planning your day, 36–37; getting tough to increase, 40–41; making a list for, 37; scrutinizing your reading to increase, 38–39; three ineffable conditions regarding, 36

Tithe to yourself: discretionary time as, 92–93; financial, 95–96; health and, 97; personal space/spirituality and, 93–95

"Tonight Show" (TV show), 221

Top Management Strategy: What It Is and How to Make It Work (Tregoe and Zimmerman), 20n.4

"Tough love," 191–192

Tregoe, B., 20n.4

Trust, 154n.7

Trust (life-balance essay), 219–221

V

Vacations, 87, 93

Value: based rewards on real, 103; deliverables vs., 18

Value-Based Fees: How to Charge—and Get—What You're Worth (Weiss), 38n.1, 54

Values: attitudes and, 146; corporate, 145–146; defining, 145; NO MEANS MAYBE principle, 170; personal, 146

W

The Wall Street Journal, 38

"Wants" vs. "musts" interests, 144–145

Warne, T. R., 108

Watson-Weir, T., 164

Weakness corrections: importance of, 62, 64–65; tips on navigation fixes for, 63

Wheatley, M., 215

When Pride Still Mattered (Coughlin), 207

"Whom Do You Trust?" (TV show), 221

William of Occam, 26

Wilsey, C., 139

Winning. *See* Playing to win

Woolley, K., 117

Woolley, M., 117

Work life assessment, 35–36

"Workaholic" imagery, 34

Working too hard: assessment of, 35–36; beyond perfection as reason for, 32–36, 33*fig*; working smart instead of, 30–32

Z

Zealotry (life-balance essay), 207–208

Zest (life-balance essay), 204–206

Zimmerman, J., 20n.4